Doing Local Theology

FAITH AND CULTURES SERIES
An Orbis Series on Contextualizing Gospel and Church
General Editor: Robert J. Schreiter, C.PP.S.

The *Faith and Cultures Series* deals with questions that arise as Christian faith attempts to respond to its new global reality. For centuries Christianity and the church were identified with European cultures. Although the roots of Christian tradition lie deep in Semitic cultures and Africa, and although Asian influences on it are well documented, that original diversity was widely forgotten as the church took shape in the West.

Today, as the churches of the Americas, Asia, and Africa take their place alongside older churches of Mediterranean and North Atlantic cultures, they claim the right to express Christian faith in their own idioms, thought patterns, and cultures. To provide a forum for better understanding this process, the Orbis *Faith and Cultures Series* publishes books that illuminate the range of questions that arise from this global challenge.

Orbis and the *Faith and Cultures Series* General Editor invite the submission of manuscripts on relevant topics.

Also in the Series

Faces of Jesus in Africa, Robert J. Schreiter, C.PP.S., Editor
Hispanic Devotional Piety, C. Gilbert Romero
African Theology in its Social Context, Bénézet Bujo
Models of Contextual Theology, Stephen B. Bevans, S.V.D.
Asian Faces of Jesus, R. S. Sugirtharajah, Editor
Evangelizing the Culture of Modernity, Hervé Carrier, S.J.
St. Martín de Porres: "The Little Stories" and the Semiotics of Culture, Alex García-Rivera
The Indian Face of God in Latin America, Manuel M. Marzal, S.J., Eugenio Maurer, S.J., Xavierio Albó, S.J., and Bartomeu Melià, S.J.
Towards an African Narrative Theology, Joseph Healey, M.M., and Donald Sybertz, M.M.
The New Catholicity, Robert Schreiter, C.PP.S.
The Earth Is God's: A Theology of American Culture, William A. Dyrness
Mission and Catechesis: Alexandre de Rhodes and Inculturation in Seventeenth-Century Vietnam, Peter C. Phan
Celebrating Jesus Christ in Africa, François Kabasele Lumbala
Popular Catholicism in a World Church: Seven Case Studies in Inculturation, Thomas Bamat and Jean-Paul Wiest, Editors
Inculturation: The New Face of the Church in Latin America, Diego Irarrázaval, C.S.C.
The Bible on Culture: Belonging or Dissenting?, Lucien Legrand, M.E.P.

FAITH AND CULTURES SERIES

Doing Local Theology

A Guide for Artisans of a New Humanity

Clemens Sedmak

ORBIS BOOKS

Maryknoll, New York 10545

Founded in 1970, Orbis Books endeavors to publish works that enlighten the mind, nourish the spirit, and challenge the conscience. The publishing arm of the Maryknoll Fathers and Brothers, Orbis seeks to explore the global dimensions of the Christian faith and mission, to invite dialogue with diverse cultures and religious traditions, and to serve the cause of reconciliation and peace. The books published reflect the opinions of their authors and are not meant to represent the official position of the Maryknoll Society. To obtain more information about Maryknoll and Orbis Books, please visit our website at www.maryknoll.org.

Library of Congress Cataloging-in-Publication Data

Sedmak, Clemens, 1971–
    Doing local theology : a guide for artisans of a new humanity /
Clemens Sedmak.
        p. cm. — (Faith and cultures series)
Includes bibliographical references and index.
    ISBN 1–57075–452–7 (pbk.)
    1. Theology—Methodology. 2. Catholic Church—Doctrines. 3.
Community—Religious aspects—Catholic Church. I. Title. II. Series.
    BR118 .S395 2002
    230'.09—dc21
                                                2002008718

Contents

Foreword

Robert J. Schreiter, C.PP.S.

Doing local theology, Clemens Sedmak reminds us in his Introduction, is about waking up. Authors before him, such as Simone Weil, have made the same contention: theology is simply a mindfulness of God, an attentiveness to the action of God in creation. Those who engage in theology are truly aware of the world as it is.

One of the things that the development of local theologies has brought about is a much keener sensitivity to the dimensions of the theological enterprise itself. The very fact that attention is paid especially to the immediate, the concrete, and the specific is bound to make us more aware. Specifically, this has become evident in four areas: theology's contexts, its addressees, its agents, and its methods.

Perhaps most obviously, local theologies are attuned to the contexts in which they arise. It was an incongruence with the context that prompted the first efforts at local theologies, because the kind of theology that was being developed lacked a firm fit with the environment in which it was being expressed. It seemed out of place. It did not address the burning questions of that place. As a result of local theologies, most theologies today are more aware of the environment in which they operate.

Second, the addressees of the theology also came more into focus. Theology produced by academically trained theologians runs the risk of becoming an exclusively in-house game of theologians talking to other theologians. That has its own time and place but can hardly be the sum total of the theological enterprise. Talk about God is intended to be more than an academic exercise. It must address, first of all, the people of God and, by extension, all who have ears to hear. Local theologies help the theologian put a face on the audience of theology. They have also made theologians much more sensitive to reception: How is a theology being received and understood by its intended addressees? Theology is intended for communities, and for the building up of communities. Or, to put it in Sedmak's words, theology is a "solidarity of the friends of God."

Third, local theologies make us aware of who is doing theology, that is, the agents of the theological enterprise. While "the theologian" usually evokes images of someone who has received graduate training in theology, usually to the doctoral level, local theologies have attuned us to the fact that the making of theologies can be much more complex than that. Anyone speaking of God in a reflective manner is somehow involved in the theological process. The form that such speaking takes is not always a theological tract. It also can be expressed, as Sedmak reminds us here, in poetry, in proverbs, and in stories.

Finally, local theologies have made us attend to the methods involved in doing theology. They have attuned us to the mix of experience, of cultures, of tradition, of quests for identity, and of the need to address social change. Local theologies, for this reason, seek somewhat different canons or criteria for authenticity, since generalization or universalization is not their primary focus.

It is especially these last two areas—who is "doing" theology and how they are doing it—that Sedmak addresses in this book. He is not interested in providing a compendium of local theologies that have been created in the past three decades—although he does draw examples from around the world. He seeks rather to engage people in doing local theologies, or "little theologies," as he so aptly terms them. He wants to guide ordinary believers in the process by which these little theologies emerge. He wants to assure them that doing theology is something well within their grasp. It is more a matter of waking up to the reality around them than spending extended lengths of time learning new skills.

To help them, he draws on the philosopher Ludwig Wittgenstein's understanding of "language games." Doing theology, Sedmak asserts, is akin to language games. He does not mean by this that theology is a fictive undertaking, or something meant as diverting entertainment. The point is rather that local theology, even though it speaks of an infinite God, speaks in a local tongue, in language that can directly engage the hearts and minds of its hearers. It does not pretend to universality, even though it may cause resonances in the hearts of others. Just as one cannot play a game without knowing the rules, so too theology functions within a framework guided by certain rules. The rules are not complicated. They help give structure and direction to the theology that emerges.

This little book, then, will help give confidence to local theologians as they ply the trade of theology in their communities. It makes an excellent introduction to the doing of local theology, guiding those trying their hand at theology for the first time. It accompanies them with practical suggestions at each turn. I am grateful to Clemens Sedmak for having produced such a useful guide into the world of local theologies.

Preface

This book is a guide book. It does theology by way of example. What it means to emphasize is to be drawn from the particular examples and not from a general theory. In order to help the reader make sense of the jumble of stories and examples I tell, I summarize the important points of the book in fifty theses. These theses are highlighted throughout the text. Some of the theses contain tools, simple tools for doing local theologies. Whenever a tool is introduced, there will be an example and an invitation to practice this tool in an exercise. In this sense, this book is a practical book.

I am indebted to Professors Stephen Bevans and Robert Schreiter for their help and support. I am particularly grateful to Bob Schreiter for accepting this book into the *Faith and Cultures Series*. I want also to express my gratitude to Orbis Books, especially to its managing editor, Bill Burrows, for the first-class treatment this first-class publishing house has extended to me. I also want to thank Joan Laflamme for her thorough and competent editing support. Words of thanks to my family will be given face to face and do not appear in the preface.

Introduction

Waking Up

THESIS 1: Theology is an invitation to wake up: to be mindful and attentive.

Do you remember the scene? After his prayer in the garden Jesus came again and found his disciples sleeping, "for their eyes were heavy" (Mt 26:43). It is too bad that our eyes are heavy. It is unfortunate that we need so much sleep. We need the sleep of watching television, we need the sleep of relaxation and distraction, we need the sleep of following our routine. We need a lot of sleep. "We wake up, take our morning showers, leave home for work. We run into people we know and people we don't know. We obey the traffic lights: If they are green, we cross the streets; if they are red, we stop to wait. We do all this without ever once asking ourselves why we do it" (Freire 1998, 77).

Theology is about waking up. It is amazing what a person who is fully awake can do. A person like Mahatma Gandhi or Pedro Arrupe can make all the difference in the world. Theology pays special attention to the few, the "Abrahamic minorities" that can change the world by being attentive to the cries of the people. Dom Helder Câmara, the bishop of Recife in Northern Brazil for many years, did not get tired of talking about these minorities that can be motivated to become agents of change, artisans for a new humanity.

It does not take much to be part of an Abrahamic minority. It is not a matter of resources or infrastructure. It is merely a matter of waking up. A mindful person can make all the difference in the world. This is what theology is about—it encourages people to wake up.

Theology is about mindfulness. It is wonderful to have mindful people who see the world with ever new eyes. Those who have ears can listen, and those who have eyes can see. And those who sleep can wake up. This is part

1

of the good news proclaimed by Jesus. It is a shame that theological studies put us to sleep more often than not. What a tragedy that we rarely preserve a child's attitude of asking questions: Why? How come? It is through these simple questions that we penetrate important truths. Ann Hope and Sally Timmel speak about the importance of the "but why method" (Hope and Timmel 1995, 1:79):

> "The child has a septic foot."
> "But why?"
> "Because she stepped on a thorn."
> "But why?"
> "Because she has no shoes."
> "But why has she no shoes?"
> "Because her father cannot afford to buy her any."
> "But why can he not afford to buy her shoes?"
> "Because he is paid very little as a farm labourer."
> "But why is he paid so little?"
> "Because the farm labourers have no trade union.", etc.

Waking up is about going to the roots of matters. This is what theological questions are about. Doing theology is a matter of being sensitive to concerns and of asking the right questions. Doing theology requires qualities that go beyond a merely intellectual profile. A good theologian, one might say, is a person who is close to people, who has a creative imagination and the gift of listening, who shows a commitment to hard work, who accepts the risk of making a mistake, who is a person of self-renewal: a person dedicated to overcoming routine and considering theology as an ongoing task and a responsibility rather than a job to be done. Being a theologian is more about who one is than about what one knows.

Theology is about life, and doing theology is part of living a responsible life. Life is a big school and there are billions of people in its classrooms, the classrooms of the open spaces of our lives. These are the classrooms where Jesus taught. And these are the classrooms where Jesus learned as well. Again, Jesus invited us to wake up from sleep. He woke up the daughter of Jairus (Mk 5:40-43) and he woke up Lazarus (Jn 11:39-44). He asked his disciples not to sleep (Mt 26:41, 45), he urged them to stay awake (Lk 22:46) and to watch (Mk 14:35). Jesus talked about being attentive in the parable of the ten virgins (Mt 25:1-13). He exhorted us to be vigilant (Lk 12:35ff.), to learn from the birds of the air and the lilies of the field (Mt 6:26-28). He healed the blind and the lame and the deaf.

Jesus wanted people to wake up. Sometimes it took time to heal (Mk 8:22-26). Waking up might take some time. Waking up is a journey. Jesus invited people to this journey. He wanted people to be opened (Mk 7:34). As Dutch theologian Edward Schillebeeckx put it: "Anyone who does not listen to the gospel is deaf and dumb" (Schillebeeckx 1989, 10-11). Following Jesus means overcoming blindness, deafness, and the inability to speak. Doing theology is a way of following Jesus. It is an invitation to wake up.

In this book I would like to reflect on this invitation. Wake up! Waking up is not the privilege of scholars. In fact, being awake in a world full of wonders is the privilege of children. Doing theology in the spirit of children means seeking God in all things, being aware of God's presence, listening to God's voice, and being attentive to the signs of the times. We can do that only if we wake up.

THESIS 2: Theology is done locally. In order to be honest to the local circumstances theology has to be done as local theology, as theology that takes the particular situation seriously. Local theology can be done with basic theological means. It can be done by the people, and it is done with the people.

Theology has been on loan from the people of God to professional theologians for a long time. Theologians have become rich, and they have amassed intellectual property. This wealth is to be found in libraries and on our book shelves. It is about time to make explicit efforts to share and to live an intellectual life of solidarity—acknowledging the treasures and gifts of everyone and making the theological resources available to all. Professional theologians as well as non-academic theologians can wake up if they realize the riches of their questions and the wealth of their cultures and their church's tradition.

This book should be a contribution toward this solidarity of the friends of God. Doing theology is a call to wake up. Waking up means learning how to listen, learning how to see, learning how to discover, learning how to speak. Waking up means seeing differences between times and places, cultures and peoples. When we sleep we close our eyes. Jesus wants us to open our eyes. Come and see! (Jn 1:39). Doing theology as a person who is not sleeping means being attentive to the particular circumstances. Doing theology in this sense means doing theology where you are—in other words, doing *local* theology.

There is a growing awareness of "local theologies" and "contextual theologies." There is a growing awareness that theology is not an instant product that we take from the shelf and put some (local) water in it in order to have an enjoyable drink. Theology is a specifically local adventure if it wants to be relevant for a particular culture. As Michael Amaladoss says, "The flowering of local theology is a sign of the rootedness and maturity of a particular church" (Fung 1992, xi). And also a sign of the rootedness and maturity of theologians. Whenever we do theology, we do theology from somewhere. We are somewhere, and we take positions. We are embedded in a form of life, here and now. This is our human situation. "*Religion only exists in the vernacular*, or to adapt a biblical phrase, the 'treasure' only exists in 'earthen vessels' (2 Corinthians 4:7)" (Mullins 1998, 3).

The same applies to theology. Doing (universal) theology locally is not quite the same as doing local theology. We know that Filipino theology, Ghanaian theology, Thai theology, Polish theology, and North American theology taste different. We know that the context within which theology takes place shapes the form and influences the contents of theology. Doing theology in a political setup of suppression, exploitation, and structural injustice will lead to different results than a theology that comes out of well-protected academic research situations. The priests' barrack in Dachau has encouraged a different kind of theology than Professor Hans Küng's academic research institute in Tübingen. Doing theology with sick and old people will take a different form than doing theology with managers or business people.

In preparing a sermon we all know that we have to take into account the community with whom we want to share our thoughts—are we talking to university students or a kindergarten class or a rural community? When we write a letter we think of the addressee first. This is a matter not only of politeness but of mere common sense. In this sense, there is nothing—nothing whatsoever—spectacular about the concept of local theologies and the idea of doing local theology. Whenever we do theology, we do theology "from somewhere."

This book wants to contribute to the growing awareness that theology is not the privilege of those who are formally trained. On the other hand, we do not want to level the differences between those who keep their nose "to the painful grindstone of study" (as George Tyrrell put it) and those who do not engage in this conversation with the tradition and the scholarly community. However, the one way of doing theology is not superior to the other. The most important thing is to see that these two cultures of doing theology are in need of each other and have to strive for solidarity.

"Christians have generally rejected a division between esoteric and exoteric theologies: intellectuals and church leaders are not to hold one set of beliefs about what Christians properly say and do, and the masses another" (Tanner 1997, 84). Whenever academic theology wakes up, it realizes that it needs the many colors and sounds of the whole world. Nothing human can be alien to the theologian. Whenever nonprofessional theology wakes up, it realizes that it needs the caution and some distinctions of the scholarly mind.

This book wants to be a contribution to this kind of solidarity. It is not a "how to" book, a book of seven steps or ten points or "learning how to do theology in two weeks." It is a book that tries to show, by way of example, how simple and colorful theology can be. The examples cannot give recipes, but they can be inspiring. Theology cannot be learned in the same way a person learns how to bake a cake or to make an omelet.

A hammer in the hands of a wise person is still a hammer. And a nail is a nail. A hammer in the hands of a sleeping person is more (and at the same time less) than a hammer, and everything becomes a nail. A wise person will use tools like knowledge and insight wisely; a sleeping person will use tools with eyes closed. We would not give a dangerous tool to a person who is half asleep—whereas those who are fully awake can make their own tools. Again, it is all about waking up.

1

Walking, Talking, Doing Theology

THESIS 3: Doing theology is a way of following Jesus. Theology seeks friendship with Jesus and communion with God.

Following Jesus means walking on a path of hope. Doing theology expresses the hope that we can work in God's vineyard by way of study and reflection. A theologian is full of the hope of bearing fruits in the vast gardens of creation, the hope to serve God through intellectual honesty. A theologian is full of trust in the gifts of reason, imagination, and trust in the guidance of the Holy Spirit. This trust in God and the community outweighs our intellectual self-confidence. In the words of José Maria Arguedas: "What we know is far less than the great hope we feel." This is especially true for a theology that works with the mystery of God's presence in the world.

Ultimately, theology wants to bring people closer to God. Doing theology is a way of listening to God. God's voice is often a whisper. God's presence is often hidden. Theology asks for an attitude of attentiveness, awareness, mindfulness. Doing theology is a spiritual act. Theology reads the book of the world, looking "in between the lines." That is why theology is not a mere intellectual exercise. It takes sensitivity and tact to do theology. Theology is not talking about God but talking to *people* about God, or talking about God in the light of God's presence in the world.

Life is ultimately about communion with God. Because of that, doing theology, just like the church, is not an end in itself; it is not of ultimate importance. We do theology because we want to serve God and the people of God. In the first two chapters I reflect on some basic questions, and I invite the readers to study under Jesus, the great teacher. What can we learn from Jesus and his life about theology? Instead of raising our heads to look up at the impressive tree of theology with its many branches, we will bow our heads to look at the roots.

THEOLOGY: THE WHY, HOW, WHAT, WHO, AND WHERE

THESIS 4: Theology talks about life. It looks at our lives as if how we live makes a difference.

Theology talks about us, the people of God, and about our friendship with God. The basic truths are simple: "To be a Christian is to be a friend of the author of life, Jesus the Christ" (Gutiérrez 1991, 19). Theology is an expression of this friendship. "Theology simply defined is 'the study of God in relation to persons'" (Fung 1992, 3). Theology talks about *our* identity in the light of who God is. Theology talks about *our* lives in the light of God's creation, and it talks about God's creation in the light of God's life with us. That is why theology talks about life.

Theology is not talking about a far-away country or a vast and dead object. The theologian is not like an adventurer who explores unknown places. There are no scientific expeditions to heaven or hell. However, there is theological fieldwork. It deals with our human situation. Theology is about us, not about measuring an object the way a butcher scrutinizes a piece of meat. Theology is not an unbiased look at a distant subject matter. It is about us.

Theology looks at our lives from a point of ultimate concern, *as if how we live makes a difference.* Theology talks about our lives as if our lives matter. The question is not about how to describe the Trinity, but about how to be friends with the triune God. The question is not about how many angels there are, but about how we can see the presence of God's friends in our lives.

"The crucial question . . . is not whether God exists, but who or what this God is whose existence we either affirm or deny. Some gods are better dead than alive. Humankind did not lose a great deal when Huitzilopochtli and his cohorts lost their power to require human sacrifices, or when the crocodiles of the Nile lost their divinity" (González 1990, 89). Theological questions are questions of life and death (Dt 30:19). The theological perspective is not detached and unbiased. Theology is about life. Doing theology is part of our religious life. It is part of answering the question of who we are as humans, as believers, as community.

Let us start out by asking a few simple questions. We will keep in mind that asking questions is a challenging art and that the simple questions are the most difficult. Let us look into the following questions: *Why* do we do theology? *What* kinds of theology can be distinguished? *How* can we do theology? *Who* is doing theology? *Where* do we do theology?

WHY? VISIONS AND WOUNDS

THESIS 5: We do theology because we share a vision and we experience wounds.

This vision we share is a promised hope—the hope, as Julian of Norwich put it, that "all shall be well, that all manner of things shall be well." Saints are people moved by a vision of a context larger than our lives.[1] It is the vision of a promised land, the vision of unbroken closeness and unthreatened community. The vision of theology is a communal vision, the vision of community and the vision of a community.

We do theology based on the conviction that this is not a private struggle. A private struggle would be a struggle of idiots (*idiots* taken in the classical Greek sense of a private person who does not share in the public thought of the community). But theology is not a project of idiots; it is about building up a community of friends of God. We do theology because we share a vision with Jesus.

In the Middle Ages there was no doubt that the ultimate goal of a life of faith was the vision of God, the *visio beatifica*. Our vision is the vision of God. In recent years theology has emphasized that this vision is not the relationship between the isolated soul and "my" God. This vision is the vision of a community. This vision is not only a distant prospect or a vague promise; it is very down to earth. To love a person is to see God's face. Mystics have communicated a taste of this vision in which the human soul comes to rest.[2] It is a vision of community. Heaven is community, and salvation is the healing of the wound of loneliness.

Doing theology means reflecting on this vision in the light of the "signs of the times" (Mt 16:3). This reflection expresses the commitment to keep the flame burning and the vision alive. We have to bring the vision to ever new and ever changing places and times, thus renewing the face of the earth.

---

[1] "A saint is a person so grasped by a religious vision that it becomes central to his or her life in a way that radically changes the person and leads others to glimpse the value of that vision" (Lawrence Cunningham, *The Meaning of Saints* [New York: Harper & Row, 1980], 65). Since "a people without vision perishes," we need to have saints to keep the flame burning. Daniel Berrigan calls these people who stand out in every culture and time "the only justification for the human enterprise at all. . . . The absence of saints is among the greatest of losses to the consciousness of a whole culture" (Daniel Berrigan, *The Dark Night of Resistance* [Garden City, N.Y.: Doubleday, 1971], 42).

[2] We can think of Augustine's famous insight from the beginning of his *Confessions* (1,1) here: "Our hearts are restless until they rest in You."

Doing theology is an attempt to renew the face of the earth. It is an invitation to dream a courageous dream.

We share a dream of freedom and full life. In the words of Brazilian theologian Clodovis Boff: "Behind all action toward liberation there's a dream, a love, an ideal, a madness, a spirit, a mystique—whatever word you want to use. It's what makes you 'hang in there' in the middle of the storm." We do theology because we share a vision and have a dream. It is a dream of life, of life in abundance, a dream of joy that does not die. It is the vision of a new face of life. And it is the commitment to renew the face of the earth.

We do theology out of a vision of resurrection. We might think of the open tomb as our symbol, but we must not forget the symbol of the cross. We do theology also out of an experience of the cross. We do theology as wounded people, sometimes because of our wounds. No one can go through life without getting wounded. No human soul leaves life without wounds, humiliations, and experiences of injustice and rejection. We all carry wounds.

Our deepest wound is the fact that we do not want to be healed. The famous German-American psychologist Erich Fromm talked about our "escape from freedom." Fromm said that we are afraid of being liberated because freedom means responsibility (Fromm 1969). Similarly, we are afraid of being touched by God. God could upset our lives, plans, and projects. Healing can be painful. We are afraid of saying, truly from the heart, "Thy will be done." Ignatius of Loyola, the founder of the Jesuits, remarked that most of us have no idea who we could be if we surrendered totally to God.

God wants to heal our wounds without making them magically disappear. The wounds are still there, like the wounds of the risen Lord. But they might become origins of growth and springs of new life. We do theology not because of hope in a magically liberated sorrow-free and happy life. We do theology because we hope that wounds may be the source of strength, that the cross may be the source of new life. That is why we need to be aware of our needs, and we need to see the wounds of our people.

Jesus brought his redemptive message to a struggling and oppressed people. He ministered to the wounded of his society, the blind and lame, the proud and the corrupt. We do theology because of wounded people who have touched us. Jesus surrendered his power and became vulnerable, defenseless and wounded. We do theology out of the experience of the cross.

We all have our cross to carry. We do theology because people suffer. Doing theology is a way to attend to the wounds of our time. There are the wounds of ignorance and stupidity, the wounds of broken promises and unrealized dreams, the wounds of innocent suffering and of guilt, the wounds of open questions and burning concerns. We all do theology as wounded healers, as people in need of healing and comfort, and as people who can share the life-giving strength of our wounds.

Without glorifying in any way the many forms of suffering, I want to say that there is an incredible power in wounds. We could not do theology without this trust in the power of our wounds and the wounds of our fellow creatures. This is the power of the poor in history, the power of the children, the power of the powerless.

What is the power of the powerless? Let us look at the story of Rebecca Jonas (Jonas 1996). Rebecca was born prematurely on July 29, 1992. She was too weak even to open her eyes. She lived for only three hours and forty-four minutes and then died in the arms of her father. Her life outside of her mother's womb was fragile, and the flame of her earthly life was flickering. Four hours is not a long life. Rebecca did not experience much happiness in the sense of those who think that human life is about maximizing utility. But in these three hours and forty-four minutes Rebecca transformed the face of the earth. She touched all the people who knew of her by the power of the powerless. She made the people who knew about her softer, gentler. She turned them into people who cared. She turned them into people who came to think about what life is all about. This is the power of the powerless.

Doing theology means listening to the voices of those without voice, seeing the power of those without power, honoring the life of those without life. We do theology because we see and feel the wounds of the times. Cardinal Bernardin from Chicago reminded us: "As Christians, if we are to love as Jesus loved, we must first come to terms with suffering. Like Jesus, we simply cannot be cool and detached from our fellow human beings" (Bernardin 1997, 49). We cannot do theology but through wounds. It takes courage and honesty to face the plight of the earth.

Theology is about being honest to reality. And the face of reality can be painful and ugly. It is the face of slavery and famine, cancer and war, tears and blood. We do theology in the middle of the storm. There is no genuine theology without wounds. Following Jesus has always been an invitation not to be afraid of wounds and of getting wounded. Doing theology is also a way of becoming vulnerable and wounded.

Felix and Mary Barreda were killed by contra-rebels on January 7, 1983, because they had taken part in a coffee harvest in northern Nicaragua. They had made a conscious decision to go and pick coffee in order to rebuild the fragile country and build a future for the children of this country (Brockman 1985). This decision was based on their faith. It was a theological decision. We do theology because we experienced wounds and have a vision. The wounds of confusion and the vision of truth have led many people to a life committed to serving the people.

In his novel *Ah, But Your Land Is Beautiful*, South African writer Alan Paton describes the courage a young black South African displays by becoming involved in the social and political struggle against apartheid. He is well aware of the risk he takes and the possible wounds that might be inflicted on him, but he says: "I don't worry about the wounds. When I go up there, which is my intention, the Big Judge will say to me, Where are your wounds? and if I say I haven't any, he will say, Was there nothing to fight

for? I couldn't face that question" (Paton 1996, 66f.). We do theology because we experience the cross and hope in resurrection, we experience
suppression and hunger for justice. This is the powerful message of the
beatitudes. That is why we do theology: We experience wounds and share a
vision.

How? What? The Many Forms and Colors

**THESIS 6: There are many ways of doing theology. Theology is
like a family of many different activities centered around friendship with God.**

Teaching theology is not about conveying *the* right way of doing theology. Studying theology is not about getting to know *the* theological method.
On the contrary, the more we know about theology, the more we come to
appreciate its many forms and colors.

There are many forms of theology. Theology is taught and written, danced
and sung, sculpted and painted, even dreamed and cried. Think of Karl
Barth's famous theological dream—the dream that he was to examine Mozart
in dogmatics; think of the use of dreams in discernment processes or the
newly discovered importance of dreams in religious communities. Or consider the beauty of the ability to cry. When Henri Nouwen visited the grave
of a sixteen-year-old boy, the only son of his mother, together with the grieving
woman, he could not invite the boy to rise from the dead like Lazarus. "I
realized that my ministry lay more in powerlessness than in power; I could
give her only my tears" (Nouwen 1992, 91).

Theology can be done with gestures: embracing, kneeling, blessing. Henri
Nouwen experienced the power of gestures at the bed of a dying child: "I
showed Ray's father how to make the sign of the cross on Ray's forehead.
He had never done this before and cried as he signed his son in the name of
the Father, the Son, and the Holy Spirit. A father's blessing is so healing"
(Nouwen 1988, 43). In Luke 15:20 we find the loving father "moved with
compassion," running and falling upon his son's neck and kissing him. No
spoken word is mentioned. Indeed, the experience of people who have difficulties expressing themselves helps us to appreciate the value of gestures.
An Austrian bishop confirming mentally handicapped children did not
preach, but he touched each and every one and said, "The Holy Ghost is
caressing you and you and you. . . . " This is a "little theology" by way of
gestures!

Movies, novels, buildings, paintings show implicit theologies. Describing his impressions of Rembrandt's *The Pilgrims of Emmaus*, Henri Nouwen
comments: "The bare feet of Jesus and the two pilgrims were painted with
great detail. Not so the feet of the servant. Rembrandt obviously wanted us

to know about the long, tiring walk they had just made. The large door and the cape on the coat stand were also there to remind us of the journey. These men truly came from somewhere" (Nouwen 1988, 33).

American missiologist Stephen Bevans draws our attention to the point that theology need not be verbal. "Theology has always been embodied in ritual, as the rule *lex orandi, lex credendi* points out, and some of the most eloquent faith-seeking understanding the world has ever known is expressed in artworks ranging from paintings on catacomb walls, through the *figure* of Joachim of Fiore, to the sculpture of Michelangelo" (Bevans 2002). Theology needs to be local theology, using the materials suitable for the local context, in order to be meaningful.

Local theological expressions may be found in sculpture and drama and used for the construction of local theologies (Oduyoye 1986, 50; Cupitt 1977; Sofola 1979; Mahoney 1994, 65). The traditional Korean mask dance, to give another example, can be understood as a means of expressing Korean *minjung* theology.[3] Art and architecture are also valuable forms of expression of religious beliefs that have to be appropriated to local contexts. Peter Schineller writes: "One senses a tremendous gap between traditional African art and the art and statues of most Catholic churches. Instead of coming from the local soil, much church art has been imported from Europe; thus the local crucifix likely depicts the Jesus Christ of Ireland or Germany, and the Sacred Heart is a drawing from Italy or America" (Schineller 1990, 85).

Even silence might be an adequate way of doing theology. Ivan Illich talks about silence in the context of an attitude of respect and listening: "The silence of the city priest on a bus listening to the report of the sickness of a goat is a gift, truly the fruit of a missionary form of long training in patience. . . . Ultimately, missionary silence is a gift, a gift of prayer" (Illich 1970, 47, 49). Similarly, we may recall the advice to be silent "after Auschwitz," and Theodor Adorno's famous statement that no poems can be written after Auschwitz.

There are many forms of doing theology, and consequently there are many ways of understanding theology. The many colors and forms of theology are reflected in the many definitions of *theology*: "speech or reasoning about God" (Augustine), "faith seeking understanding" (Anselm), "wisdom"

---

[3] "Through the mask dance, the people make fun of the ruling classes of the old Korean society" (David Kwang-sun Suh, "A Biographical Sketch of an Asian Theological Consultation," in *Minjung Theology: People as the Subjects of History*, ed. Commission on Theological Concerns of the Christian Conference of Asia [Maryknoll, N.Y.: Orbis Books, 1981], 27). Mask dances have a simple plot and express feelings of suppression and frustration with the political and social situation through jokes and ridicule. Even dirty jokes are part of the game of exposing the social disorder. It is through the mask dance that people can transcend the factual situation and reflect on the context in which they live.

(Bonaventure), "rational knowledge" (Thomas Aquinas), "critical reflection on praxis" (Gutiérrez). There is a danger in definitions, of course. If we eat beans and rice every day, we might think they are the only foods. If we go to a fast-food chain every day, we might assume this is the way it should be. Any dietary regime includes certain items and excludes others. Likewise, any definition includes certain aspects and excludes others.

Since I am trying to take the many forms and colors of theology and the incredible variety of local theological landscapes seriously, I will abstain from giving a definition. Rather than saying what theology is, I suggest looking at the many ways theology is being done. As Wittgenstein advised, "Don't think, but look!"[4] Don't try to come up with a universal and abstract definition! Look at what is *happening* in theology!

When we take a look at the theological activities, we find a number of related activities: teaching and preaching, counseling and planning, writing and discussing, studying and exchanging. The desk, the lectern, and the discussion table are part of the whole project of doing theology, as are the conference hall, the counseling room, the living room, the dining room, and even the shade of a tree. Thinking of diverse examples of doing theology broadens our view.

WHO IS DOING THEOLOGY? "WE, THE PEOPLE"

THESIS 7: Since doing theology is as natural as walking and talking, we all do theology, both as individuals and as a community. There is, however, a difference between explicit and implicit theologies, between trained and untrained theologians.

In the broadest sense, everyone does theology. Everyone asks theological questions, questions of origins and ends, questions of meaning and hope. All of us have at least implicit theologies if not explicit theological positions.

Asking theological questions, questions of ultimate concern, is too important a task to be left to professionals. "Not only professional, scientifically

---

[4] Ludwig Wittgenstein, *Philosophical Investigations* (Oxford: Basil Blackwell 1967), §66. The context of this quotation is Wittgenstein's reaction to the reproach that he talks about all sorts of language games but never says what the essence of a language game and hence of language is. He does not speak about the general form of propositions. Wittgenstein restricts himself to the indication that all the activities that we call games "are *related* to one another in many different ways" (§65). It is because of this sort of "family resemblance" (§67) that we call a whole set of activities "games." Similarly, we could say that there are family resemblances uniting the various fields of theology and the various activities we call "doing theology."

trained theologians but also others more directly engaged in the effort to transform their lives and society motivated by the Christian Faith can make valuable contributions to the elaboration of a theology relevant to our situations" (Balasuriya 1980, 16). And it is not even only people of faith who can contribute to theology, as we have seen. Theology is a natural part of religious praxis; that is, theology does not enter from the outside but is part of what we do in expressing our faith.

From the very beginning the proclaiming of the good news and the justification of our hope was part of religious practice itself. Nancey Murphy stresses the fact that theology finds its origins in amateurs rather than professional theologians (Murphy 1990, 196). Doing theology is indeed a Christian imperative. A famous passage in the first letter of Peter reminds us to be always ready with an answer to everyone who asks a reason for the hope that is in us (1 Pt 3:15). It is because of the witness of life and the ability to answer that we can testify to the depth of our hope and the foundations of how we understand ourselves and our lives.

Again, this is not a luxurious act that comes in addition to living faith. Understanding the faith is part of our faith life. "Living faith calls for and demands theology. Theologizing is an imperative of Christian (and, I would say, simply human) existence" (Clodovis Boff 1987, xiii). Asking fundamental questions is part of who we are. That is why *everyone* does theology, at least implicitly, however rich or poor our implicit theologies may be.

The fact that everyone does theology has certain consequences. First, everybody is, at least implicitly, concerned with theological questions. This could be an invitation to do theology as if all people, believers and nonbelievers, mattered. Second, professional theologians cannot deny a mandate to nonprofessional theologians. Professional theologians do not have a monopoly. Even more so, professional theologians have to concede theological competence outside of professional theological reflection. There is theological wisdom outside of (professional) theology. Third, explicit theologies have to work with implicit theologies and consider them a very important theological source.

However, not everybody is equally talented (or "called") to do theology. It makes sense to talk about the "vocation of the theologian" (see Jennings 1985). A person who has embarked on a long journey of theological studies is able to make a contribution that is clearly different from that of a person who can draw only from personal experience. And a person who has encountered many different forms of theology is in a good position to place particular theologies in a larger context.

This does not mean, however, that professional theologians receive special forms of revelation. Theologians have no special channel to God. The doctor of theology is not like Doctor Dolittle, who could speak the language of his animal patients. The theologian does not speak the language of God in the way Italians speak the language of their country. Actually, it is not so much the ability to talk but the abilities to listen and to observe that make a good theologian. Moses, Aaron, and Jeremiah were not famous for their rhetorical skills before they became prophets.

There are different tasks in theological reflection and different skills required, but there must not be a gap between professional and nonprofessional theologians. They belong to the same community and share the same concerns and priorities, namely, bringing about the kingdom of God. Against this background, another idea has been brought forward: the image of the good theologian as a good companion. J. J. Mueller characterizes the theologian as a disciple who is journeying with fellow disciples (Mueller 1988, 92-97). As a companion, local theologians should be able to speak the language, sing the songs, and recite the poems of the people they live with and the culture of which they are a part.

There is another important point. Our community of faith helps us to make experiences and find words. Sometimes theologians are like a voice in the wilderness, lonely prophets. But even then they speak the language of their people. We take from the treasure of a rich tradition. We sing songs other people have written, we share stories other people have told, we use insights other people have gained. Theologians are called to serve a community of believers.

Genuine theology, then, is "Fuenteovejuna theology." Justo González talks about the communal nature of doing theology by referring to Lope de Vega's play *Fuenteovejuna*. Fuenteovejuna is a small town in Spain. The town is under tyrannical rule; the knight commander is murdered; an investigation is held into who did it. Again and again the question is asked, "Who killed the commander?" And again and again the investigators receive the same answer: "Fuenteovejuna." The judge asks for instructions from Isabella and Ferdinand, who conclude that, given such unanimity, there must have been just cause for the commander's death (González 1990, 28f.). Theology unites individuals in a common struggle, the struggle for the kingdom of God. Theology is a communal enterprise.

Where? Theology and the Village

THESIS 8: Theology is always done from a certain perspective within a particular context.

The first answer to the question "Where is theology being done?" has to be "In the village." The idea is simple. Theology is done "from somewhere," from a particular perspective, out of a particular context. Theology can be done under the shade of a tree, at a street corner talking to a homeless person, in a bus talking to the person in the next seat. John Mahoney gives an account of his theological work in Fiji: "Much of our best discussion took place in small villages while drinking yaqona, discussing immediate problems, celebrating festive occasions, preparing for sacraments" (Mahoney 1994, 8). Theology is done where people care about life. And theology is always done by people who are "somewhere"—somewhere in a context, somewhere in a net of relationships, somewhere in their lives, somewhere in their intellectual and spiritual journeys.

Theology is always done with a "backpack." In this backpack we find all the things that our family and friends, our culture and tradition, our training and experience have packed for us. We have packed only a few things ourselves. We hardly know about all the things we carry. No question: it is a mess. Our backpack is full of things we do not use, and it lacks other things we need. It contains the proverbs we have heard, the books we have read, our memories of people and encounters and experiences, and our favorite words and ideas. No two theologians have the same backpack!

The practice of theology takes place at a certain time, at a certain place. We are always "somewhere."[5] Theology is done from a village and not from the clouds. Austrian philosopher Ludwig Wittgenstein remarked at some point in his notes that the gospels talk about cottages, and that only Paul creates a palace. There is a stable and not St. Peter's basilica. There is a small village and not the Eternal City.

The origins of Christianity are found in an unspectacular local setting. Jesus grew up in a village. He was familiar with the local customs. His life was lived *somewhere*. In Jesus, in the incarnation, God became human in a particular local culture. "God became flesh in a human person of such and such a height, with particular color hair, with particular personality traits" (Bevans 2002, 8).[6]

Jesus, human and divine, accepts the challenge of the local culture with its chances and limits. He raises his prophetic voice after having been introduced to the local culture. He does not start from scratch. Genuine prophecy has to use familiar concepts in order to have an impact. "Only a theology firmly rooted in a culture can be genuinely prophetic in that same culture.

---

[5] There is no view from nowhere except as a normative ideal that has both its value and its limits in the sciences. The American philosopher Thomas Nagel asks the simple question, What is it like to be a bat? We can, of course, imagine how it would be to fly around in the dark, equipped with certain sensory capacities, but we can never imagine what it is like for a bat to be a bat. There is a certain theological point hidden here. I am a white, male, European theologian. I always look at things through my glasses, I always climb mountains with my backpack. See Thomas Nagel, *The View from Nowhere* (New York: Oxford University Press 1986); idem, "What Is It Like to Be a Bat?" *Philosophical Review* 83 (1974) 435-50.

[6] "If God really became man, then God neither did become nor could become universal man, for universal man does not exist" (Virgil Elizondo, *The Future Is Mestizo: Life Where Cultures Meet* [Bloomington, Ind.: Meyer-Stone Books, 1998], 76). See also C. H. Dodd, *The Founder of Christianity* {New York: Macmillan, 1970), chap. 3, where Jesus is described as a unique person with individual traits.

. . . Prophecy is effective when it reorganizes knowledge already part of the culture. To stand completely outside is to be ignored. Thus, the more contextually rooted a theology, the more acute can be its prophetic voice and action" (Schreiter 1991, 24). Theology has to refer to the well-known in order to communicate God's message. That is why the parables Jesus uses are rooted in local life.

Theology is done "in a village," within a particular local culture. St. Paul tries to do locally appropriate theology. He tries to live in the village with the people and tries to speak their language. He preaches the gospel "not with eloquent words" (1 Cor 1:17). He adapts to the language of the local people (Rom 3:5; 6:19; 1 Cor 3:2). He adapts to the lives of his hosts (1 Cor 9:20-22; Phil 4:11). The circumstances of life determine the measurement with which to judge (Rom 2:12; Mt 7:1-2). "Give no offense to Jews or to Greeks or to the church of God" (1 Cor 10:32; see 1 Pt 2:12f.). These thoughts are important not only for mission theology but also for theology in general. At the roots of Christianity there is a village. Humility is the art of living in a village, the art of being down to earth, close to the ground *(humus)*. Doing local theology is a service, like washing feet. You have to be close to the ground to do that. Local theologies are village theologies, theologies that are created within a village, using the available material. Local theologies, however, are also constant invitations to leave the village, to think beyond the village traditions and rules. Theologies that simply conform to the local rules are not doing justice to the local context.

A GUIDING IMAGE: THE LOCAL THEOLOGIAN AS VILLAGE COOK

THESIS 9: Many different images capture the work of a theologian. The idea of local theologies can be expressed through the image of the theologian as village cook. Doing local theology is like cooking with local ingredients.

After having asked a number of questions about the nature of theology, let us take a further step. It can be very useful to express a "guiding image" when talking about the nature of something. Jesus used such metaphors in talking about the kingdom (Lk 13:18-21; Mt 22:1-14; 18:23ff.). After having reflected briefly upon the why, how, what, who, and where of theology, I would like to develop a simple image—not primarily as an illustration, but as a contribution to the understanding of theological work. The guiding image gives us nuances and a "feeling" that a definition could not convey.

There are a number of images that could be chosen to describe the role of the local theologian. We could use the image of the doctor (dealing with the well-being of people just as Jesus did),[7] or we could choose the image of the repair person (repairing problems of religious practice) (see Dulles 1992; Sedmak 1999), or we could talk about the image of an artist (drawing pictures of unknown horizons and talking about utopias), the image of a pilgrim on a pilgrimage toward the Holy City, together with fellow-pilgrims, or the image of the listener to the word (the word of God, the word of community and friends, the word of culture).

The image I choose for the theologian, however, is the image of the cook. We should not forget that Jesus fed people, talked about the bread of life and the hunger and thirst for justice, and used the banquet as a metaphor for the kingdom of God. Jesus used the images of food and eating to express his message. We are called to take part in these feeding and nourishing activities Jesus speaks about. Theologians are called to be creative cooks. The local theologian can indeed be compared to a cook, and not to an employee in a pizza delivery where he or she delivers ready-made products. The theologian, however, is not free to cook anything he or she likes. A local theologian is not working in a "divine deli," where "anything goes."[8]

---

[7] Bernard Häring, who served as a medical helper in the Second World War, comments: "My wartime service as medical helper brought me to a deeper understanding of Christ as savior, as physician, as the one who comes not to judge but to heal" (*Embattled Witness: Memories of a Time of War* [New York: Crossroad, 1976], 9). This image is useful to emphasize the need for professionalism and detachment. Doctors are concerned with people's well-being, but in doing their work they cannot give in to all emotions. "Anthony de Mello liked the image of a surgeon. He called it the perfect example. The surgeon applies all his skills, powers and interest to the operation he is performing, but is at the same time without any emotion, bias or attachment that would precisely impair his work. Do your duty and stay calm. That attitude serves lives" (C. G. Valles, *Unencumbered by Baggage: Tony de Mello, a Prophet for Our Times* [Gujarat: Gujarat Shitya Prakash, 1987], 44).

[8] See John H. Berthrong, *The Divine Deli: Religious Identity in the North American Cultural Mosaic* (Maryknoll, N.Y.: Orbis Books, 1999). There is a richness in having choices and there is a danger. In any case, there is a variety of choices, and more and more people make individual selections from various menus. "We can learn how to handle chopsticks and knives, spoons, and forks as we sample the divine deli. The divine reality has provided all of us with a truly cosmic gastronomic range of choices" (xxiii). In view of all the possibilities given we have no choice but making choices. In *The Heretical Imperative* Peter Berger talks about modern people being forced into heresy. He speaks about the "heretical imperative," that is, the necessity to choose a religious faith among many offers on the "religious market" (*The Heretical Imperative: Contemporary Possibilities of Religious Affirmation* [New York: Anchor Press, 1979]). We can see the price we have to pay for religious pluralism. Considering some of the implications of the "divine deli" (privatization of religious beliefs, destruction of unity and community, religion as just another commodity), it is important to stress limits. Local theologies are called to respect the framework of a community with its traditions.

The local theologian is part of a community that provides ingredients and shares the food. The local theologian can be regarded as a cook in a kitchen that also has nonprofessional cooks (theologians) at work.

Kosuke Koyama talks about the Thai theological kitchen and the Aristotelian pepper and the Buddhist salt used there. He talks about the implicit theologies that can be smelled from the kitchen while you are sitting in the living room. "My experience in peeping into the kitchen is sometimes like watching a great Chinese chef throwing six different ingredients into a heated oiled kwali. I can smell a most delicious aroma and I can see smoke, but I cannot identify the ingredients!" (Koyama 1999, 83). There are so many nuances and "inside aspects" that are hardly accessible to an outsider. Sometimes outsiders are not even able to see the differences (have you ever been in the company of a connoisseur who talks about the many different kinds of wine?). It is meaningful to compare doing local theology with cooking and the product of local theology with food:

- we eat because we are hungry (we do theology out of hunger and thirst)
- food is to be served (theology has a service function)
- food is necessary but always found within a cultural context (doing theology is natural but always takes a particular cultural shape)
- food nourishes and energizes (theology empowers)
- sharing food can be a purpose in itself (like sharing theological discussions)
- sharing food ties a community together (theology is community-building)
- food is, next to language, *the* local cultural product par excellence; there is Thai food and Filipino food and Kenyan food and a cuisine française and a cucina Italiana and so forth. Each family has its favorite recipes (local theologies have particular nuances and particular flavors).

Doing local theology is like preparing local food. Food can be prepared by professionals, or by people who love to cook, or by people who have to cook. But everyone relies on prepared food. We distinguish between edible and inedible. But this distinction is not a sharp one (an authentic Bhutanese meal is so spicy that most Westerners are unable to eat it). There is a general framework of food in terms of the materials available on our planet. Similarly, there is a framework for local theology.

Ingredients can be imported, but they have to be adapted to the local purpose. A whole bag of potatoes can't be used the way it is. You have to select some potatoes, wash them, peel them, and prepare them. You will probably combine them with local ingredients and spices. And be aware of the tastes of your guests! If you prepare European food for Asian guests, for example, they might find it tasteless and boring. The question of how to avoid food poisoning is one of the key questions in constructing local theologies.

Cooking is done at a certain place. It has to be that way. That is why we invented the kitchen and the fireplace. Cooking, just like theologizing, takes place at a certain time, within a particular context. Cooking, just like doing theology, can be learned by way of courses and books—but good cooks, just like good theologians, do not always follow the recipes; they create recipes of their own, know how to cook without a book, know how to utilize locally available ingredients. Cooking can be creative without end.

If a new cook arrives in a village, he or she introduces the people to new recipes, to new ways of preparing and eating food. Can we understand the deep meaning of the idea that Jesus taught us a new way to eat? Isn't it significant that Jesus tells us: "When you give a banquet, invite the poor, the crippled, the lame, and the blind" (Lk 14:13)? What does this tell us about our theological cooking and our theological (soup) kitchens?

Exercise: Think of an image for the theologian. Unfold the different aspects of this image. Which aspects would you like to emphasize? Does the image you choose consider the many forms of theology?

2

Jesus

Teacher of Theology

THESIS 10: Jesus is our great teacher. Since he was talking about God, he was doing theology. It is helpful to look at the way Jesus did theology. We will take this look without an elaborate Christian theology. We will look at Jesus "B.C."

Obviously there is a difference between a meal that we can enjoy and a meal that is not enjoyable at all. How should we cook in our theological kitchen? Which ingredients should we use? For whom do we cook? It might be a good idea to go back to the foundations and look at Jesus, who nourished and taught, healed and celebrated. The image of Jesus as the host who invites us to his banquet is familiar. The image of Jesus, bread of life, is well known. What about Jesus as the village cook?

What can we learn from Jesus about theology? Jesus did not teach courses in a classroom. He had no syllabus. He didn't write a book. This is significant. It took quite some time to record some of Jesus' sayings and deeds. Jesus' life was a series of personal encounters. The portrait we find in the gospels shows how much Jesus' theology depended on the people, on their pains and wounds, questions and concerns.

There can be no doubt that Jesus was doing theology. He was proclaiming the good news, teaching and preaching, talking about God. He answered questions about our attitude toward life as such and toward the world as a whole. Jesus challenged his friends and encouraged his community. In the same voice with the disciples who asked Jesus "teach us to pray" (Lk 11:1), we could ask Jesus: Teach us how to do theology!

Jesus' life has often been judged from a Christian perspective using Christian categories. Albert Nolan, in contrast, wrote a widely acclaimed book taking a look at Jesus before Christianity. When we try to reconstruct Jesus' life from this perspective, we see the local categories and images used to describe Jesus' life. He is depicted both as a citizen of his local culture and as a local theologian fulfilling the task of challenging his local culture.

The gospels describe Jesus in order to show his *relevance* for local human existence: "The four small books that we call the gospels are not biographies and were never intended to be. Their purpose was to show how Jesus could be relevant to people who lived *outside* Palestine a generation or two *after* Jesus' death" (Nolan 2001, 13). We have to be careful not to jump to quick and narrow conclusions, however. The sources we have reveal a certain perspective and were written under particular circumstances. The image of the Pharisees in Matthew or the image of the Jews in John or the image of women in Paul's letters must be taken with a grain of salt. However, it is indispensable to look at the foundations of our faith prior to any elaborated theology. It is important to look at Jesus "B.C."

Jesus was teaching and preaching about God. He was doing theology, and he was doing it explicitly. Let us take a look at the way Jesus was doing theology. The very first impression one gets is that Jesus must have been skeptical regarding theology. His harsh words directed against the Pharisees seem to indicate that Jesus was actually unhappy with the prospect of systematic, learned theology. "Beware of the scribes!" (Lk 20:46). Jesus denied a sign to the scribes and Pharisees (Mt 12:38-42).

This impression that Jesus is no friend of academic theology becomes stronger when one thinks of church officials and professors of theology today—aren't there in a number of cases striking similarities between them and the Pharisees as they are presented in the gospels? Doesn't that mean that the whole enterprise of theology is suspect? Are the shoes that professors and church dignitaries wear too big for the small path of Jesus?

Let us be optimistic. It is understood that the accounts of the Pharisees that we find in the gospels are filtered through special interests and perspectives. Jesus taught in the Temple (Lk 21:27) and the synagogues (Mt 4:23; 9:35). These were the official teaching institutions at that time. So, Jesus was doing theology in more than a private and merely informal manner.

The way Jesus dealt with scriptures shows his respect for these texts, and the way he argued reveals a high esteem for intellectual skills and the capabilities of human reason. In fact, he astonished people with his theological arguments at an early age (Lk 2:41-52). He did not despise studies and scholarship. It is significant that Saint Paul was made an apostle of Christ. Hence, I would not say that Jesus was in any way against theology. But the example of his life points in a very particular direction. Looking at the whole context of Jesus' life, we can ask how Jesus did theology.

THE LOCAL LIFE OF JESUS, THE CHRIST

THESIS 11: Jesus' life is described as a human existence within a certain local culture. He was rooted in the religious traditions of his time and place. Jesus' life is described as a sequence of face-to-face actions on a local (especially rural) level. Jesus is, however, also described as a person challenging local cultural standards and raising a universal claim.

Jesus was "somewhere"; his genealogy, his place in history is clearly described (Mt 1:1-17). Jesus started at the very beginning as does any human being—as a baby. Everyone who has some experience with babies knows what this means: helplessness, dependency, and a need to learn, grow, and mature. Jesus was "born into a little people, a nation of little importance by comparison with the great powers of the time" (Gutiérrez 1991, 86).

Jesus is also made part of a local tradition by the many references to the prophets throughout the gospels. This shows the attempt to describe Jesus as a legitimate citizen of a local tradition. Jesus is placed by the public in the local cultural context (see Jn 7:40-44). The circumstances of his birth are told in a very detailed way (Lk 2).

The first aspect of the local life of Jesus, the Christ, is Jesus' situatedness in a particular local culture. Jesus was rooted in a local culture, expressing himself in the local language, using local experiences and local images in his parables (Denzinger 1991, 4332, 4404; Soares-Prabhu 1988, 109-10).[1] He was a member of his cultural community. Jesus shared the hopes and fears of his people (Denzinger 1991, 4611). It can be argued that Jesus had a home and local roots (Nolan 2001, 46). The famous passages Matthew 8:20 and Luke 9:58 might have been taken too literally in the past. "Besides it is difficult to understand how Jesus could have been accused of entertaining sinners (Lk 15:2) if he did not have some kind of a home in which to do so" (ibid.; see Mk 1:29, 35; 2:1-2; Mt 4:13). Finally, the most important period in Jesus' life for the project of doing local theology is Jesus' "middle period," the so-called hidden life of Jesus.[2]

---

[1] "Jesus taught with imagery taken from his culture, pointing to the birds of the air, the lilies of the field, the sower and the seed, and so on, to explain the mysteries of the kingdom" (Peter Schineller, *A Handbook on Inculturation* [New York: Paulist Press, 1990]).

[2] Charles de Foucauld, appropriating the perspective of Jesus, wrote: "What was the meaning of that part of my life? I led it for your instruction. I instructed you continually for thirty years, not in words, but by my silence and example. What was

We do not know anything about Jesus after the story about the twelve-year-old Jesus in the Temple and the beginnings of Jesus' public activities. There are almost twenty years in the life of Jesus that are missing in the acknowledged gospels. It is this period of time that gives rise to the assumption that Jesus was very much rooted in his time. Otherwise, the historians of his time and the authors of the gospels might have found it important to mention details of that period of Jesus' life. The very fact that this is not the case can be taken as an indication that Jesus' life during that period was locally rooted and unspectacular.

"Jesus was a Jew. He was born into Judaism, subject to the law of Moses, and lived within the limits of that law. The movement he founded stood in the tradition of the Old Testament prophetic movement and that of John the Baptist (Ukpong 1994, 57).[3] Jesus used important Jewish sources in his ministry himself (for example, Mt 11:10); he was a law-abiding citizen. He asked the healed leper to show himself to the priests and offer for his cleansing "what Moses prescribed" (Mk 1:44). Jesus' family followed the local laws. This is shown in the passages that retell the circumcision and the presentation of Jesus (Lk 2:21-40). His parents followed the Jewish customs, and Jesus and his disciples themselves respected the Jewish feasts and rituals. Jesus did not intend to abolish the law (Mt 5:17).

There can be no doubt that the localness of Jesus' life is a key to understanding Jesus; Jesus was doing theology "in the village." Jesus' life was a life full of local encounters. It is significant that Jesus did not live in the urban context of New York City in the twenty-first century! Jesus is described as a "country person" who taught mainly in rural areas (Soares-Prabhu 1988, 98-100). With the exception of Jerusalem, Jesus seems not to have preached in any other significant town in Galilee or Judea. We encounter Jesus at quite insignificant places like Nazareth (Mt 2:23; Mk 1:9), in remote fishing villages like Bethsaida (Mk 6:45; 8:22; Lk 9:10), and in little provincial villages like Capernaum (Mt 9:1; Mk 1:21; 2:1; 9:33; Lk 10:15).

Jesus' disciples are also countryfolk. Peter betrayed his identity, possibly through his rural accent (Mt 26:73). Jesus is described as walking through the villages and towns and meeting many people, his life a series of personal encounters (Rayan 1984, 83). Jesus was dealing with "little people." This is significant because history is usually written about the powerful, rich, and

---

I teaching you? I was teaching you primarily that it is possible to do good to men . . . without using words, without preaching, without fuss. . . . I was teaching you to live by the labor of your own hands" (*Spiritual Autobiography of Charles de Foucauld*, ed. J. F. Six [New York: Kenedy & Sons, 1964], 82f.).

[3] See B. H. Young, *Jesus the Jewish Theologian* (Peabody, Mass.: Hendrickson Publishers, 1995). Young describes Jesus as a theologian who is deeply rooted in the Jewish tradition. He depicts the Jewish roots of Jesus' kingdom theology (part 2) and the Jewish theology in Jesus' parables (part 3).

famous (Nolan 2001, 28). In the light of his very unspectacular life for many years during his life time we could say that Jesus led the life of a worker (Denzinger 1991, 4332).[4] As a woodworker, Jesus belonged to a social class even below the peasants, since woodworkers did not own land. It is indicative that Jesus was not a member of the highest classes.

The localness of Jesus is one aspect of his life. On the other hand, Jesus challenged the local tradition. He became a stumbling block for many people. He was not well received in his hometown as a prophet (Mt 13:53-58); this indicates that there is a contrast between the ordinary life of Jesus within his local culture and his public ministry. The tension expressed in that passage is the tension between Jesus' local existence and his invitation to transcend the local context.

Jesus introduced new categories like "being born from above" (Jn 3:5-8) or "freedom" (Jn 8:34-38) or "living water" (Jn 4:10-14) and caused confusion and amazement. Jesus challenged the perception of the people around him by talking about the official's daughter and Lazarus as "sleeping" (Mt 9:24; Jn 11:11). His parables are challenges and, although in familiar language, are frequently misunderstood, even by his disciples (Mk 4:10; Mt 13:36; 16:11-12). Jesus wanted the law to be understood at its deepest level. So he placed the fasting (Mt 9:14) and the Sabbath law (Mt 12:1) in a new, deeper, more human context in which the law served the well-being of people and was not an end in itself.

Local cultures, like individuals, are in need of transformation, in need of conversion. This is part of our concept of the kingdom of God. It is this invitation to "go beyond," to walk the extra mile, to risk the exodus. Jesus questioned local norms, invited outsiders and sinners, and redefined social borders; we can see this in the encounters with the Samaritan woman (Jn 4) and with his family (Mt 12:46-50) (Nolan 2001, 27-36; Cunningham 1988, 127f.; Senior 1992, 61-73). Jesus gave new value to old traditions by reinterpreting them; he reinterpreted the Paschal meal through the institution of the eucharist, and he reinterpreted the Sabbath. Respecting local traditions means reappropriating them in the light of change and new challenges.

Jesus is not only the cornerstone but also the stumbling block. Jesus talked about the seriousness of following him (Mt 16:24-28) and used the image of sheep among wolves (Mt 10:16). He challenged the local contexts of his time to transcend the village, to refound the village, to discover differences and alternatives. Jesus had a universal claim, crossing the threshold of his

---

[4] The image of Jesus the worker has been influential for the worker-priests in France and the Catholic Worker Movement in the United States. "Christ Himself was a worker. St. Joseph, His foster father, was a worker. A man who works with his hands as well as with his head is an integrated personality. He is co-creator, taking the raw materials God provided and creating food, clothing, and shelter, and all manner of beautiful things" (Dorothy Day, *From Union Square to Rome* [New York: Arno Press, 1978], 150).

local culture. There is a paradox between the universal savior and the provincial teacher (Smith 1969, chap. 4).

What can we learn from Jesus about doing theology? We can, first of all, see that it is not easy to take our tradition seriously and to consent to it. Appropriating the tradition is a creative act that asks us to uncover its true concern rather than merely follow its external form. We also learn that theology has to be rooted, that we as theologians have to be rooted in a village, in a community of reference. And we also learn that we must not consider our village the ultimate norm. We cannot expect all villages to be structured in the way our own village is organized. Jesus was rooted in a village, but he did not stay there!

THE AUTHORITY OF JESUS

THESIS 12: Jesus did theology with authority that was not his. The basis of Jesus' doing theology was his relation with God. That is why he sought out spaces for prayer and solitude. He did theology as one sent, and he used this authority to serve God and the people.

Jesus started his theological mission after accepting the baptism of John the Baptist, after a time of probation (the temptations), and after a time of prayer, meditation, and solitude (Mt 4; Mk 1:35-36). It is important to see that Jesus took up the task of doing theology publicly only after a process of spiritual formation. Furthermore, Jesus is described as a person who withdrew for prayer and meditation (Mt 14:13; Lk 4:42; 5:16; 9:10-11; Jn 8:1). Jesus prayed and meditated before making decisions; it was after a night of prayer that he summoned the Twelve (Lk 6:12-16). He also went with his disciples to deserted places to reenergize them (Mk 6:30-33; Jn 11:54).

Jesus was doing theology to show the way to someone other than himself. Both the foundations and the message of Jesus' theology were life in God. This is the basis of Jesus authority, a basis he touched again and again in prayer and solitude. Only out of his intimacy with God could Jesus teach and preach. Their relationship is so close that Jesus used the word *Abba* to talk to and about God.[5] The intimate relationship with God was the basis

---

[5] "The word [*Abba*] implied deep intimacy. Now the Old Testament had spoken of God as Father. God was the Father of orphans and the Father of the nation. Jesus' usage was remarkable on two counts: It uses 1) the diminutive form 2) in personal direct address to God. The sense of intimacy with God expressed in the term *Abba* exceeded the generally accepted limits in Judaism" (D. A. Helminiak,

for Jesus' prophetic language, which is grounded in a deeper, mystical language.

It is on this basis that Jesus was able to teach with authority. Among the attributes Brazilian theologian Leonardo Boff uses to describe Jesus, I would like to mention the very astute observation that Jesus is a person who had the courage to say: "I" (Leonardo Boff 1987, 115-18). He had the courage to stand up against the tradition ("You have heard . . . but I say to you" [Mt 5:21f., 27-28, 33-34, 38-39, 43-44]). Jesus was doing theology "with authority" (Mt 7:29) (see Grollenberg 1978, chap. 7). He ratified this authority in practical deeds, by healing (Mt 9:5) and feeding (Mt 15:37). Jesus pointed at the fruit as the ratification of his mission (Mt 11:5). We could say that he was one with his message. Jesus' message also gets authority by the witness of his whole life. He was willing to endure the consequences.

Jesus used his authority to serve—to serve God in fulfilling God's will and to serve the people in being their servant. Daniel Berrigan discovers "tenderness, majesty, and above all, personalism" in Jesus (Daniel Berrigan 1979, 19). Jesus was exercising his authority in a tender and personal way. People were astonished at his teaching because he was teaching "with authority" (Lk 4:32). The question "By what authority are you doing theology?" (see Lk 20:2) is an important question, until now.

People knew that Jesus' authority was not the authority of the scholar (Jn 7:15). Jesus' answer to those questioning his authority is very clear: "My teaching is not mine but his who sent me" (Jn 7:16). He was doing theology by way of imperatives because he was clear about the fact that his mission was not his. Jesus was authorized by the Father (Lk 3:21-22). Jesus did not go out to preach on his own; he was sent (Jn 5:23; 7:28-29). Jesus explicitly mentioned that if he glorified himself his glory would be nothing (Jn 8:54-58). There are similarities between Jesus and prophetical speech (Helminiak 1986, 68-71). Jesus was doing theology in a prophetic way— talking about a future and a hope for his people. The God of Jesus is the God of the kingdom Jesus proclaims (see Lois 1993, 179-82).

The center of proclaiming God is our relationship with God. Jesus teaches us that theology is theocentric, God-centered, and that it serves both God

---

The Same Jesus: A Contemporary Christology [Chicago: Loyola University Press, 1986], 74). "The central and decisive fact in the appearance of Jesus was the renewal of the sense of the present immediacy of God" (John B. Cobb Jr., *The Structure of Christian Existence* [Philadelphia: Westminster, 1967], 111). Jesus "knew God as the presently active reality that had incomparably greater reality than the world of creaturely things. He lived and spoke out of the immediacy of this reality" (ibid., 112). This relationship was new and is a key to understanding Jesus: "The research of J. Jeremias . . . has placed it beyond all doubt that Jesus addressed God as *abba*, that he taught others to do the same (Lk 11:2) and that no one else had ever done this before" (Albert Nolan, *Jesus before Christianity*, twenty-fifth anniv. ed. [Maryknoll, N.Y.: Orbis Books, 2001], 97).

and the people. Theology is not about self-promotion and seeking one's own glory.

THE PASTORAL THEOLOGY OF JESUS

THESIS 13: Jesus was doing theology with common sense. He invited people to use their own judgment and trusted in the capabilities of human reasoning. This can be illustrated by the parable of the good Samaritan.

Jesus was doing theology as a pragmatic person. We can see Jesus' appeal to common sense in the way he talked about the Sabbath law (Mt 12:1-14). Jesus talked about priorities and human needs (see Lk 13:10-17; 14:5; Jn 5:1-19). He trusted that human beings are capable of making judgments. He invited John's disciples to make up their mind by looking at the fruit of his ministry (Mt 11:4-5). He knew that people can make valid judgments (Lk 12:54). He argued logically against the Pharisees (Lk 11:14-52). He asked those he healed what they wanted him to do.

Jesus honored common sense and sound reason. We can think of his sayings on discipleship: "For which of you, intending to build a tower, does not first sit down and estimate the cost, to see whether he has enough to complete it? . . . Or what king, going out to wage war against another king, will not sit down first and consider whether he is able with ten thousand to oppose the one who comes against him with twenty thousand?" (Lk 14:28, 31). Jesus invited people to use their common sense.

The common-sense attitude of Jesus is a pastoral attitude that permeates his sense of ministry and interaction. It can be traced in the parable of the good Samaritan (Lk 10:30-37). This parable points to the way to do local theology.

- The good Samaritan is not expecting the situation. He is moved by the occasion, changes his schedule, and adjusts to the needs of the situation. His ministry is service in context.
- Compassion is the primary motivation of his ministry.
- He takes care of the victim according to his means; after that, recognizing his limits, he delegates the task of attending to the man to a local professional, the innkeeper.
- The good Samaritan continues his journey as planned; he does not give up everything because of the emergency situation.
- The good Samaritan accepts the responsibility and promises to return to the innkeeper on his way back to pay whatever more is due.

This is an impressive model of doing local ministry. It provides an example of ministry based on common sense and on compassion. It is important for our understanding of theology to see that Jesus honors reason, judgment, and common sense. Being down to earth can be an expression of humility. It is vital for our theological efforts to recognize the trust Jesus puts in human capabilities. But it is equally vital to see his emphasis on life. Jesus looks at what people do rather than what they say. Jesus even gives the message that the common understanding of "orthodoxy" ("know your faith") is not the ultimate thing. We should not forget that the Samaritan was not a person of "right faith" but a Samaritan, one whose faith was considered "unbelief" by Jesus' Jewish hearers!

THEOLOGICAL OCCASIONS

THESIS 14: Jesus did "situational theology." He had an eye for detail, the small things and the "little people." Jesus used occasions to do theology, and he respected the dynamics of particular situations. We could see this as an invitation to do "leaflet theology" rather than "book-length theology."

Jesus did not give formal courses. With the exception of a few passages that portray Jesus teaching in the synagogues, the gospels talk about Jesus as teaching and preaching in villages, in fields, on mountains, and on the road. Jesus was using *occasions*. Jesus was flexible in doing theology; he changed his pastoral approach according to the situation, thus living the parable of the good Samaritan. This is shown in the encounter with a centurion in Capernaum (Mt 8:5-13). Jesus was doing theology according to the "signs of the times" (Mt 16:3-4).

It is remarkable that Jesus is very often depicted as the addressee of people's demands: sick people are brought to Jesus, people call Jesus for help. We could say that Jesus reacts to local needs; his theology is "user oriented." Jesus respected people in need and asked them what kind of ministry they were seeking (Mt 20:29). On the other hand, he was not willing to "sell" his ministry for the sake of demonstrating something (Mt 16:1-4; Mk 8:10-12); he refused to give a sign, he refused gratifications such as fame, money, and power.

Jesus did local theology also in the sense that he did not use prefabricated notions. He did not impose ready-made theological categories on people. This can be illustrated by looking at the story of the man with the withered arm who was cured by Jesus on a Sabbath (Mk 3:1-5). Uruguayan theologian Juan Segundo comments on this passage: "Jesus rejects

the possibility of forming any concrete judgment on the basis of theology or
its realm of competence. One cannot begin with certitudes deduced from
revelation. . . . To paraphrase Gutiérrez once again, theology is the second
step in the methodology of Jesus and the first step in the methodology of the
Pharisees" (Segundo 1976, 78).

Jesus went with the tide. That is why he was willing to learn in the encounter with the Canaanite woman (Mt 15:21-28). That is why he adjusted
to the needs of the times: he took time to stay two days with the Samaritans
(Jn 4:41); he took time to stay with friends who needed him (Jn 11:6-7).
Jesus lived in the present, in the here and now. There is an amazing local
attentiveness in Jesus.

Jesus also used the local material to heal and cure. He did not carry
ointments or powders. He used the soil and his spittle (Mk 7:31-37; Jn 9:6-
7). Jesus characterized those who are part of his mission as householders
who bring forth from their storerooms things new and old (Mt 13:52); this
could be understood as a statement saying: Everything you need is there;
everything you need for your mission is in your hands. Jesus respected local
theological resources. This is also shown in the mission of the disciples,
who are to go forth without taking much baggage (Mt 10:5).

Jesus used local observations as a starting point of his teaching, as he did
in the experience of the widow's offering (Mk 12:41-44). Jesus respected
the dynamics of a situation and did not impose rote judgments; an illustration of his readiness to listen and see is the encounter with the woman
caught in adultery (Jn 8). Jesus is depicted as a person who listened and
perceived rather than talking and judging. He did not react to the situation
with a general judgment but with an unexpected and unprecedented response.

Jesus' eye for detail is also shown in the way he dealt with people. He
treated everyone with dignity. He respected people's privacy and did not
permit anyone except Peter, James, and John to enter with him into the
house of Jairus to see Jairus's daughter (Lk 8:51). Jesus respected small
things and "little people," like children and social outsiders, the sick and
marginalized. Jesus had a special compassion "for the little ones" (Mt
10:42;11:25-27; 18:5-6, 10; Mk 9:41-42; Lk 7:13).[6] He emphasized that
his wisdom was revealed to the "little ones" and kept from the wise and

---

[6] See Gustavo Gutiérrez, On Job: God-Talk and the Suffering of the Innocent
(Maryknoll, N.Y.: Orbis Books, 1987), xii. Gutiérrez underlines that Jesus took a
position contrary to the cultural expectations and against the mainstream. Who are
"the little ones"? "The 'little children' are related to the poor, the hungry, and the
afflicted (Luke 6:20-23); to sinners and the sick (who are despised on this account)
(Matt. 9:12-13); to sheep who have no shepherd (Matt. 9:36); to the little ones
(Matt. 10:42; 18:1-4); to those not invited to the banquet (Luke 14:16-24). All
these categories form a bloc, a sector of people; they are 'poor of the land'" (ibid).

prudent; he blessed the children as living parables of the kingdom (Mt 19:13-15; Lk 10:21).

These are key ideas for understanding theology as a series of local theologies. Jesus seems to encourage local theologies that rise to the particular circumstances. He teaches us to do theology "unencumbered by baggage." He challenges our ideas of general theories. Jesus invites us to wake up—to see the small things and to discover the dynamics and proper weight of situations. Theology becomes an art, the art of looking at details, the art of responding to the "little ones."

Theology is always in the making, reading the signs of the times. Jesus is walking, not standing; he is always on the road. Jesus teaches a "theology of leaflets" rather than a "theology of books." Jesus encourages oral theology and "little theologies" for particular occasions. He suggests that the particular situation rather than the full "backpack" of prefabricated notions should serve as a source for theology.

A THEOLOGY THAT BUILDS COMMUNITY
"AS IF PEOPLE MATTER"

THESIS 15: Jesus did theology to build up community. He called everyone into community, a community that is constantly "on the move." Doing theology as Jesus did is a community-building enterprise.

Jesus called people into community and redefined the borders of the local communities of his time. Service to God cannot be rendered if one's communal life is in disorder (Mt 5:23-25). Jesus called people to community (Mt 4:18-22); he instituted disciples with authority and created new social networks (Mt 10); he introduced forms of fraternal correction and an order of life valid for his disciples (Mt 18:15-18). In this way Jesus instituted a community.

It is remarkable how often Jesus is depicted in the company of his friends. "One of the most touching and revealing aspects of the gospel story is that of Jesus in the company of his disciples. They are an almost constant presence, gaping in awe at his acts of power. They are confidants of his most important teaching, at his side as his mission drove him through the crowds of Galilee. . . . All of the gospels relate that one of the first things Jesus did was to gather disciples" (Senior 1992, 51). Jesus proclaimed the good news and brought people together. The crowds that Jesus attracted were amazing. People came together to be healed and nourished. Jesus was a wise community leader. He distinguished between his close disciples and the crowd. He felt responsible for the crowd as well, attending to them and being present, but he spoke differently to his disciples, more intimately—the language of friendship.

Jesus did theology by bringing people together, by building community, and by living friendships. Consequently, the Jesus-disciples differ significantly from the rabbi-disciples at that time. Thus, Jesus offered a new way of community building. The following characterized Jesus' way of building community, of forming a "Jesus community":

- Jesus chose his disciples; he was the founder and the center of the community; it was not primarily the disciples who chose him (Jn 15:16; Mk 3:13; Lk 9:59).
- The community of life with Jesus is an end in itself; it need not be justified with reference to other external factors (Mt 10:24-25).
- Jesus empowered and sent his disciples to proclaim the kingdom of God and to make its presence felt (Lk 9:60; Mk 3:14).
- Jesus called everyone to become his disciple; his community is "an open society"; he even called the rich and the outsiders (Mk 1:16-20; 2:14; Lk 6:15). Jesus called disciples rather than accepting demands for discipleship (Mt 4:18).
- Jesus exhorted his disciples to humility and service and did not promote strict hierarchies within the structure of his disciples (Mt 23:5-12).
- The disciples of Jesus in turn did not form their own disciples (Mt 5:19; Mk 6:30) (see Fuellenbach 1998, 91f.).

We could say that the community that Jesus founded is to be characterized by its intrinsic tendency to overcome local contexts. Second, the Jesus community is characterized by its localness in the sense that it is rooted in a person, Jesus. It is the itinerant person, not a place, that gives the community its local identity. The way Jesus showed was a way open to everyone. He called everyone and invited everyone to convert and be transformed. The Jesus community is "on the road." Jesus described the way of following him in terms of an ongoing journey (Mt 8:18-22). The follower of Jesus can never complacently sit down; the story of the transfiguration of Jesus (Mt 17:1-13) depicts this refusal to get too comfortable very impressively.

Jesus refused to settle down. He did not choose buildings in which to institutionalize his community. The Jesus community is defined by a person, not by a location. He called his disciples out of their ordinary life and invited them to a new way of life. Jesus' way of doing theology changed the life of his followers entirely.

When we think of our understanding of theology, we can see the importance of friendships and of bringing people together. Doing theology is an attempt to build communities, to strengthen the ties of a community. It is not surprising that Ignatius of Loyola emphasized the criterion of community building in decision making (Does the decision contribute to strengthening the community and to promoting unity?). This is an important consideration for theology. There is the invitation to build up and not to divide, to create unity and not conflicts. That is why John XXIII talked about the "medicine of mercy rather than that of severity" to be applied by the Second Vatican Council. Jesus' invitation to build community can be seen as an invitation to use the same wisdom in choosing the right medicine to attend to the wounds of the community.

THESIS 16: Jesus did theology with self-respect and with respect for others; he did theology "as if people matter." Healing and feeding, forgiving and teaching formed a unity in Jesus' way of doing theology. We can see this feature of Jesus' way of doing theology as an invitation to theologies that are vulnerable, modest, and a response to people's questions and needs.

Jesus was doing theology as if people matter.[7] He treated his fellow human beings with respect. As we have seen, Jesus had no doubts that humans are capable of making judgments (Lk 12:54-59) and decisions. It is in this spirit of empowerment and trust that Jesus called and commissioned his disciples. Jesus' way of doing theology was holistic in the sense that teaching, preaching, and healing went hand in hand (Mt 4:23-24; 9:35-36). Doing theology meant forgiving sins, instructing people, and healing human illness. Jesus fed the crowds, thus dealing with their basic needs (Mt 14:13-15; 15:32-33); he did not separate basic physical needs from the spiritual needs of the people.

Jesus was so committed to his ministry that he accepted the responsibilities involved; he took it as part of his responsibility for his sheep to feed the crowd when they had nothing to eat. Taking part in the mission of Jesus means to serve, to do ministry as if people matter, to render service to people. In this regard Jesus compared his mission with the responsibility of a physician (Lk 5:32).

A deep motivation and driving force for Jesus' doing theology was compassion for people. Jesus was compassionate. He was not afraid to touch people or to be touched. He touched the leper (Mt 8:3) and allowed the

---

[7] This phrase refers to E. F. Schumacher's *Small Is Beautiful*, which is a study in economics as if people matter. Schumacher wanted to stress the fact that economic systems (like the Sabbath and all religious norms [see Lk 6:6-11; 14:1-6]) are constructed because of the people and that they can serve this purpose only if their size is human and can be handled by the people.

woman suffering from a hemorrhage to touch him (Mt 9:20). He used his own saliva to heal (Mk 7:31-37; Jn 9). Jesus encountered people with tenderness (Nolan 2001, 37). Seeking the personal encounter was part of Jesus' *theological method* (Rayan 1984, 81; see Fuchs 1990, 31-45).

Jesus healed people, but he did not create dependencies. Again and again we find the invitation: Go! Go your way! Jesus did not heal people to have followers; he did not heal people to become famous; he was discreet about his healing ministry (see Mt 12:16) and healed people for their own sake. Jesus empowered the sick by telling them that the healing power was within them ("Your faith has made you well!" [Mk 10:52]). Jesus did theology as if people matter—irrespective of his own reputation and the categories of political correctness of his time.

Let us look at the spirit in which Jesus did theology. Christian spiritual life is life lived in the spirit of Jesus (Sobrino 1985, 2). Hence, it is important to analyze not only the deeds of Jesus but also the spirit in which Jesus acted.[8] Leonardo Boff, in an attempt to approximate the spiritual profile of Jesus, describes him as "a person of extraordinary good sense, creative imagination, and originality" (Leonardo Boff 1987, 11-15). Millar Burrows talks about the following "outstanding characteristics" of Jesus: devotion to the will of God, sincerity, patient endurance, love for the Father, consciousness of sonship, authority, insight into human nature, keenness of intellect, sense of proportion, rejection of asceticism, friendship with outcasts, relations with women, love of children, love of nature, humor, tolerance, anger, grief, compassion, mysticism, and prayer (Burrows 1977, 280-95). The following features must be considered when trying to understand the spiritual profile of Jesus:

- Jesus is consistent in his life—he accepts the consequences of his actions and his actions follow his convictions.
- Jesus does not want to say something new merely for the effect and whatever the cost.
- Jesus wants to understand; he appeals to sound reason.
- Jesus does not paint the world better or worse than it is. He is honest to reality, the visible, and the invisible.
- All that is authentically human is seen in Jesus: anger and joy, goodness and toughness, friendship, sorrow, and temptation.

---

[8] Knowledge about Jesus in a theological perspective, consequently, is practical knowledge: "Knowing Christ . . . is something we achieve not intellectually, but in doing. We know him to the extent that we understand what he did through experience, and by assimilating this and making it ours, we come to be more fully in tune with his cause and his person, which complement one another. . . . The best setting for really knowing Jesus is simply carrying out what he did, following him" (Pedro Casaldáliga and J. M. Vigil, *Political Holiness* [Maryknoll, N.Y.: Orbis Books, 1994], 65).

What does that mean for theology? What does it mean to do theology as if people matter? There is certainly the aspect of wholeness. Doing theology as if people matter cannot separate the hunger for God from the hunger for life. The bread of life and the daily bread cannot be separated in our theological work. There is certainly the aspect of responsibility: it is the responsibility that we see in the parable of the good Samaritan. Doing theology as if people matter means responding to people. There is certainly the aspect of authenticity. Doing theology as if people matter is a call for spiritual and intellectual honesty. Good theology is not judged by the *finesse* of its rhetoric but by its truthfulness.

GOOD THEOLOGY

THESIS 17: Jesus talked about the criteria for good theology. The most obvious criterion is the criterion of the good fruit, but he also saw this fruit coming from modest beginnings. Jesus taught that the full variety of good fruits came from a variety of sources or ministries (theologies). Jesus did theology according to the criteria of sustainability, appropriateness, empowerment, and challenge.

The criterion of good theology is the kind of fruits it bears (Mt 7:15-20; 12:33-38). Jesus stressed that the kingdom starts small (Mk 4:30-32).[9] Any natural fruit begins small. Jesus, when asked about his credibility, offered the fruits as the criteria by which to judge the way he did theology: the blind see, the lame walk, the lepers are cleansed, the deaf hear, the dead rise, the poor have the gospel preached to them (Mt 11:5-6). The fruits are the main criteria.

There are many good fruits by many good trees. We can think of the different local theologies as a garden full of trees. There are apple trees and

---

[9] Gerald A. Arbuckle took up this point in requiring the quality of a commitment to small beginnings as an important quality of a pastoral change agent (Gerald A. Arbuckle, *Out of Chaos: Refounding Religious Communities* [New York: Paulist Press, 1988], chap. 5). The readiness to work with small beginnings is alien to the contemporary academic culture of intellectual competition. The Centro Bartolomé de las Casas in Lima attempts to live a different culture, a culture of small beginnings. In the words of Xavier Iguíniz: "We are not interested in creating a new theology, we are not trying to confront traditional church structures. We are not hoping for quick radical changes. No, we want to listen carefully and patiently to the movement of the people and slowly identify those elements that lead to progress" (Henri Nouwen, *¡Gracias!* [Maryknoll, N.Y.: Orbis Books, 1992], 163).

plum trees and pear trees and cherry trees. They need different kinds of soil, have different flowers, and bear different fruits. There are better and worse ecological conditions for a particular tree. It is amazing that Jesus acknowledged a plurality of ministries (see Mt 11:7-19). This is an invitation to accept a plurality of theologies, a richness of the many ways of doing theology. At the same time, this is an invitation to generosity for each local theology, an invitation to be open to the gifts of others. Many trees—one garden; this is true for ministries and theologies. Jesus had no problems with other people casting out demons (Lk 9:49-50). He saw his mission and the mission of John the Baptist as complementary missions in the common task of building the kingdom.

Let us try to be a little more specific about the criteria by which to evaluate theologies. I suggest that we take a prominent passage from the gospel of Luke, the one in which the disciples are sent out. This is indeed an important gospel passage for our topic. Jesus tells his disciples how to proclaim the good news:

> After this the Lord appointed seventy others and sent them on ahead of him in pairs to every town and place where he himself intended to go. He said to them, "The harvest is plentiful, but the laborers are few; therefore ask the Lord of the harvest to send out laborers into his harvest. Go on your way. See, I am sending you out like lambs into the midst of wolves. Carry no purse, no bag, no sandals; and greet no one on the road. Whatever house you enter, first say, 'Peace to this house!' And if anyone is there who shares in peace, your peace will rest on that person; but if not, it will return to you. Remain in the same house, eating and drinking whatever they provide, for the laborer deserves to be paid. Do not move about from house to house. Whenever you enter a town and its people welcome you, eat what is set before you; cure the sick who are there, and say to them, 'The kingdom of God has come near to you.' But whenever you enter a town and they do not welcome you, go out into its streets and say, 'Even the dust of your town that clings to our feet, we wipe off in protest against you. Yet know this: the kingdom of God has come near.' I tell you, on that day it will be more tolerable for Sodom than for that town" (Lk 10:1-12).

This gospel passage illustrates Jesus' way of doing theology. We can look at the criteria that Jesus suggests in doing theology. One way to do that is to see whether the criteria we normally use to assess local initiatives are used by Jesus: sustainability, appropriateness, and empowerment.[10] Let us take a

---

[10] These criteria are taken from the field of development. The criteria of sustainability, empowerment, and appropriateness emerged in the 1990s and are an attempt to respect local knowledge, local cultures, and local initiatives. It is because of this background (respect for localness) that these criteria seem to be fruitful for our context of local theologies.

look at Jesus' mission statement in the light of these three criteria. Does Jesus make use of the ideas expressed in these criteria?

First, let us look at sustainability. It is obvious that Jesus was interested in the sustainability of his mission. That is why he sent disciples out in the first place; that is why he spoke about the kingdom as the ultimate goal, challenge, and task; and that is why he encouraged endurance and strength (Mueller 1988, 28f.). The very idea of mission is a sign of Jesus' interest in making his mission sustainable. The gospel passage is a call to mission, a situation in which disciples are sent to multiply the fruits of Jesus' mission. Jesus was rooted in a local culture, but his claim transcended the local context and became universal. This is also expressed by the symbols that he used—word, life, light, water, bread, shepherd. He touched upon the really human (Amaladoss 1984, 33). It is part of the Christian message to hope and strive for the salvation of all.

Jesus extended his mission to people who were not part of his own cultural community. "Jesus extended one's neighbor to include one's enemies. He could not have found a more effective way of shocking his audience into the realization that he wished to include all people in this solidarity of love" (Nolan 2001, 75).

The central symbol of this claim that Jesus' message is a lasting one is the message of the kingdom of God. The church (after Christ) clearly realizes and acknowledges the claim of sustainability. Actually, the very foundation of the church is the idea of the sustainability of Jesus' mission. Jesus' mission was the annunciation and the restitution of the kingdom of God (Denzinger 1991, 4105, 4224, 4571f.). Jesus both announced and realized the kingdom of God (Denzinger 1991, 4611; Brown 1994, 60-70; Leonardo Boff 1978, chap. 4). The kingdom of God described by Jesus has to be extended and preserved (Denzinger 1991, 4123). Jesus wanted his words to bear fruit (Mt 7:24-27). The key symbol for the claim of sustainability of Jesus' mission is the institution of the eucharist and the command to celebrate it in memory of him.

Second, let us look at the criterion of appropriateness. In the gospel passage mentioned, Jesus tells his disciples to accept the local conditions that determine both the welcome or acceptance and the way of life. That is why he warns them not to take too many things with them. They are to eat and drink what is available in the local culture and become rooted in a local culture as much as possible ("remain in the same house"). They should not arrive with ready-made tools and concepts; instead, they should first assess the situation and accept the local quality of life.

The idea of appropriateness is a key message of the gospels. Many things that could be mentioned under the word *appropriateness* have been mentioned already in the characterization of Jesus' ministry. Let us repeat some of the main ideas: Jesus accepted the local laws and hierarchies to the extent possible. He asked the leper to go to the priests and offer the gift that Moses commanded (Mt 8:4); he was diplomatic about the tax (Mt 22:15-22). He talked in local images.[11] Jesus emphasized that norms and laws must be locally appropriate; they are instituted for the sake of the well-being of human beings (see Mt 9:14-17; 12:1-14).

Jesus dealt with many different people in many different ways. And the people approaching Jesus had many different reasons to be with him: some wanted to be cured, others were seeking forgiveness and consolation, some wanted to be fed, others hungered for a vision, some might have been only curious. Jesus gave himself in many different ways.

Doing theology in a way that is appropriate to a local context can also mean accepting local challenges; we do see passages in which Jesus was challenged by the local culture, especially in the encounter with the Canaanite woman (Mt 15:21ff.). Jesus respected the dynamics of situations and human encounters; he accepted the specificity of a situation and measured each situation separately. He did not apply ready-made standards to situations, as we can see in the story of the anointing at Bethany (Mt 26:6-13) or the story of the centurion's servant (Mt 8:5-18). Jesus adapted the mode of healing to the circumstances. This is part of who Jesus was. Jesus Christ, "*the* model of incarnation and inculturation, became incarnated in one particular time and place. Even there he spoke differently to his own apostles than he did to the scribes and Pharisees, differently to the Samaritan woman than to Peter. He could be stern or gentle. He knew when to speak and when to be silent. He was sensitive to the generosity of the widow at the temple, and to the need for affection on the part of the children who sought his blessing" (Schineller 1990, 7).

Third, we look at the criterion of empowerment. Jesus did not hold on to his powers—the power of healing, the power of evangelizing, and even the power of forgiving sins—but shared them. The gospel passage quoted above (Lk 10) continues with reports of the disciples returning full of excitement and joy that their powers had worked. We can see this kind of empowerment at work in all the situations describing Jesus healing people. It is on that basis that Jesus could send his disciples and the people he healed to "go out and do the kingdom," because the kingdom has to be "done."

The concept of empowerment can be traced throughout the gospels. The images Jesus used to describe the responsibility of the people are images of empowerment (salt of the earth, light of the world, fishers of men). Jesus encouraged his disciples to be part of the mission (Mt 10:26ff.). Jesus

---

[11] There is a revealing passage in Ernesto Cardenal's recordings of Bible discussions in Solentiname, in which the group discusses Matthew 25:14-30. They do not like the fact that Jesus uses the image of money to make his point. One participant suggests that this is probably what people understand best, and another says, "Like here among ourselves we give examples of hens and corn and kidney beans, which are the things we understand best, so it'll be seen clearer, in the people's words. Well, that's the way Jesus was talking too" (Ernesto Cardenal, *The Gospel of Solentiname*, 4 vols. [Maryknoll, N.Y.: Orbis Books, 1984], 4:39).

invited people to come to him with their sorrows and burdens (Mt 11:28-30). He called people to mission and commissioned his apostles (Mt 28:16-20); he talked about the efficacy of faith and the works that can be done on the basis of faith (Lk 17:5-6). Jesus empowered people by telling them that everything is possible for God (Lk 18:27). The invitation not to be afraid can be found in many places throughout the gospels (see Mt 8:26; 9:22; 19:27). This is as much empowering as the invitation not to worry about material needs (Mt 6:25) and the reassurance of the power of prayer (Mt 7:7-12; 18:19-22).

Again and again Jesus made clear that it is the faith of the healed person that has brought about the healing (Mt 8:13; 9:29; Lk 7:50). Jesus empowered people. Again and again it is mentioned in the gospels that Jesus invites people to go their way. This is indeed a core element of Christian ministry. Ricardo Rezende talks about Acts 3 and the healing of the crippled man through Peter. "No longer did he have to ask anyone for favors." Rezende connects this story with a Brazilian experience, the experience of the farmers of Itaipava who wanted the bishop to solve their land problems: "Bishop Hanrahan read this passage from the Acts of the Apostles to them. The farmers, on hearing the reading, understood that they had to walk with their own feet. They returned to the land. They were evicted again. They persisted and won the rights to the land" (Rezende 1994, 46). This is an example of empowerment.

Jesus did not use his healing powers to create dependencies or to exercise power; he empowered the people he healed to live their lives (Mk 10:52; Lk 7:10; 8:38-39; Jn 4:50; 8:11; 11:44). He tried to make clear to his disciples that their ministry, that doing theology, is not a matter of power (Lk 10:17-20).

Sustainability, appropriateness, and empowerment are three standard criteria. In the light of what we said about the invitation to go beyond the local context I would like to add a fourth criterion: challenge. Jesus makes it clear that good theology challenges local cultures. This is the criterion that talks about the counter-cultural force of the message of Jesus.

Let us look at the criterion of challenge. Jesus was not absorbed by the local culture. He did not totally surrender to the local culture. Time and again he posed counter-cultural challenges to the local culture. Jesus challenged people to take a different look at reality; the judgment that the ruler's daughter had died was challenged by Jesus (Mt 9:18ff.), and people laughed him to scorn. Jesus uses different categories that are incompatible with the traditional, local categories, for example, talking about "rebirth" (Jn 3:5-8) or "freedom" (Jn 8:34-38). Jesus indicated that there is a significant difference between knowledge of earthly things and knowledge of heavenly things (Jn 3:10-13). We are talking about *different categories*.

Jesus challenged his disciples when they tried to measure his mission in secular categories—it is in this sense that he rebuked Peter (Mt 16:23). We can see the same challenging harshness in Jesus' approach toward cultures that try to find a "way out" similar to the escape suggested by Peter. For cultures not willing to accept the counter-cultural challenge, "it will be more tolerable on that day for Sodom" (Lk 10:12). Counter-cultural challenges were part of his very mission. Because of his lack of formal education (Jn 7:15), the very fact that Jesus was teaching could be seen as a counter-cultural challenge to the local cultures of his time.

The core of Jesus' teaching is in the beatitudes. The beatitudes are a strong expression of Jesus' counter-cultural challenge to established categories of power and fame. In the beatitudes Jesus contrasted the old law with the new law (Mt 5:17ff.), thus explicitly indicating that he would introduce new ways of looking at reality and human life. The beatitudes show a transformation from external criteria. This is also clearly shown in the new law of divorce (Mt 5:31-32; 19:3ff.).

Jesus' mission called for transcending local social boundaries (Mt 8:22; 12:46-50); the community he founded is not compatible with the established social order, as the cleansing of the Temple showed (Mt 21:12-17). Jesus talked about the mission of his disciples as explicitly counter-cultural: "Behold, I am sending you forth like sheep in the midst of wolves" (Mt 10:16). There is a price to pay for the kingdom, Jesus said: the cross. Jesus did not promote "cheap ways to salvation" (Mt 16:24-28).

The price for the counter-cultural challenge of Jesus is a certain loneliness. Jesus did not entrust himself fully to the local cultural community (Jn 2:25); his fate clearly showed the price of counter-cultural engagement. Jesus talked about his own mission as a counter-cultural challenge that would bring the sword, not peace (Mt 10:34). Jesus did not hesitate to threaten local cultures by talking condemnation and disaster (Mt 11:20). Being counter-cultural was part of what the Jesus community was.

The message of the kingdom of God is the core of Jesus' message. The kingdom provides us with a vision of a new society, a contrast society. The kingdom of God is not simply an opposition to secular kingdoms. The structure of the kingdom of God, as described by Jesus, is entirely different from those structures that are familiar to us. Power in the kingdom, for example, is essentially different; it is not the case that the rich and the poor simply change places (Nolan 2001, 84).[12]

Christianity is a constant invitation to go beyond the local. This call has been heard from the very beginning (see Rom 1:14; 1 Cor 9:22). People whom we call saints are those who have transcended their local village, left the safe harbors, and sailed the open sea. What does this mean for theology? The challenge Jesus poses to local cultures is ongoing. As Tony Walsh says, "The Gospel needs to keep its shocking effect. You can never claim to

---

[12] Juan Segundo speaks about the "counter-theology" of Jesus as opposed both to capitalism and to socialism (Juan Segundo, *Capitalism-Socialism: A Theological Crux*, *Concilium* 96 [1974], 118).

have fully understood the Gospel. It always should keep you on edge and never satisfied" (in Nouwen 1976, 117). The gospel must not lose its counter-cultural force. It remains the engine of theology and of the church. Rodney Stark explains that a "movement must maintain a substantial sense of difference and considerable tension with the environment if it is to prosper" (in Mullins 1998, 167).

Thus, we have four criteria for judging local theologies. They need to be applied jointly, since they counterbalance each other (for example, the criterion of appropriateness and the criterion of challenge). These four criteria imply a trust in human growth and the depth of cultures. They express the fact that not all theologies are equally good, and that it is important to distinguish between more adequate and less adequate (or bad) theologies.

A THIRD LOOK AT JESUS

THESIS 18: An important tool for doing local theology is taking "a third look at Jesus." It is an invitation to ask the question: Who is Jesus for you? This question can be answered by identifying the key moments in the life of Jesus as depicted in the gospels.

Filipino theologian Carlo Abesamis talks about the necessity of taking "a third look at Jesus" (Abesamis 1991). The first look is the way Jesus saw himself and perhaps the way all those who had face-to-face encounters with Jesus saw him. The second look is that of the Western world, which normatively appropriated Jesus. The third look is from a local perspective, the local appropriation (reappropriation) of Jesus. This can be done by asking a simple question: Who is Jesus for you?

The question is simple but demanding. German theologian Dietrich Bonhoeffer asked "Who is Christ for us today?" in the Nazi prison of Tegel (Bonhoeffer 1953, 279). Questions of identity are delicate. I remember being asked by a friend who did not know my wife, "What kind of person is Maria?" I sat there thinking about an appropriate answer, an answer that would do justice to my wife. How could I describe her? What key features and character traits did I want to communicate? Should I use the word *caring* to describe her? Or *gentle*? Should I tell stories about her? Which stories, which experiences? These are difficult choices. The same applies to this third look at Jesus.

A good way of taking this third look might be to ask which story we would tell about Jesus. Another way is by picturing a day in the life of Jesus, the Christ. We might find Jesus praying in the early morning, walking on the road in midmorning, resting at a well during lunchtime, attending to the people's needs in a village in the afternoon, celebrating in a friend's house in the evening, and, again, praying at night.

Who is Jesus for you? How would you depict Jesus in a painting? Is it significant that the majority of Jesus representations depict Jesus as an innocent, helpless child or as the suffering Jesus on the cross?

Another challenging way of taking the third look at Jesus is to rewrite gospel passages in the first person, from the perspective of a face-to-face observer, or from the perspective of Jesus. Who is Christ for you? Dom Helder Câmara writes, "Although for some people it may seem strange, I declare that, in the North-east, Christ is called Jose, Antonio, or Severino. *Ecce homo*! Here is Christ the Man! Man who needs justice, has the right to justice, deserves justice!" (in Mary Hall 1980, 75). Who is Jesus for you?

The discovery and construction of local images of Jesus have been identified as central topics of theological research and pastoral work. In the African context Jesus is depicted as the chief, the ancestor and elder, the healer, and most especially as the master of initiation. Who is Jesus for you? is a key question for inculturation. Robert de Nobili presented Jesus as a guru. There are many different local images of Jesus. Different social groups will come up with different reappropriations of Jesus.

Who is Jesus for you? is a key question if not *the* key question in the framework of the Christian religion (see de Mesa 1987). Every culture has to receive Jesus Christ in its own special way. There are Asian faces of Christ, and there are faces of Jesus in Latin America; there are faces of Jesus in Africa and there are faces of Jesus in high schools and convents. The special way of receiving Jesus should be an invitation to freedom and dignity. This special way has to be liberated and cleansed from colonialism: "Christ the liberator can hardly look like the colonizer (Williams 1994, 152). This is not easy, as Kosuke Koyama points out for the Thai context: "The first question our Lord posed to his disciples at Caesarea Philippi was: 'Who do people say the Son of Man is?' To this question, Thailand today is likely to answer, 'Jesus Christ is a god of the Americans'" (Koyama 1976, 82).

There is the reappropriation of Jesus as superstar, pal, pacifist, new man. Virgilio Elizondo discovers Jesus as a mestizo liberator and a human sufferer (Elizondo 1988, 79ff.). Who is Jesus for you? Receiving Jesus according to the culture presupposes a personal encounter with Jesus and a translation of Jesus' message in a way that makes this message relevant for the everyday life of the people. It is only at that point that theology can fulfill its practical purpose and its service function.

Exercise: Take "a third look" at Jesus. What are the most important words that Jesus spoke, according to the gospels? Which of the recalled actions of Jesus impresses you the most? Which image would you use in order to understand Jesus? Can you describe a gospel scene in Jesus' words? Or can you describe it in your own words as a close observer?

3

Reappropriating Our Tradition

THESIS 19: Doing theology is a way of following Jesus. We follow Jesus as a community of believers, a community built on a tradition. In order to do local theology we have to reappropriate the tradition of our community. This is a challenging task because there is a series of little traditions rather than one great tradition.

Jesus can teach us how to do theology. Jesus teaches us (1) to reappropriate our tradition, (2) to do theology as if people matter, and (3) to base our theologies on our relationship with God. Doing theology is a way of following Jesus. It is a ministry. It is not an end in itself, but a means that serves a higher goal. Theology is to be characterized through the service it renders. It serves the kingdom of God. In this chapter we look at reappropriating the tradition. Then, in the following chapters, we look at what it takes to do theology as if people matter, a call to respect the local context in its cultural and social dimension. Thus we look at the relationship among theology, culture, and social structure. In each case we look at the context that shaped our community.

In order to understand our community we need to understand its tradition. Looking at the tradition that has shaped our religion is difficult and sometimes painful. Whenever we do theology, we do it within the context of a community and the tradition of that community. There is a long and rather confusing tradition that provides the foundations for our theologies. This tradition has given birth to many concepts and ideas, some of which seem difficult and hard to understand. Rather than talking about *the* Christian tradition, we might feel more comfortable talking about many little traditions that have shaped Christianity—many small rivers that come together in the sea of the great tradition of Christianity.

Missiologist Andrew Walls suggests the thought experiment of a Martian scholar of religions who would do research on the state of Christianity on earth. He would come at the beginning of Christianity, return after the establishment of Christianity as a state religion, then the Council of Trent, and yet again for the Second Vatican Council. This Martian scholar would not assume that he was always looking at the same religion! (Walls 1996, 3-15). We should keep this diversity and the incredible richness of history in mind because they sometimes make our tradition difficult to grasp.

OUR TRADITION:
ASKING QUESTIONS

THESIS 20: Reappropriating our tradition means seeing its relevance for our contemporary situation. We need to ask these questions: What is the key message of our tradition? How do we understand this message today?

Jesus respected his local tradition but also challenged the context of his time. He was rooted in his village but did not consider his village the ultimate norm. By putting traditions in a larger context, Jesus rediscovered the history of his people. We, for our part, are called to reappropriate the tradition of Jesus.

A very useful way to go about this reappropriation of traditions is to ask the question: How do we understand the key message of Jesus, the Christ? The identification of the key message of our religious tradition may vary from person to person. For some, the key message of Christianity may be love of enemies or being like children. For others it is salvation or holiness. For still others it is solidarity with the poor or obedience to the pope.

We can ask: How do I understand these ideas in my particular situation? How do I understand love of enemies or being like children in my context? Let us take an example: How do I understand the concept of salvation? There are many different connotations that determine the meaning of this important concept. The Greek term *soteria* connotes "being rescued from shipwreck," the Latin term *salus* means "health," a Latin term, *redemptio,* means "being ransomed from slavery." The Hebrew *Yasha* signifies primarily the possession of space and the freedom and security that are gained by the removal of constriction. A pastor in the Philippines found out that his parishioners associated "being free" with "having no debts." A teacher at a Western high school found out that salvation for her students meant being free from peer pressure. What does salvation mean for us?

Filipino theologian José de Mesa has collected some short but elucidating examples of the concept of salvation in various cultures (de Mesa 1996, 92-111). The concept of salvation was translated into a symbol for Jesus as the savior. De Mesa distinguishes three phases: the question of salvation, the phase of projection of this concept onto Jesus, and the phase of "regauging." Let us take the example of Australians, who, it is said, long for a sense of personal and national integrity, they long to be a "fair dinkum" people. This idea of fairness contrasts mainly with hypocrisy. "If Jesus brings about 'fair dinkum-ness' to people, then he can be fittingly called 'The True Blue,' which means 'a really good bloke' or 'a fair dinkum person'" (ibid., 110). In the phase of regauging the participants relativized the concept: "'The True Blue' person suggests excessive independence and self-reliance that comes from the need to be that autonomous, rugged, macho individual. This needs to be counteracted with the ability to be truly interdependent which allows mateship" (ibid., 111). In doing so, the participants were in a position to think about the utilization of this Australian interpretation for the category of salvation in pastoral contexts. How can the image of Jesus, the True Blue, be communicated? How can the church provide experiences that make this inculturation of the concept of salvation and the person of Jesus tangible?

In this way we can reappropriate our tradition by working toward an answer to the questions: Who is Jesus for us? What is the key message of Jesus? What is the core of our Christian religion? What does Jesus mean to us in our local situation? A look at the roots of our faith will help us to put current phenomena into perspective. It is the reference to Jesus that can guide us in our attempt to understand our own tradition. This is a challenging task.

The gap between our local situation and the history that determined our context can be painful and confusing. Kathleen Norris, a spiritual writer who was alienated from the church and found her way back, wrote a famous book entitled *Amazing Grace*. It is subtitled *A Vocabulary of Faith*. Norris describes the shyness she felt when returning to religion; there were so many big and difficult concepts like sacrifice, infallibility, sin, blood. She decided to try to make sense of all these concepts by relating them to her own life story, trying to find insights or experiences that might help her to understand. This is an impressive example of trying to reappropriate the tradition.

It is useful to "spell the vocabulary of faith." We have been looking at "spelling the word *salvation*." We can do the same with other big concepts of the Christian tradition. Let us take another example—the concept of the resurrection of the flesh. It is a difficult concept. How could we make sense of it? I remember a story about two children, Jacob and Catherine. They play in the mud and really enjoy it. Catherine asks: "Do you think God knows how it feels to walk with bare feet in the mud or on the sand or in the water?" And

Jacob replies: "I don't know. But I am sure that if God did not know, God would want to know all these things." These experiences are important to God. This is a simple illustration for the theology of resurrection of the flesh—people treasure their experiences and they trust that these experiences are important to God. We trust that God knows how it feels to walk on this earth, to play in the mud, to swim in the water. And these experiences are precious and are part of being human, which is God's gift. Resurrection of the flesh then means that all these experiences will not lose their significance. Whatever we experience here on earth will remain precious and valid and an experience we can relate to. Resurrection of the flesh means that the new body of the new life is not a jump into a new form of existence without connections to our previous experience. The experience of walking in the mud will still be precious and remembered.

In this sense we try to reappropriate the big concepts and concerns of our religious tradition. To translate the big concepts of our theological tradition into our life experience is to create "little theologies."

Exercise: Try to answer these two questions: What is the key message of our tradition? How do you understand this message today? Choose one key term of your religious tradition (for example, justification, final judgment, Providence) and try to translate this concept into down-to-earth language.

REDISCOVERING THE MESSAGE OF JESUS

THESIS 21: Events in the life of Jesus can serve as a reference point for our judgments in the present. When thinking about ideas, concepts, or values of our own culture, we can assess these elements by looking at how Jesus responded to facets of his own culture and times. This is a useful theological tool to connect contemporary challenges with the praxis of Jesus.

As with the big concepts of our religious tradition, we can think about the key ideas of our culture in the light of the gospel. It is well known that each culture and every cultural tradition have key ideas that shape the identity of this tradition.

The way we order the world around us is influenced by our culture. We can think about these categories in the light of the message of Jesus. Kosuke Koyama describes an experience during his mission years in Thailand: "One of my students told me that the idea of *good* in Thai culture can be portrayed as clothing washed, neatly ironed and placed in a closed, undisturbed drawer. Don't wear it! It will get dirty! The clothing must stay 'detached' from the dirty world" (Koyama 1999, 84).[1] Doing local theology in this context may mean asking the questions: Does the fact that Jesus was faced with the accusation of impurity have an impact of how we approach this category? Is the fact that Jesus sided with outsiders and people who were "out of place" important in this context? Can we make use of this concept of goodness when looking for images for the kingdom of God or for images of salvation?

Locally available ideas and concepts can be used for doing theology. Children's respect for their parents, which can be found in Chinese culture, can be understood as a tool to do Chinese theology (Chang 1984, 36-40). Similarly, the Holy Spirit in Chinese theology can be interpreted based on the category of the *ch'i* (ibid., 116). *Ch'i* can be understood as "clouds"; "breathing in"; "breathing out"; "a force that works at the generation and at the shaping of things"; "vitality"; "a certain aspect of the will" (ibid., 116). These ideas are relevant for all local cultures because every culture develops key concepts for viewing the world.

Similarly, William Stolzmann talks about the Lakota use of categories, which is different from Western categorizations:

> Different actions have different effects upon different people. Particular actions are normally not bad in themselves but bad insofar as they have a negative impact on other people and the relationship the doer has with other people. Certain relatives and people deserve greater respect than others. . . . Thus what may be recognized as "good" in front of one person may be considered "bad" in front of another. The notion of sin is associated with a standard that God has applied equally to all. The notion of "sin" normally concentrates upon the *action* of the doer to the receiver rather than the *relationship* of the doer to the receiver (Stolzmann 1986, 70).

Looking at Jesus will help us to place the key concepts of our culture within a context. The look at Jesus may serve as a reference point when we are confronted with the many different ideas and concepts that the many cultures offer. Entering a different culture changes the way we see the world and the way we see ourselves. The categories we use change. We may get confused. Michael Lapsley, a priest from New Zealand who has worked for many years in South Africa, remembers: "Before I went to South Africa, I thought of myself as a human being. On arrival in South Africa, my

---

[1] Similar questions can be asked in different local contexts. Malaysian Jesuit J. J. Fung, for instance, discusses the concept of "dirt" in his local context: "There is a popular belief attached to the removal of one's shoes. Some Malaysians consider shoes not only literally 'dirty' but also figuratively 'dirty.' By wearing shoes into homes or places of worship, one has 'dirtied' the ground" (J. J. Fung, *Shoes Off: Barefoot We Walk* [Kuala Lumpur: Longman Malaysia Sdn. Bhd, 1992], 13).

humanness was removed and I became a white man" (Worsnip 1996, 34). In the midst of these changes and the resulting confusion, a look at Jesus can help orient us. The stable point of reference for the concepts we encounter can be Jesus, the example of his life.

We can translate the big ideas of our culture into little theologies by looking at Jesus. This turning back to Jesus seems particularly important for the idea of doing local theology. Otherwise, there is the danger of getting lost in the tradition.

The problem of reappropriating the tradition is a problem known to all religious movements. There is a dynamic in the development of religious movements. First, there is a person. This person has a message. This message attracts disciples. As soon as there is a small community of disciples, some social order becomes necessary to tie this community together, an "order of life" established by the founding figure. In many cases it is at this moment that the founding figure, after these four primary steps in the emergence of a social/religious movement, dies. Soon afterward the first disciples die. The community asks, How can we preserve the message of the founder? Two things seem inevitable: The message of the founding person can be preserved only if it is translated into a systematic doctrine. And second, the idea of the small community can be preserved only if the movement develops structures.

Faced with this dynamic, many followers of Jesus experience frustration. They do not encounter Jesus and his message; instead, they are confronted with the structure of the church and with a body of doctrines. That is why it is of vital importance to go back to the roots. What can the example of Jesus teach us about current issues?

The gospel does not tell us how to live in the third millennium. But the gospel can give us guidelines for where to look and what to consider. We can look at Jesus' words and deeds. When dealing with contemporary challenges, we can ask, What are relevant aspects of Jesus' life for this situation?

Let us look at two concepts—ambition and friendship—from a theological perspective, taking into account the example of Jesus.

A THEOLOGICAL REFLECTION ON AMBITION

One of the key concepts of our time is ambition. Let us take a theological look at this concept in the light of the life of Jesus.

An ambitious person is a busy person, always doing something, always running. The roots of the word *ambition* mean "walking around." They call to mind the image of a politician who goes around hustling votes. This is not a very pretty image. There is an ugly face of ambitiousness. In *Henry VI* Shakespeare writes of Mortimer, who was "chok'd with ambition of the meaner sort." This is the kind of ambition that makes a person pursue something whatever the cost.

Ambitious people have an "engine" that keeps them going. No one would deny that Ignatius of Loyola, the founder of the Society of Jesus, was an ambitious man. He was an ambitious soldier, and this ambition shows also in his strong intention to be a good Catholic and obedient to the pope. No one would deny that Albert Schweitzer was an ambitious man. He had the ambition to excel in what he did—music, theology, philosophy, humanitarian service.

Archbishop Oscar Romero once said: "I believe that the saints were the most ambitious people. This is my ambition for all of you and for myself: that we may be great, ambitiously great, because we are images of God and we cannot be content with mediocre greatness." Ambition is also the will to be good and to do good. Most of those we call saints were definitely ambitious, at least ambitious in the sense that they wanted to do something well.

The lack of ambition shows a dark side of human life. We need challenges and we need motivation. There is a famous example in sociology. In the 1930s there was a small Austrian village, Marienthal, where most villagers made their living by working in the local factory. In the course of the painful recession of that time, the factory shut down. Practically the whole village was unemployed. And there was no realistic hope of ever finding work in that village. Sociologists carried out a well-known study about the effects of unemployment in Marienthal. Among their findings was the discovery that these unemployed people had lost their self-esteem, their energy, and even their sense of time. They walked much slower on the street than other people; they had all the time of the day at their hands and were still late for meals! They had become "a slow village," a "tired society," as the sociologists called it. And even the little things they had to do were too much for them, little things like taking out the garbage or helping with household chores. This is significant. A life without challenges, a life without any sense of success, is empty.

On the other hand, if society were built exclusively on ambitious, dynamic, successful people, where would we be? Jean Vanier, the founder of L'Arche, the network of living communities of people with and without mental handicaps, talks about how much we can learn from persons with handicaps. They are not "successful" in the terms of our society, but they can teach us to be human.

Life is about relationships and freedom and a good heart. Jean Vanier says: "People with mental handicaps, so limited physically and intellectually, are often more gifted than others when it comes to the things of the heart and to relationships." They can help us to see what it means to encounter another person without looking at status or image, family or educational background, color of skin or language.

In our competitive society, people with mental handicaps are the excluded, the unwanted, the weak. Yet, as Jean Vanier reminds us, "in their thirst and their gift for friendship and for communion, the weaker people in society can touch and transform the strong, if the strong are only prepared to listen to them." We become more human by allowing ourselves to be led by the weak.

It is significant that Jesus approached those who were not successful by the measures of his society. He approached the weak and the sick. He approached the "losers" of the society of that time. Jesus had a visible tolerance of failures. He did not pick the brightest and most successful people of his time to become his disciples. Peter, the foundation of Jesus' community, is not depicted in the gospels as a particularly brave or smart person. And yet Jesus chose him and was faithful to him even after Peter's betrayal. Jesus himself was not really successful. In fact, in a certain sense he too was a loser. He lost the struggle with the political authorities of his time, and he lost his life. Martin Buber once said, "Success is not one of the names of God." And this expresses a deep truth.

Jesus was not opposed to the idea of pursuing goals. It seems that Jesus was a well-motivated person. Jesus wanted to do the things he did well. He was driven by a mission. But Jesus was not ambitious in the sense of seeking his own glory. He was not pursuing his own private mission but was following a call. And he followed this call with all his strength and all his conviction. Jesus teaches us that ambition can be unhealthy. We can think of the time when he is unhappy with the jealousy among his disciples and their desire to have privileged places next to him. Jesus teaches us perspective. "Strive first for the kingdom of God and his righteousness, and all these things will be given to you as well" (Mt 6:33).

A THEOLOGICAL REFLECTION ON FRIENDSHIP

With regard to the concept of friendship, Jesus again can show us the way. Friendship is one of the most important experiences in a person's life. How can we develop a "little theology" of friendship based on the example of Jesus' life?

Aristotle said that a mark of a good person is the ability to make friends. This is an interesting idea. And, we can continue, it is the mark of a good person to distinguish between close friends and others. Jesus called his disciples "friends." He said that they were his friends because they knew what he was doing.

Jesus shared friendship with his disciples, and he shared some particular and beautiful friendships with special people: the disciples Peter and John, and Mary, Martha, and Lazarus from Bethany. The depth of these friendships is shown in the trust Jesus puts in Peter, knowing Peter's weaknesses and still trusting him to be able to do great things. This trust is also shown in the secrets Jesus shares with his friends, personal mysteries he would not share with just anybody.

The depth of these friendships also is shown in the affection Jesus shows for John and in the shared pain Jesus suffered with Martha and Mary after the death of his friend Lazarus. In this friendship Jesus is committed to action when it is needed—so, it is told, Jesus raises Lazarus from the dead.

There is trust, affection, shared suffering and joy, and commitment in Jesus' friendship. But there is also something else. There is the scene in the gospel when Peter wants Jesus to be spared future suffering and he urges him to be unfaithful to his mission (Mt 16:22-23). Jesus is adamant in this situation and rebukes Peter with strong words. This is not a sign that their friendship is weak but rather shows Jesus' commitment to their friendship. Friendship means wanting the other person to be well, even at the price of his momentary hurt. Friendship is not about making the other person feel good all the time. A true friend invites us to be the best person we can be. And a true friend believes that we can be that best person, even if most people do not think so. A true friend discovers our wonderful sides and invites us to cultivate them. A good friend wants our well-being, even if this means being painfully honest. Father Arrupe, the superior general of the Jesuits, said in an interview that he encourages his fellow Jesuits to have "virile relationships"—relationships in which they can face reality, be honest with one another—as opposed to "diplomatic rapports." Being a friend can sometimes be painful.

It is not always comfortable to be friends with Jesus because he challenges his friends for their own sake. He reminds his friends who they could be. It is in this sense that we could say that a good friend is someone who knows the melody of our soul and can sing it to us. And Jesus was not afraid to be friends with outsiders, he was not afraid of entering relationships. Entering a relationship means becoming vulnerable. As the saying goes, Nobody can be a hero to his valet. Likewise, nobody can be a hero to his or her true friend. Admiration is not the basis of true friendship. Jesus refused to be called "master" by his disciples.

Being a friend means taking an interest. Jesus did not always enter people's lives when they were "at their best." Jesus came to people, sometimes quite unexpectedly and in moments of frustration. He became friends with Peter when Peter was frustrated after a whole night of useless fishing!

True friendship requires effort. Making a phone call or writing a letter or making a visit (let us say, in a hospital) is not always fun. It is not pleasant to sit next to a friend who has been diagnosed with cancer or to have a conversation with a friend who is angry and hurt because her partner just left her. And it is not fun to answer the phone or open the door in the middle of the night because your friend needs you. Friendship involves commitment.

Friendship is an art. People who are really good at the art of friendship are creative and full of surprises; they like to find new ways of expressing their friendship, the unexpected parcel, the surprising invitation. In a book on the art of loving, Erich Fromm describes love as an art that can be cultivated and practiced (Fromm 1963).

Friendship is part of the art of life, an art in which a person can grow and blossom. As with any other art, it takes time. It takes time to grow into the art of friendship. And it takes time to become friends. A good friend is not made in a day. Friendship is a journey undertaken together. Friendship is about having something in common. As Antoine de Saint-Exupéry wrote in

The Little Prince, "Love does not consist in gazing at each other but in looking outward together in the same direction."

True friendship can only exist between people who can share a balance of giving and taking. Friendship is different from ministry. There is no doubt that unequal people can become friends and that these friendships can become enriching and deep. But there has to be the respect for what the other person has to give. What did Jesus receive from his friends? He received their communion when he was announcing the kingdom of God; he received their trust and their hope; he received their tears when he suffered and died.

True friendship is a commitment to caring about another person. It is in this sense that friendship involves responsibility. It is another lesson we can learn from *The Little Prince*: Becoming friends is a journey with a small beginning, step by step. And with each step (which de Saint-Exupéry called "taming"), the responsibility grows. We are responsible for the people we have "tamed."

Jesus accepted this responsibility and consoled his disciples. He promised they would never be alone. Through these examples we can see what it means to think about our culture and its concepts and to look at the example of Jesus and his life for a reference point. This turning back to the roots can, of course, also be done in a more systematic way by looking explicitly at biblical sources.

Exercise: Take a current debate or a key phenomenon of your cultural context (such as the concept of impatience or the discussion on genetic engineering or the phenomenon of pluralism) and develop a theological sketch of this issue by referring to the example of Jesus.

REAPPROPRIATING THE THEOLOGICAL TRADITION

THESIS 22: Our community of faith has developed a theological tradition. It is a matter of intellectual honesty to respect this tradition when doing theology. As theologians we are members of a community and accountable to this community. That is why we are called to make an effort to reappropriate the theological tradition of our community. It gives guidelines and norms on how to do theology. It is an important theological task to "translate" the theological tradition into a local context by looking at the concern of a particular element of this tradition.

The history of theology is a treasure house of insights and thoughts. It is a matter of intellectual honesty to pay attention to this tradition. As a source of norms, this tradition can also give us guidelines for doing theology today.

Reappropriating the theological tradition means placing our own theology in a larger intellectual context. If we play a game, we have to follow its rules. If we want to play chess without the queen, then we are not playing chess anymore but a different game. Of course, doing theology is not a game like chess, rather a family of different games, but all of which in their specific local contexts have something in common. There are rules to the game of doing theology. And these rules are connected with our theological tradition and with the authority of that tradition.

As Barbara Brown Taylor writes: "Faith may be an imaginative act but the Bible reminds us that we are not free to imagine anything we like. . . . By keeping us rooted in our historical tradition, the Bible helps us to know the difference between imagination and delusion; by tethering our own imaginations to that of the whole people of God, the Bible teaches us to imagine the God who was and is and who shall be" (in Tisdale 1997, 94). Theologians are accountable to a community, a community that was there before them and will be there after they are gone. Chesterton talked about tradition as a democracy including the dead, giving a voice to those who cannot speak for themselves any longer. Tradition is a dialogue with a larger context than the immediate context of our actions. This dialogue changes both the present and the view of the past; the tradition has preserved the memory of the past, but it is also subject to growth and change through the work of new generations who face new situations that require reconsideration of their heritage. Tradition is being produced by people who are involved in the struggle of life. Traditions are collective memories of key events that have shaped our self-understanding and identity. That is why it is vital to enter into a dialogue with tradition.

This dialogue with the tradition gives us a sense of identity. "Theology is basically the dialectical drawing together of two experiences, our present-day experience and the history of faith experiences which we find expressed in our Judaeo-Christian tradition" (de Mesa and Wostyn 1984, 67). Or, as American theologian David Tracy writes: The theologian has the task "to show the appropriateness of his/her own categories (and, by implication, the categories of the later tradition) to the meanings expressed in that collection of texts called Hebrew and Christian scriptures" (Tracy 1975, 73). Local theology brings different times and different places together. Thomas Merton talks about this "importance of being able to rethink thoughts that were fundamental to men of other ages, or *are* fundamental to men in other countries" (Merton 1996, 42). Respect for the theological tradition is also a sign of respect for other cultures.

This commitment to our theological tradition ensures that theology is done not in isolation, but as a community. Theologians respecting the authority of their community find themselves part of a community and are willing to be corrected by their community. Reading the works of the great theologians opens the eyes to deep insights and influential ideas. Reading the church fathers gives a sense of the basic questions of the Christian tradition in the formative centuries of Christianity.

However, the theological tradition has to be reappropriated. We have seen that we have to make an effort in order to understand central theological concepts like the resurrection of the flesh or salvation. And this reappropriation must have a cultural face. It is one thing to believe in the truth of theological statements and another to believe in their relevance. Securing the relevance of the theological tradition is the task of cultural workers. Theologian Maurice Wiles has made this point: "A 'true' doctrinal statement (though the phrase is less simple than appears on the surface) can, it may be admitted, never lose its truth, but it can lose its relevance. A statement whose truth or falsity can be determined only in terms of a world view that is dead and gone can hardly be a statement of direct relevance to subsequent ages" (Wiles 1975, 9). That is why the theological tradition has to be reappropriated.

Reappropriating our theological tradition means to look at the local context of its main elements; the elements of the theological tradition have come into existence within a particular cultural and historical context. The documents of the church's teaching or the books of the Bible cannot be fully understood without the history that made a certain clarification necessary. Second, we have to follow an invitation to look "beyond" the text into the concerns underneath. This is part of giving a positive meaning to normative texts.

Let us look at an example. The public reacted with bitter opposition to the contested encyclical *Humanae vitae*, which prohibited all means of artificial contraception. American and German bishops stated the possibility of legitimate dissent from church instructions that are binding to a certain degree but still subject to error. They stated the legitimacy of such dissent under three conditions: (1) One must have seriously tried to give a positive meaning to the teaching in question and one must have made the effort of personal reappropriation; (2) one must seriously question one's own theological competence and expertise to disagree with a certain teaching on the basis of intellectual honesty; and (3) one must examine one's conscience for traces of conceit, pride, or selfishness. These guidelines tell us how to reappropriate the difficult elements of our theological tradition. In this case we have to ask: What is the concern behind *Humanae vitae*? How could we formulate this concern in a way that is acceptable to us and to our local context?

Where are possible points of friction between the theological tradition and our local context? Theologian Elizabeth Achtemeier proposes four questions to be asked in bringing together the Bible and the world of a particular community. We can ask the same questions about texts of the theological tradition:

1. What would people doubt in this text?
2. What do people need to know or to be reminded of by this text?
3. With what inner feelings, longings, thoughts, and desires does this text connect?
4. If this text is true, what kind of world do we live in? If this text were not true, what would be the consequences? (in Tisdale 1997, 105).

It is hard theological labor to understand the concerns of the theological tradition and to interpret it in a way that can render it meaningful for a concrete situation. Different contexts are sensitive to different aspects of the theological tradition. Let us look at a few examples of how the traditional theological teaching on Jesus as both human and divine has been reappropriated.

The theological discipline of Christology talks about Jesus, the Christ. The way this is being done depends on the concerns that are emphasized: "The specific christological problem lies in the fact of a male savior, the significance of the maleness of Jesus, and the uses and effects of the male Christ symbol for the lives of women" (Carr 1990, 163). These are feminist concerns with the image of Jesus.

Brazilian theologians Leonardo and Clodovis Boff interpret the Council of Chalcedon in 451. This council has stated the two natures of Jesus Christ, human and divine, and the unity of these two natures in one person. The Boffs reappropriate this key idea of our theological tradition in their emphasis on liberation. They interpret the formulation of Chalcedon as a statement about how salvation and liberation are interrelated. The teaching that Jesus is at once God and human and that Jesus is from two natures (Denzinger 1991, 302, 293) shows that Jesus is indissolubly conjoined with God: "This schema has a . . . meaning for the problem of the salvation-liberation relationship. Salvation and liberation are distinct; but they are united, without confusion and without separation" (Leonardo and Clodovis Boff 1984, 59). This is an attempt to reappropriate this theological tradition for a local context. Different christological statements have different status for different groups.

Let us look at a last example: Nestorianism was rejected by the Christian tradition. It claimed that Jesus Christ was both human and divine but not in the unity of one person, that the two natures of Jesus Christ were separate. Hispanic theologian Justo González reappropriates the idea of Nestorianism and its rejection to the context of his culture:

Nestorianism has never been a temptation for Hispanic Christians. The reason for this is that we feel the need to assert that the broken, oppressed, and crucified Jesus is God. A disjunction between divinity and humanity in Christ that denies this would destroy the greatest appeal of Jesus for Hispanics and other groups who must live in suffering.

North Atlantic Christians have often criticized Hispanics for repre-
senting Jesus and his sufferings in gory detail. This, they claim, is a
sign of a defeatist religion, or of a sadomasochistic attitude that de-
lights in pain. But this is not the case. The suffering Christ is important
to Hispanics because he is the sign that God suffers with us (González
1990, 148).

*Exercise: Take a document from the teaching office of the church, for example,
the definition of the infallibility of the pope. Locate the definition in its context
based on historical research. Try to work out the issues and concerns at stake. Try
to identify these issues and concerns in your own context. Rephrase the definition.*

REAPPROPRIATING THE BIBLE

**THESIS 23: The main source of Christian tradition is the Bible. In
order to see the relevance of the Bible for present-day contexts
we need to reappropriate biblical texts. In order to do that we
need basic knowledge of the Bible and sensitivity toward the concrete concerns of a given biblical text.**

The main source of our Christian tradition is the Bible. How can we
reappropriate the scriptures for our particular local context? There are a
few simple points to remember when thinking about the role of the Holy
Scriptures:

- The Bible is written for people who want to be introduced to the mysteries of divine life; it is not an intellectual discussion.
- The Bible is a realistic book, a book about all aspects of life. It does
  not avoid any part of human reality: lust or greed, tenderness or care,
  cruelty or frustration, joy or hope.
- The Bible is a series of "little books" rather than one big book, and
  these books are diverse and have to be respected for what they are in
  their particularity.
- The Bible does not talk about "the innocent history of a perfect people"
  (González 1990, 75-80).
- The history of the use of the Bible is not innocent.[2]

---

[2] In many cases the Bible has been the book of the colonizers, the oppressors,
the conquistadors. "With regard to the treatment of the indigenous population by
the Spanish invaders, the biblical narrative of the divinely sanctioned destruction of

- The different books of the Bible can be seen as testimonies of local theologies.

The treasures of the Bible have to be reappropriated. This reappropriation is an invitation to respect many different ways of reading the Bible. Latin American theologian Ernesto Cardenal reflects on different agendas with which the Bible is read by the people in Solentiname:

> Not all those who did come took an equal part in the commentaries. There were some who spoke more often. Marcelino is a mystic. Olivia is more theological. Rebecca, Marcelino's wife, always stresses love. Laureano refers everything to the Revolution. Elvis always thinks of the perfect society of the future. Felipe, another young man, is very conscious of the proletarian struggle. . . . Pancho is a conservative. Julio Mairena is a great defender of equality. His brother Oscar always talks about unity (Cardenal 1984, 1:ix).

Everybody who reads the Bible has an agenda. "When a preacher says 'The Bible says . . . ,' it tells me more about what the *preacher* thinks than anything else" (Webb 1999, 101).

The Bible has to be reappropriated, taken into the reality of the people. Some books of the Bible are more challenging in this regard than others. Henri Nouwen reflects upon his experience with the psalms, some of which are rather cruel in their expression. But the language of these "difficult" psalms becomes important for him when thinking of the atrocities and tortures of the totalitarian regime in Chile in the 1970s. "I could go on and quote many . . . Psalms because after reading about Chile they become like burning prayers" (Nouwen 1976, 38). All of a sudden the psalms had a place in Nouwen's life. The main objective of local theologies "is not an interpretation of the Bible, but of an *interpretation of life,* with the *aid* of the Bible" (Gorgulho 1993, 124).[3] That is why Jean-Bertrand Aristide asked in his sermon on John 9:39-41, "Are there other instances where Jesus would repeat himself in Haiti today?" (Aristide 1991, 85). By asking this question

---

Jericho and the slaughter of the population (Josh 6) was used by the Spaniards to justify their violence against the peoples of the Americas. Luke 14:23 was used to justify the forcible conversion of those who survived sword and plague" (J.-P. Ruiz, "The Bible and U.S. Hispanic American Theological Discourse: Lessons from a Non-Innocent History," in *From the Heart of Our People: Latino/a Explorations in Catholic Systematic Theology,* ed. O. O. Espín and M. H. Díaz [Maryknoll, N.Y.: Orbis Books, 1998], 103).

[3] A farmer talks about a Bible course in a Brazilian base community: "The people like it a lot. We take the word of God and compare it to life. God is animating the path of the people in history. It's beautiful" (Ricardo Rezende, *Rio Maria: Song of the Earth,* ed. M. Adriance [Maryknoll, N.Y.: Orbis Books, 1994], 141).

Aristide invites people to connect their situation to the gospel situation, to connect their lives with a message of Jesus, which is valid beyond a particular historical context.

Particular passages and books of the Bible will be reappropriated differently in different cultures. It will make a difference whether we discuss the Book of Exodus with Israelis or with Palestinians, the Book of Job with rich or with poor people, the Old Testament in a culture with a short history of Christianity or in a culture rooted in the Jewish-Christian tradition. It will make a difference whether we read Mark 4:3-9 with urban people or with farmers, with European farmers or with farmers from the Philippines: "Though most Bible study leaders would focus their interpretation on the soil as the problem, a rice farmer would rather look at the *sower* as the problem. From his point of view a responsible farmer would not just randomly scatter seeds" (Montgomery-Fate 1997, 17). Each culture is invited to develop its way of reappropriating the Bible.

To add a further example: Virgilio Elizondo stresses the peculiar cultural identity of the land of Jesus using the experience of his own culture: "As I started to explore the socio-cultural imagery of Galilee I became more intrigued. It was a borderland, the great border between the Greeks and the Jews of Judea. . . . It was a land of great mixture and of an ongoing mestizaje—similar to our own Southwest of the United States. . . . By growing up in Galilee, Jesus was a cultural *mestizo*, assuming under himself the great traditions that flourished in his home territory" (Elizondo 1988, 76-77, 79).

Another example of the reappropriation of a biblical text in local contexts is the use of the Book of Exodus, a prominent book for many political theologies.[4] In the Korean context, to give a more specific example, a specific way of doing theology was developed against the background of the political situation. This kind of theology is called *minjung* theology because it focuses on the *minjung*, the simple people. The crowds, the masses were subject to exploitation and abuse by an elitist minority, and thus the story of the Exodus made a deep cultural and religious impact. The Book of Exodus tells a story that is familiar to the people of Korea: "On the basis of the event of the Exodus in the Old Testament, which it considers a paradigm, the Korean church understands the historical experience of the March First Independence Movement of 1919 and the liberation on August 15, 1945, as events of God's salvation of the nation" (Nam-dong 1981, 158). The story of the Exodus became a favorite story that Bible schools used to raise political conscience and to explain contemporary political situations. It is not

---

[4] An interesting liberative reading from an African perspective is to be found in Ela, *An African Reading of Exodus* (Jean-Marc Ela, *African Cry* [Maryknoll, N.Y.: Orbis Books, 1986], chap. 3). An example of working with the Book of Exodus in a rural Brazilian context is found in Rezende, *Rio Maria*, 45.

surprising that the Japanese authorities felt threatened by this book because of its powerful reception:

> Korean Christians understood the story of Moses not only as a *literal* event in the history of *Israel* but also as a *literal* event in the history of the oppressed people in *Korea*. This identification, evident in the development of the language of the Christian church in Korea, led to the subsequent resistance against the Japanese (Suh 1981, 22).

The Exodus is interpreted as proof that God cares about the *ochlos*, the common people. "In fact, some of the first words with which God is introduced to Moses in the Exodus narrative indicate that God is concerned with the *minjung*. In Exodus 3:7 God states: 'I have seen indeed the affliction of my people which are in Egypt.' God relates not just in a general way as the creator of human beings, but as concerned with specific oppressed people to whom Moses stands in a special relationship" (Moon 1985, 6). And below: "It is obvious that the revelation of the name of God given to Moses has the purpose of assuring him and the Hebrews of the very real presence of God who will act justly for the liberation of the *minjung*" (ibid., 7).

The Bible is a book about life, and it is an invitation to live. Because of its relevance for our lives the Bible speaks to each individual and it speaks to each individual differently. We know that the letter to the Romans became important to Martin Luther and Karl Barth. We know that Sirach 34:21-27 opened the eyes of Bartolomé de las Casas (Ruiz 1998, 103). Michael Lapsley's advice has to be taken to heart: "I want to suggest that all of us [should] read the gospel again" (in Worsnip 1996, 77). It does not hurt to take "a third look" at the biblical texts—again and again. With an attitude of openness and creativity we can discover new details every time we approach even familiar passages.

Let us take a look at a very impressive theological reappropriation of a particular book of the Bible: Gustavo Gutiérrez's interpretation of the Book of Job. Gutiérrez, the Peruvian "father of liberation theology," is a first-rate theologian. His reappropriation of the Book of Job is a theological interpretation on a very high level. To reach this level, one needs resources, time, and theological experience. However, even for "little theologies" we can learn a lot from looking at the example of this professional theologian's attempt to come to terms with this important book of the Old Testament.

Gustavo Gutiérrez Reappropriates the Book of Job

Gustavo Gutiérrez sets the context of his reappropriation of the Book of Job by talking about his general understanding of theology and his understanding of speaking of God in a Latin American context. He is well aware that the decision to look at the Book of Job may come as a surprise to some people. The Book of Job talks about "our relationship of faith and hope with God" (xvii).[5] Gutiérrez wants to listen to the Bible as it speaks to us today. He reads the text carefully and takes into account many works of theologians, writers, and scripture scholars.

Gutiérrez reconstructs the book from a literary standpoint as a wager: "Can human beings have a disinterested faith in God—that is, can they believe in God without looking for rewards and fearing punishments?"(1). Gutiérrez describes the situation and the first "wild words" of Job from the garbage heap; these emotional words need not be seen as a rejection of God. "In fact, it might well be claimed that this manifestation of irrepressible feeling expresses, even in an unconventional form, a profound act of self-surrender and hope in God" (10). Gutiérrez tries to read "through the text" to discover a meaning beneath the literal surface. What is this deeper message?

The deep question at the heart of the book is the question of speaking about God amid unjust suffering, a question that is of ultimate importance in a Latin American context. The Book of Job talks not so much about suffering but about our speaking of God in a situation of pain. "How are human beings to find a language applicable to God in the midst of innocent suffering?" (12). This question is taken to an existential level in the Book of Job. Job is not in doubt about whether he is a sinner or not, but about the question of whether he deserves his suffering (24). This is a question of his life experience.

"There is in fact no circumstance of human life that makes it more difficult to accept the gratuitous love of God than our own experience of suffering" (14). This is indeed the dividing line between Job and his friends: Job's experience of suffering (27). How should we speak of God in a situation of suffering? This dividing line between Job and his friends is also a dividing line of theological method: "The speeches of Eliphaz and his companions take certain doctrinal principles as their starting point and try to apply them to Job's case" (27). These speeches "have not in fact produced more than spontaneously foolish and indeed almost blasphemous responses to the situation" (12). Job's friends are firmly rooted in the traditional theology of temporal retribution. Their arguments remind us of "the wasted energy of intellectuals who get excited but do not actually do anything" (29). They do not talk to God, they talk about God (54). This is indeed a form of doing theology. Job, on the other hand, bases his way of talking to God and about God on experience.

The Book of Job describes a journey. Job experiences growth from an individualistic perception of suffering toward a view of solidarity with the

---

[5] The page numbers given in parentheses throughout this section refer to Gustavo Gutiérrez, *On Job: God-Talk and the Suffering of the Innocent* (Maryknoll, N.Y.: Orbis Books, 1987).

poor and a growth from a language of prophecy toward a language of contemplation (16-17). In the beginning he talks about his individual lot and his own personal experience. But slowly "Job begins to free himself from an ethic centered on personal rewards and to pass to another focused on the needs of one's neighbor" (31). This broadening of his view allows Job to develop a new way of talking about God.

"Now that he is sharing the lot of the poor in his own flesh, his talk of God becomes more profound and truthful" (48). He realizes "that innocence is not a matter of simply individual uprightness. It is rather a question of all of one's behavior to the poor, who are especially loved by the Lord" (39). This is one aspect of Job's journey. This growth leads him to a certain form of prophetic language, language about God's love for the poor and the imperative to live in solidarity with the poor. But the journey does not stop here.

Job must understand the mystery of God on a deeper level. Job realizes a deeper meaning of gratuitousness as a main characteristic of authentic faith in God. Gutiérrez identifies the three key passages that express this spiritual growth in Job 9:33 (need of an arbiter), 16:19 (presence of a witness demanded), and 19:25 (hope of a defender or liberator). These three roles are "three faces of one and the same God as experienced by one who suffers adversity and is searching" (56). In struggling with these faces of God, Job grows in the insight that the greatness of God "is to be identified less with power than with freedom and gratuitous love" (69). This is the key: "In the beginning was the gratuitousness of divine love, it—not retribution—is the hinge on which the world turns" (72). "God's love, like all true love, operates in a world not of cause and effect but of freedom and gratuitousness" (87).

This insight has tremendous consequences. A basic conviction—that the world has been made to be immediately useful to human beings—has been shaken. "Not everything that exists was made to be directly useful to human beings; therefore they may not judge everything from their point of view. The world of nature expresses the freedom and delight of God in creating" (74). Human beings are not the center of the universe. This insight (this experience) has the consequence that Job understands more deeply God's freedom. God's behavior cannot be calculated and foreseen.

The Book of Job criticizes "every theology that presumes to pigeonhole the divine action in history and gives the illusory impression of knowing in advance" (72). There is another aspect of God's freedom: It cannot primarily be understood in terms of power. God cannot impose his justice on humans; God's power is limited by human freedom. Gutiérrez refers to Job 40:9-14: "The Lord is explaining, tenderly and, as it were, shyly, that the wicked cannot simply be destroyed with a glance" (77). There is the face of a "weak" God. The mystery of God's freedom is linked with the mystery of human freedom.

This is the key to the Book of Job: understanding the mysterious relationship between gratuitousness and justice. "Nothing, no human work however valuable, merits grace, for if it did, grace would cease to be grace. This is the heart of the message of the Book of Job" (88-89). Job's second and final reply to God captures some key insights (Job 42:1-6). God's freedom goes beyond our concept of justice. "Job realizes that he has been speaking of God in a way that implied that God was a prisoner of a particular way of understanding justice" (87). He has tried to bind God's justice by the ideas of human justice. Speaking of God in terms of human justice does not give the final word. There is no opposition between gratuitousness and justice, there is only opposition between an anthropocentric understanding of justice and God's gratuitousness.[6]

A deep understanding of God's gratuitousness is still asking for a commitment to work for peace and justice in the world (90), a combination and growing integration of the two languages, the prophetic language and the contemplative language (94). The prophetic language attacks the misery of a situation and addresses structural causes, "the language of contemplation acknowledges that everything comes from the Father's unmerited love" (97). Gutiérrez relates these ideas with other biblical references, especially some references from the letters of Paul, passages from Psalms, and references to the synoptic gospels. At the end, Gutiérrez talks again about the Latin American context. "Job shows us a way with his vigorous protest, his discovery of concrete commitment to the poor and all who suffer unjustly, his facing up to God, and his acknowledgment of the gratuitousness that characterizes God's plan for human history" (102).

From this example we can learn that the reappropriation of a biblical text

- gains through considering other people's perspectives and insights;
- requires a careful reading of the text;
- is a profoundly spiritual and at the same time intellectually challenging task; and
- leads to a deeper understanding of other biblical texts and of our religious tradition.

Exercise: Take a passage (for example, a vocation story like Judges 13 or 1 Kings 19) or a book of the Bible (such as the Book of Micah or the Letter of James) and try to work with the text in your context as Gutiérrez did in his.

---

[6] Gutiérrez uses a beautiful image: "What he should have done was to leap the fence set up around him by his sclerotic theology that is so dangerously close to idolatry, run free in the fields of God's love, and breathe an unrestricted air like the animals described in God's argument—animals that humans cannot domesticate. The world outside the fence is the world of gratuitousness; it is there that God dwells and there that God's friends find a joyous welcome" (88).

INSPIRING EXAMPLES

THESIS 24: The tradition of our community of faith is a living tradition. It "lives" because there are people who realize the message of Jesus in their own lives. It is inspiring to look at the example of these people who have reappropriated the message of Jesus in their particular situation.

We have seen that the reappropriation of biblical texts is challenging. The Bible offers a key to the main door of our Christian tradition. Another open door to the message and tradition of Jesus is to be found in the lives of people who can inspire us. It is through these people that we can come to appreciate our tradition and its strength. In a very general sense, we can call these inspiring people saints. We can say that "holiness may be described as the whole life of a person as directed towards God" (Sheldrake 1987, 28). By their outlook on life inspiring people can give us an idea of how to reappropriate our tradition.

People who inspire us are the living tradition in our church.

> The saints aid us in developing an experiential and practical mediation of the "theology and doctrine in possession." A reading, for example, of Loyola's Spiritual Exercises will reveal much that was commonly taught in the Church and theology of his time. . . . But Loyola, like many of the other mystics, quite personally and experientially probes these beliefs and lives them out (Thompson 1996, 60).

The many faces of faith in the many saints give us a taste of the healthy pluralism in the reappropriation of the tradition. This goes far beyond intellectual reappropriation. It uncovers a spiritual reality.

Spirituality "is the mode of living, the essential disposition of the believer, and it imparts a new dimension to the believer's life. In other words, it is not only a new way of looking at human life, but a new way of living it" (Shorter 1980, 4-5). Spirituality is the certainty that our life is part of a larger context. There are innumerable examples of how this embracing of a larger context can be done, just as there are countless ways of reappropriating the tradition.

We have seen that the Christian tradition is a series of "little traditions," local traditions. Similarly, we can see that the reappropriation of the tradition and the message of Jesus can have many faces. Christian spiritual life allows a healthy pluralism of spiritualities and expressions of faith life. Jesus allowed a healthy pluralism of ministries (see Mt 11:7-19; Lk 9:49f.).

Planting only a single crop depletes the soil and leads to in-breeding. Saint Paul talks about the many gifts, the many members, and the one body (1 Cor 12). There has to be a healthy pluralism of theologies and spiritualities.

There are many trees in the Christian garden, many different trees with many kinds of fruit. Each tree grows on a special soil, a soil that is shaped by local history, local social situation, local cultural expressions, and local beliefs; a soil that is shaped by the struggle of individuals to go beyond the limits of their culture, to become prophetic voices in the wilderness, and to be messengers of the good news. Each tree needs these special conditions to grow and bear fruit.

In his keynote address to the U.S. Conference of Major Superiors for Men in 1996, Timothy Radcliffe compared religious orders to an environment, to a mini-ecosystem "which sustains weird forms of life." Each religious order provides an ecological context in which rare species can develop and can be preserved (Radcliffe 1996, no. 7). If there were not many charisms and many gifts, the church could not respond in so many different ways to so many different local situations. The communion of saints is a community of unity in pluriformity, of difference in harmony.

Jesus called different people with different gifts, backgrounds, stories, and ideas. There are many trees. There is, however, one garden (one vineyard) and there are common roots, all shared by the many trees in the garden of Christian life. Christian spiritual life shares certain characteristics:

- It is communal, the experience of a community. It serves to strengthen community ties.[7]
- It is traditional (Sobrino 1985, 1). Spirituality is not constructed or invented but handed down from generation to generation. It has depth and value because of this historical dynamic. It is ultimately rooted in a Jesus-experience.
- It is historical and incarnated and manifests itself in various ways, searching for a tangible historical expression.
- It looks for simplicity (Rohr 1992, chap. 9) and depth.
- It challenges local culture and has a counter-cultural force within any given culture.[8]

---

[7] This point is impressively made by Gustavo Gutiérrez in *We Drink from Our Own Wells*, in which Gutiérrez describes a spiritual journey as the communal experience of a people (Gustavo Gutiérrez, *We Drink from Our Own Wells: The Spiritual Journey of a People* [Maryknoll, N.Y.: Orbis Books, 1984]). Furthermore, *Lumen gentium* replaced an elitist concept of holiness (see Philip Sheldrake, *Images of Holiness* [London: Darton, Longman and Todd, 1987], 20).

[8] "Christian holiness . . . is not a search simply for tranquillity and invulnerability. Christian tradition has always emphasised that a kind of 'holy discontent' and struggle is an essential part of the journey towards fulfillment" (Sheldrake, *Images of Holiness*, 32).

These common characteristics ensure that local faces of Christian spirituality are part of a larger picture. However, there are many ways to see that picture; it is painted in local colors. Different spiritualities reflect particular encounters with particular faces of Christ. "The realisation has emerged that specific spiritual traditions are initially embodied in people rather than doctrine and grow out of life rather than from abstract ideas" (Sheldrake 1992, 33). New spiritualities arise out of responses to local situations. Spirituality develops in interaction with the natural life environment. Fishermen, for example, seek protection from the powers of the sea and thus develop special prayers and special forms of worship because of their special concerns (see Gravrand 1986, 101). Farmers will pray to different powers.

"At the root of every spirituality there is a particular experience that is had by concrete persons living at a particular time" (Gutiérrez 1984, 37). Every religious order grows out of a founding myth, the particular story of a particular person in a particular situation. The late superior general of the Jesuits, Pedro Arrupe, was moved by experiences he had in Lourdes while working with the medical service there and by the experience of being in Hiroshima on 6 August 1945. These local experiences shaped his biography, the story of a man who himself influenced Ignatian spirituality after Vatican II.

The spirituality of the "little way" of Thérèse of Lisieux is local in the sense that it reflects features of nineteenth-century French middle-class piety. Thérèse wanted to offer herself "up to the Child Jesus as a plaything, for him to do what he liked with me . . . a toy of no value—a ball, say—is all at his disposal: he can throw it on the ground, kick it about, make a hole in it, leave it lying in the corner, or press it to his heart if he feels that way about it" (Knox 1958, 171). This is a particular spirituality, rooted in a local context. Every person is going a unique way toward Jesus.

By looking at the spirituality of a person we could ask the following questions: What are the central stories in this person's life? What are the key insights I try to follow in my life, the "wisdom"? What are the central encounters? Who are the central persons? What are the guiding ideas and values? What is the vision of this life? What are the most important rituals and ceremonies, places and times, that structure this life, its rhythm?

We could ask these questions with regard to a person who has become a source of inspiration for our own spiritual life and for our attempts to reappropriate the tradition and message of Jesus. And we could ask this question for the context of our own life, trying to look into our own spirituality. Let us look at an example of such an outlook on the spirituality of an inspiring person.

Aspects of Dom Helder Câmara's Spirituality as Encountered by Mary Hall

Dom Helder Câmara was the bishop of the Diocese of Recife in Northern Brazil for many years. He was a gentle but powerful witness to a life in service to the poor. Many people were afraid of this courageous pastor, just over five feet tall. Dom Helder's power was the power of the powerless, nourished in prayer. He is known as a priest and bishop, a poet and writer, a speaker and preacher, a spiritual person of deep faith. Looking at Dom Helder's spirituality would require us to take into account his many books, poems, and reflections. Of course, we cannot do that. I suggest a more personal way to get to know Dom Helder's spirituality. In the late 1970s Mary Hall talked to Dom Helder Câmara. She wanted to find out more about him and the sources from which he drew his energy. In a very personal book she records her encounters with Dom Helder, presenting us with an assessment of Dom Helder Câmara's spirituality.

Dom Helder's way of looking at life had been shaped by experiences that became key stories for him. His mother taught him a lot about life. "One day my native town, Fortaleza, was shocked by the murder of a poet dearly loved by all. The whole town was thinking of his mother, crushed by her loss. My mother's comment was 'I don't know who I pity most—the mother of the murdered man or the mother of the assassin'" (23).[9] The wisdom to look through the surface of things and see a greater reality has always been part of Dom Helder's way of encountering situations.

He received many lessons in his childhood that would shape his later ministry. "I cannot help but remember that I myself knew hunger and misery; that I saw my mother weep and my father fall silent from bitterness when there was nothing to eat, when there was not enough to break bread among the children. I didn't like okra. Once, I stopped eating when there was only okra on the plate. Next day my mother presented me with the same plate and said with a smile: 'Helder, this business of liking and not liking is a luxury only the rich can enjoy. Eat a little and you will see that it is good.' Since that day, I eat anything" (23). His father taught him about the priesthood in a very simple statement when Helder told him that he wanted to become a priest: Priests do not belong to themselves, his father said; they belong to God and the people. Dom Helder's private teacher Dona Salome Cisne taught him the lesson "that in spite of diplomas, we must never forget that we never stop being pupils" (27). And Padre Cabral, director of the Junior Seminary, taught him a vision of love: "I never was afraid to love anything created" (28).

In the seminary he experienced the first great humiliation of his life when he was not allowed to publish articles against a professor, the sister-in-law of the vicar general. Looking back, this experience was healing: "God sends us four or five humiliations each day and four or five big, first-class humiliations during our life-time. . . . 'Humility is indeed an essential virtue, because without it we cannot advance a step in the spiritual life'" (32). These are

---

[9] The page numbers given in parentheses throughout this section refer to Mary Hall, *The Impossible Dream: The Spirituality of Dom Helder Câmara* (Maryknoll, N.Y.: Orbis Books, 1980).

stories that have shaped Dom Helder's outlook on life. Another key experience was the comment of Cardinal Gerlier of Lyons after the Eucharistic World Congress that Dom Helder had very successfully organized in 1952: "He congratulated me on the success of the Congress and praised my organizational ability, but then he said, 'Why don't you use this ability to find a solution for the favelas, the scandal of this beautiful city'" (56). This was the beginning of Dom Helder's option to use his skills for the poorest of the poor. These are some of the central encounters and some of the central people in Dom Helder's life.

Dom Helder follows the wisdom of encountering Christ in the people. "During the Congress Christ had been honoured in the Eucharist, now I was determined to honour him in the poor" (56). He was able to find Christ in his people (75). Honoring Christ in the poor cannot mean bowing down to others. Being of service is a privilege, a gift, grace. "It was St. Vincent de Paul who said, 'We must conquer by love the right to give.' We must get rid of every idea of alms. He who is helped today, is helped with the conviction that tomorrow he will be able to help" (57). A metaphor he used in the conversation with Mary Hall describes how he sees himself—he thinks of himself as the little donkey that brought Jesus to Jerusalem (60). This rich metaphor throws light on many other aspects of Dom Helder's life. He lived his priesthood in gentle, unwavering service to others. And he was happy to be a priest. "I lived my priesthood with very deep emotion. It has fulfilled all my dreams of belonging to God and to others" (36).

Dom Helder understood his own life as God's life through him: "I consider there is no need of words to talk with God, so I think to myself, 'Lord, I would like to lend you my eyes, ears, mouth and hands. Look through my eyes, listen through my ears, and speak through my mouth.' It is so good, so good to look at the world, at mankind, when one lends one's ears to Christ. There is never a possibility for hatred, never a possibility but to love, to love largely, grandly, fully" (60). And this love manifests itself in concrete actions, in a life of solidarity, in a concern for justice. Loving God means living the truth. When he came to Recife in 1964, he knew that he had to speak up: "From the beginning I knew I must have the courage to speak the truth, right from the very first moment" (76). Speaking the truth means speaking about social justice. "Because social justice is the most important issue, it is at the root of all problems" (80). This hunger for justice shaped Dom Helder's identity: "I see my role as speaking out about social justice on every occasion. . . . I would not be worthy of Christ if I remained silent. . . . Today I am becoming one of the voiceless poor of Brazil" (80).

Dom Helder's life beat to a certain rhythm that kept him in touch with the center of the universe. The essence of his life was his meditations, "the most intimate and profound records of my heart. I write them during the early morning hours" (59). Dom Helder would rise each morning at 2 A.M. and spend some hours in prayer.

I begin by saying my breviary in a very simple way. I open the window, look at the sky, read the psalms, and review the day that has passed. I recall all those I met, the people I have seen; the news I have heard of the city, the nation, the world, interests me enormously. When I meet a person the meeting is on a very personal level. If that person is Irish like yourself I think of Ireland and its problems, and I think of all the people of all religions who are doing so much good for the world. During the day, perhaps, I meet a worker, Antonio . . . I think of all the workers everywhere in the world. . . . His wife is pregnant . . . I think of all the women in the world who are expecting (60).

Dom Helder's relationship with God and with the supernatural world was very natural. "His ability to pass easily from the natural to the supernatural gives him great consolation and great courage" (68). He felt protected by the presence of God, in a very natural way. His philosophy of life was not a sophisticated theological construction. He knew that he did not live alone: "There are three persons—the Father, the Son and Holy Spirit. I enjoy all the current discussions of theologians very much, but I must admit I hold on to my own conception of the Blessed Trinity" (69). He knew that his life was a point of encounter of the visible and the invisible. This was human identity for him: "I see no dichotomy between soul and body. A man is a single undivided unit; we can't separate his 'religious part' from the rest of him" (90). He strongly believed in the presence of his guardian angel: "He is my good friend and he is there especially in moments of great joy as in moments of great suffering" (68). Dom Helder was convinced that the supernatural is tangible, that the mystery of God speaks to us through the mystery of nature and the mystery of people. He was full of imagination, a poet, a person with a dream and a vision encouraging "Abrahamic minorities" all over the world, communities of people who care about a better world. His rich imagination helped him to encounter God in all things: "You know imagination is very important in understanding creation, it helps us to understand God" (67).

He told of an encounter with an ant: "Once when the ants had eaten the leaves of my rose-bush I picked up an ant and scolded it for doing so. But the ant in my palm taught me a lesson. As it squirmed in my hand it replied: 'Why should you be the only one to enjoy the rose-bush?'" (67). Finding God in all things, seeing through the surface and touching upon God's humor, mystery, and love was Dom Helder's charism. Being a poet and being a priest were, in a way, one and the same thing for Dom Helder Câmara.

Dom Helder's philosophy of life was as simple and as deep as his life: "Such is my life . . . prayer and work" (61). His spirituality was an open book; his inner life penetrated all aspects of his actions. Mary Hall recalls "a first glimpse of Dom Helder at the airport in Washington, surrounded by a welcoming group of important officials. Suddenly he stops, the cortege also stops as Dom Helder smiles and waves at a beautiful flock of birds" (68).

> Exercise: Think about a person who has inspired you by his or her example of witnessing to the message of Jesus. Describe the spirituality of this person by answering the following questions:
> What are the central stories of this person's life?
> What are the central encounters of his or her life?
> Who are the central people in this person's life?
> What are his or her guiding ideas and values?
> What are the rituals and ceremonies, places and times, structure and rhythms
>   of this person's life?
> What if you ask these questions about yourself?

GOOD THEOLOGY

THESIS 25: Reappropriating our tradition cannot be done without good theology. Chief among the criteria of good theology are reality, fidelity to the founder, and the practical consequences that follow from a particular theological "work."

Entering a dialogue with the wider horizon provided by our tradition prevents us from being narrow-minded; it reminds us that there is more than the perspectives of which we are immediately aware; it helps us to put our thoughts into perspective.

What is "good theology" according to Jesus? As we have seen, theology is not exclusively an academic endeavor. It is about personal and communal transformation, based on a relationship with God. A person who does not pray cannot credibly claim to be a theologian. This is what we can learn from Jesus, our teacher of theology. He also taught us how to think about good theology.

Jesus emphasizes the practical consequences, the fruits. He emphasizes the spirit with which theology is done. He emphasizes the need to care for the people and to be with the people. In this light I suggest three criteria for good theology.

The first criterion is *realness*. We have to be true to the facts. We have seen how Jesus honored common sense and human reason, the ability to make judgments and to base these judgments on arguments. We have seen that Christianity is rooted in history and honors the importance of natural reality and history. We know that the natural and the supernatural work together, not against each other. Being true to reality is also an aspect of human maturity. It means acknowledging that reality cannot merely be constructed in an arbitrary manner. It has to deal with hindrances, difficulties, and impediments. "The test of reality is the resistance it offers to the otherwise uninhibited course of my own thinking, desiring and acting. Reality is what 'I come up against,' what takes me by surprise, the other-than-myself which pulls me up and obliges me to reckon with it and adjust myself to it because it will not consent simply to adjust itself to me" (Baillie 1962, 33).

Jean Vanier talks about the importance of being present in reality: "Often I go off in dreams about living and being with the poor, but what the poor need are not my dreams, my beautiful thoughts, inner reflections, but my concrete presence. There is always the temptation to replace real presence with lovely thoughts about being present" (in Nouwen 1988, 83). There is always the temptation to deny the truth, to deal with it only partially, to paint an appealing picture, to cushion the truth. There are the hard facts of suffering and suppression, death and evil. But, indeed, it is a spiritual challenge to see even these hard facts in a soft light without betraying them. Henri Nouwen describes a film he has seen about the atomic bomb over Hiroshima: "Among all the scenes of terror and despair, emerged one image of a man quietly writing a word in calligraphy. All his attention was directed to writing that one word" (Nouwen 1992, 63).

American psychologist Rollo May attacks a false religiosity that acts as a means of preventing real confrontations with evil by protecting us in an artificial world (state of pseudo-innocence), a state of being fixed in a childhood mentality that is mistaken for goodness. In this sense "honesty to reality" also means the readiness and ability to be exposed to reality (May 1998).

I would like to understand this criterion in the sense of Jon Sobrino: "Any genuine spirituality will demand in the concrete: (1) honesty about the real, (2) fidelity to the real, and (3) a certain 'correspondence' by which we permit ourselves to be carried along by the 'more' of the real" (Sobrino 1985, 14). The third point talks about growing into a larger reality, into seeing more and hearing more.[10] Based on the criterion of realness, there must be no dichotomy between the vertical and the horizontal dimensions of spirituality, between the dimension oriented toward "the untouchable" (vertical, supernatural, sacred, God) and the dimension oriented toward the "tangible" (horizontal, social, community).

---

[10] We can also understand the Ignatian criterion as part of this criterion of realness: "Does [the spirituality at stake] bring a greater sense of consecration, an integration of life through holiness, and at the same time the need for purification, the sense of our distance from God?" (J. R. Sheets, "Profile of the Spirit: A Theology of Discernment of Spirits," in "Notes on the Spiritual Exercises of St. Ignatius of Loyola," ed. David L. Fleming, *Review for Religious* [1981], 221).

The second criterion for good theology is the criterion of *fidelity to the founder*. In the Christian tradition we are talking about fidelity to Jesus. We have seen the importance and the possibility of looking at Jesus. Christian theology has to be faithful and honest to the mission and message and person of Jesus. We have seen that there are many faces of this loyalty to the founder. We have come to acknowledge the pluralism of local theologies and the many local responses to the invitation of Christ. A genuine response to Jesus will always be a personal response.

The third criterion is the criterion of *practical consequences*. What are the fruits of our theologies? To which form of praxis does this theology lead us? Is the spirituality at stake confirmed in the course of human and social praxis? Theology is a way of following Jesus. It has to be measured in the terms of an apostolate. "The sincerity of our conversion to the Lord is to be judged by the action to which this concern leads us" (Gutiérrez 1984, 103). Jon Sobrino mentions fortitude, impoverishment, creativity, solidarity, and joy as fruits of a valid spirituality (Sobrino 1985, 96-102). These ideas are important for our understanding of good theology. The emphasis on practical consequences can also be found in the framework of Ignatian spirituality: Does the theology at stake contribute to the building of communities, to the unification of communal structures? Does it tighten the bonds of unity in the community? (Sheets 1981, 223). We do theology as if people matter—in order to build up community. We have seen that the building of community is a key in Jesus' way of doing theology.

The question of the criteria for good theology is no idle one. We want to do theology, and we want to create good theologies. The three criteria above remind us of Jesus. He was doing theology as if people matter and as if facts matter. He was doing theology in fidelity to the One who sent him, and he was doing theology that forged community ties and brought people together. The practical consequences of Jesus' way of doing theology were sustainability, empowerment, appropriateness, and challenge. These are guideposts for our endeavor to do theology. In short, good theology is theology following the example of Jesus.

A THEOLOGICAL APPRAISAL OF AN ANTI-SEMITIC LOCAL PRACTICE

After having described three criteria of good theology, I would like to show the application of these criteria in the praxis of Christian life. We can make use of these criteria in situations where we are called to assess and evaluate implicit theologies or particular spiritualities. We will look at an example of a theological assessment of an implicit local theology embedded in a particular local practice in Southern Austria.

In a particular Tyrolean village people told of events that supposedly dated back to the fifteenth century. The legend centered around a group of traveling Jews who killed a little boy named Andreas Oxner (who was later called Anderle von Rinn). In fact, this story is one of many stories of ritual murders by Jews that haunted Europe in the seventeenth century. In our particular village, in the year 1670 a chapel was built to honor Anderle of Rinn; by its very existence as a shrine it inculcated a spirit of contempt for Jews. In the retelling of the story, Anderle von Rinn was made a martyr and venerated. Pilgrimages were organized. Representations of the alleged martyrdom showed the bloody murder of the little boy by Jews and became part of the décor of the parish church. A supposed relic of the boy was even placed in the altar. In the mid 1980s, however, the local bishop asked for a theological assessment of this local devotion, and when it was finished, he strictly forbade public continuation of this local "spiritual" practice (Fresacher 1998).

The theological assessment, first of all, acknowledged that there was a vital local spirituality involved. Even in a situation such as this one, the bishop recognized that there has to be an appreciation for local culture and that practices that appear blatantly aberrational must not be simply condemned on an a priori basis. Instead, a careful theological evaluation had to be made. In an application of our first criterion, concerning the *reality* of the events on which a practice is based, a historical investigation found that in this particular case there was no factual basis to the legend upon which the devotion was based. Therefore, there was no fidelity to real events. In fact, it was shown that the legend is an example of baroque fictional literature.

Applying the second criterion—*fidelity of the devotion to the spirit and teaching of Jesus as the founder of Christianity*—we know that Jesus was a Jew himself and that he did not encourage any form of anti-Semitism. In spite of his conflicts with the leaders of the Jewish people over the proper interpretation of Judaism, the essence of his teaching was a call for life in unity and a love that embraced everybody. Similarly, Jesus respected facts and taught people to be careful in making judgments, especially in making judgments that were critical of others. Jesus also taught that God is the center of human worship.

Taking the third criterion—that of the *practical consequences* of a theological belief and practices stemming from it—one needs only point to the anti-Semitic representations, songs, prayers, and emotions. This local spirituality led to anti-Semitic feelings and practices that caused pain among the Jewish people. Because of its failure to meet our three criteria, a theological evaluation had to challenge this particular local spirituality.

Exercise: Examine a theological work of which you are aware (for example, a devotion promoted by a religious order) and evaluate it using the three criteria.

4

Theologies
and Local Culture

THESIS 26: Local cultures are expressions of God's continuing creation. Theology begins with the human situation. It is a "second step." The human situation has a cultural face. The concept of culture, which touches all levels of human existence, is one of the most difficult and yet basic concepts and needs to be considered in local theologies.

CULTURE AS A LOCAL REALITY

"Culture is what we make of creation" and "a metaphor that has come to stand for what humans have made of their particular corner of the earth" (Dyrness 1997, 58, 62). Bernard Meland gives us a colorful description rather than a definition of culture when he characterizes culture as

> the human flowering of existing structures and facilities, becoming manifest as an ordered way of life in the imaginative activities and creations of a people, their arts and crafts, their architecture, their furniture and furnishings, their customs and designs, their literature, their public and private ceremonies, both religious and political. It is in their formative ideas, giving direction to their educational efforts and customs, as well as to their religious notions and practices, their social graces and manners; in their habits of eating and body care; in their modes of livelihood and the social organization that follows from them (Meland 1962, 212).

Culture is the way we live and at the same time the framework within which we live as social beings. A few familiar characteristics that shape the modern concept of culture are the following: Culture marks the difference between human and nonhuman forms of life; culture is multifarious and varies with geographical, social, and historical context; the way cultures are shaped and come into existence is contingent; culture is learned and passed on, constantly changed and modified; a culture forms "a whole" that can be construed either on an expressive level (various features of a particular culture as the expression of the same idea or worldview) or a logical-semantic level (various features of a particular culture are interlinked in relations of implication and dependency); culture is expressed in many observable ways; culture touches all levels of human existence (see Tanner 1997, 25-28).

Cultures are expressions of our attempts to come to terms with life. Cultures express the human need for security and meaning and the human fear of chaos. Cultures help to answer the question, Who am I? This question is also one of the basic questions of theology. In this sense we do theology all the time, because we constantly try to find our place in our community, in society, in the world. Questions of identity are theological questions. "The complete loss of one's identity is, with all propriety of theological definition, hell" (Murray 1960, 6). And being known for who we really are is heaven.

Questions of identity are questions that make our heart burn. Virtually anything can become the object of theology, anything can be treated from a theological point of view. Every aspect of life can be related to God, to a matter of ultimate concern. Theology is about the whole human situation. "Any and every theological question begins with the human situation. Theology is 'the second step'" (Segundo 1976, 79). The first step is the human situation. Theology is a way of reflecting on human life in the light of human experiences with God. Theology is secondary; it depends on our human experience. Gustavo Gutiérrez writes, "What Hegel used to say about philosophy can likewise be applied to theology: it rises only at sundown" (Gutiérrez 1973, 11). The journey of theology can only begin once you have embarked on the journey of life. And the journey of life is difficult.

The human situation provokes questions because it is fragile. Without warning someone loses a job, gets involved in a car accident, is diagnosed with cancer. None of us can program our life as a straight line. We cannot predict what is going to happen tomorrow. The rich man built a larger barn and died (Lk 12:16-21). We cannot plan the exact outcome of our lives. Whoever lives, takes risks—the risk of failing, for example. That is why we ask these burning questions of identity and meaning all the time. These questions pervade our cultures and shape our cultural expressions. In this sense our cultures are shaped by implicit theologies.

IMPLICIT THEOLOGIES

THESIS 27: Doing theology is a matter of being honest with ourselves and others. We do theology because we are inevitably faced with burning questions of life (beginning, end, purpose, choices) in our human situation. Everybody is confronted with these questions and develops "implicit theologies," which can be dangerous and should be made explicit for the sake of the community.

Implicit theologies are our attitudes toward life as such and toward the world as a whole. Implicit theologies are our attempts to deal with the burning questions of life. Because we all experience wounds we all ask questions. Nobody can assume a "view from nowhere," looking down on life from an ivory tower without ever getting involved.

There is an implicit theology hidden in our form of life and in our way of looking at things. Our cultures are shaped by implicit theologies, implicit beliefs about what counts in life. The businessman will hear the noise of a falling coin in a busy street, but he will not hear the singing of a bird. A mother will hear her baby. Where some people see a beggar, others see a loser, and still others see a person in pain. Our cultures teach us how to listen and look.

American anthropologist Edward T. Hall has drawn our attention to the "silent language" and the "hidden dimension" of cultures (Hall 1959; Hall 1982). We are raised to organize our space in a particular way. Each culture teaches a particular concept of time. What constitutes a "long silence" depends on the culture. How close we can stand to another person without making that person feel uncomfortable depends on the culture. What is public space and what is private space depends on the culture. We might recall the example of the Filipina girl who was sent to a host family in the United States. Right after her arrival in the house, the host mother showed the girl to her room and closed the door. She assumed that the girl needed some rest and privacy. The girl felt miserable—what had she done wrong to be so excluded?

Culture teaches us a way of facing reality, space, time, and people. In one of Chesterton's stories a person testifies that no one came to the house that morning. No one? It turns out that there was a man delivering something and the postman. But they do not count; we do not even "see" them usually, certainly not as visitors. Whom do we see? What do we see? What are our implicit theologies, shaped by our cultures?

Our implicit theologies are like silent languages that shape our way of life. These implicit theologies are sometimes more important than the explicit ones because they are hidden, deeper, more powerful, and less controllable. Colonization has introduced implicit theologies, thus colonizing the mind. Theologies are silent languages of our cultures. There are innumerable cultures, and there are many silent languages within each culture.

The silent languages of cultures are revealed in details. Colors may "mean" something (See Mveng 1979). An example comes from Africa:

> Victory, in my culture, for example, is marked by white. If you see people with white clay *(hyirew)* marks on their bodies, you know that they have been successful in one of life's battles, be it childbirth or a case in court. Red *(ntwoma-Laterite)* markings spell gloom, disaster, and even despair. The choice of white clothes by Methodist Church Ghana for communion service and Easter and New Year celebrations is not fortuitous. White clothing is the raiment of a people who trust in the victorious God (Oduyoye 1986, 50).

The analysis of signs can point to important dimensions of cultures, "depth" dimensions. Semiotic analysis can have an impact on the organization of pastoral set ups: "In the West black is traditionally associated with mourning, but in other parts of the world, like China, white is the color of grief" (Chupungco 1992, 91).

These silent languages can reveal wounds. Virgilio Elizondo observes from a Hispanic perspective: "From birth we are conditioned to see angelic beauty in the white, the blond, the blue-eyed. The liturgical colors sacralize our color coding: white is pure and festive while black and brown are negative and non-existent. White baby Jesus and blonde Virgin Mary" (Elizondo 1988, 54).

People normally have a good idea of what the "good life" means for them. This idea depends on their culture. Let us look at an example:

> Two American volunteer development workers on a South Pacific island, who were worried by seeing the ladies in a village washing their clothes in a distant river, decided to build washing tubs. Having built the tubs—according to the specifications from America and with imported cement—the volunteers invited the women to use the tubs. The following day, the women were back at the river and the volunteers were hurt and angry. On being asked why the tubs were no longer used, the women replied: "We like to gossip about the men. If we wash at the tubs, the men will hear. Also, our backs are sore from standing at the tubs. We like to squat when we do the washing" (Arbuckle 1987, 130).

Anybody doing local theology has to respect the implicit theologies of the local culture. An explicit theology can only strike roots if the minister, community leader, or professional theologian respects and honors and considers the existing implicit theologies.

Implicit theologies can be inconsistent, unjustifiable, or even dangerous. Because of the consequences of our implicit theologies, we have to do explicit theology. We can say about theology what Karl Popper wrote about philosophy:

> We all have our philosophies, whether or not we are aware of this fact, and our philosophies are not worth very much. But the impact of our philosophies upon our actions and our lives is often devastating. This makes it necessary to try to improve our philosophies by criticism. This is the only apology for the continued existence of philosophy which I am able to offer (Popper 1973, 33).

We do theology to acquire some distance from the heat of our implicit theologies. We step back and take a look.

"VALUE STORIES"

THESIS 28: A way to unveil biases or to trace hidden values and implicit theologies is through the use of stories that present ambiguous situations with actors who act on the basis of different value systems. These "value stories" are a useful theological tool when we ask which actors in this story are justified in acting the way they do.

Value stories invite us to think about the appropriateness of various behaviors. An open discussion of the story can reveal silent assumptions and interpretations of the text as well as moral standards we live and judge by.

THE STORY OF LO-TSEN AND KA-PO

Lo-Tsen has been in the capital for a few days visiting friends and having fun. On the way back to the village, Lo-Tsen is traveling with Aku, the best friend of Lo-Tsen's partner, Ka-Po. Late at night Lo-Tsen and Aku are stopped by a group of criminals, threatened with weapons, and brought to a cave. One of the group, Ra-Tschung, is put in charge of the prisoners. Aku is sleeping. Ra-Tschung approaches

Lo-Tsen and says, "I do not know what is going to happen to you tomorrow. Anything can happen. They might kill you both. I have a suggestion. If you spend the night with me, I will let you and your travelmate go tomorrow and tell my people that you managed to escape. I will come back to you once all my friends have fallen asleep." Lo-Tsen is confused and does not know what to do. After some time Ra-Tschung comes back. Lo-Tsen spends the night with Ra-Tschung, and the next morning Lo-Tsen and Aku are set free. Aku asks Lo-Tsen what happened. Lo-Tsen tells the story. Finally they reach the village. Lo-Tsen and Ka-Po are happily reunited. During the night, however, Ka-Po senses that there is something wrong with Lo-Tsen. Lo-Tsen does not say anything. The next morning Ka-Po turns to Aku and inquires what happened during their stay together. Aku thinks of a friend's duty and tells Ka-Po the whole truth. Ka-Po is angry, sad, and disappointed. Ka-Po knows that there is only one way out: the criminals have to be killed. Aku has to promise to keep silent. Without saying a word to Lo-Tsen, Ka-Po leaves the village to look for the criminals. Ka-Po has never been seen again.

Of whose behavior do we approve?

THE STORY OF KIKO AND ONO

Kiko is married to Ono. Ono falls ill and cannot work anymore in the factory, the only employer of their village. Kiko's wage has to sustain the whole family—Kiko, Ono, and their two children, aged five and seven. Kiko's wage has to cover Ono's medical bills as well. Kiko's wage in the factory is low. So Kiko approaches Zaza, the boss of the factory. Kiko urges Zaza to assign a different type of work in which Kiko can earn more money. Zaza promises to think about it. The next morning Zaza calls Kiko and says, "I am willing to help you. But I need your help, too. There is a military training camp where my children have been called to go for three months. The people at the camp are nasty. I do not want my kids to go there. If you send your kids to the camp instead of mine, I will take a risk and give you a much better paying job even though you are not qualified for it. Think about it." Kiko does not know what to do. Kiko goes to Runu, a wise person, and seeks advice. Runu thinks about the question and says, "This is a decision where any advice would be dangerous and wrong. You are mature and adult. You will have to make the decision on your own!" Kiko becomes more and more confused. Kiko turns to Ono and tells Ono about the dilemma. Ono says, "This is no question. We will not expose our children to the military camp. I will die soon and then you will be free to marry again, perhaps to a wealthier person." Kiko is desperate. While Ono is sleeping, Kiko takes the children to Zaza, then lies to Ono about their whereabouts. Kiko gets the well-paid job and with expensive medical treatment Ono slowly gets better. After three months the children return. They tell Ono what has happened. Ono is angry and wants to divorce Kiko. But Ono is still not well enough to take care of the children. Ono decides to say nothing and wait till the situation has improved. Then Ono will leave Kiko and take the children.

Value stories leave much space for interpretation. There are no exact indications of place, time, background, age, sex, religion, and so on. They are written solely to help us to think about our hidden values, about our implicit theologies.

Exercise: Assess the behavior of the actors in one of the stories told above. Which (if any) acted in a way you approve of? Discuss your opinions with others. Are there differences? What major arguments are brought forward? Would it make a difference if all people in the story were male? if they were all female? Would the time or the place of the story make a difference? What implicit judgments (assumptions) concerning their sex did you make? What about time and place?

THEOLOGY AND THE DIALOGUE WITH CULTURE

THESIS 29: There is a need for a dialogue between our understanding of theology and our concept of culture: Theology reflects upon culturally embedded forms of religious life. Theology has to reappropriate the message of Jesus from its cultural context into local cultural context. There is, however, no "super-cultural theology" or "universal Christian culture."

As we've seen, implicit theologies shape our cultures. Doing theology is an attempt to bring the implicit theologies to the surface, to make our hidden values explicit. In order to do that, theology needs to take a careful look at the many faces of a particular culture. Local theologies are invitations to enter a serious and respectful dialogue with a particular local culture. "Those cultural realities that cluster around the theological concepts of creation, redemption, and community are of paramount importance for a theologian wishing to listen to culture" (Schreiter 1985, 40). The pastoral constitution of the Second Vatian Council, *Gaudium et spes*, tells us that understanding culture is necessary for a full understanding of the human (no. 53). It is a genuine theological task to analyze local cultures from a theological perspective. This is part of the prophets' tradition in the Old Testament.

Theology touches upon the deepest layers of human existence; it touches the point where we seek to understand our life and where we seek to come to terms with the world as a whole. These attitudes are shaped in cultural ways. Second, theology needs to look at cultures because the origins of Christianity are to be found in a particular culture. Theology has to talk about culture when trying to understand the person and message of Jesus the Christ in particular and of the Holy Scriptures in general. Third, theology is itself part of a culture. Doing theology takes place within the framework of a particular culture. This has an impact on the language we speak, the categories we use, the experiences we rely on, the problems we deal with, the assumptions we make.

We also need the dialogue between theology and culture because Christian identity is constantly negotiated within local cultures. Christians live within local cultures. They do not live within a Christian culture. There is no such thing. Nor is there any Christian religion on a culturally neutral ground. "Human beings are 'situated' beings. They can begin only with what they have received. There is no 'ideal Christianity' on this earth" (Kabasélé 1994, 80). In this sense Japanese theologian Uchimura Kanzo said in 1926:

> I am blamed by missionaries for upholding Japanese Christianity. They say that Christianity is a universal religion, and to uphold Japanese Christianity is to make a universal religion a natural religion. Very true. But do not these very missionaries uphold sectional or denominational forms of Christianity which are not very different from national Christianity? . . . Is not Episcopalianism essentially an English Christianity, Presbyterianism a Scotch Christianity, Lutheranism a German Christianity, and so forth? (in Mullins 1998, 37).

Christian identity is always shaped in dialogue with particular cultures. Christian identity in a country where the majority is Hindu is different from Christian identity in an environment where the majority is Christian. But we are still talking about Christian identity. Christian identity has to be understood in terms of a task and a responsibility rather than in terms of something we "have," "own," or "possess."

Furthermore, Christian identity cannot be based "purely on the gospel" (not to speak of the many cultures we refer to when we talk about the gospel): "Christian social practices are always forced to incorporate material from other ways of life if they are to constitute a whole way of life themselves" (Tanner 1997, 112). This basically means that we cannot understand our Christian identity without understanding particular cultures. This is what Jesus did: By reappropriating his own tradition he was trying to make sense of his own culture.

LOCAL LANGUAGE

THESIS 30: Local theologies need to pay attention to the particularities of local language. Concepts are powerful because they reveal a culture's way of seeing the world. Concepts convey value systems. An elementary linguistic analysis is a useful tool for local theologies. Using local language is a sign of respect for the local culture.

The most important expression of culture is language. There are not only many different languages and many dialects of one language, there are also many ways of talking, many ways of making use of a particular language. This colorful variety is of vibrant interest for local theologies that attempt to take the many forms and faces of a cultural context seriously.

Austrian philosopher Ludwig Wittgenstein has called to mind the many ways of using language. He compared the function of words with the function of tools: "Think of the tools in a tool-box: there is a hammer, pliers, a saw, a screw-driver, a rule, a glue-pot, glue, nails and screws.—The functions of words are as diverse as the functions of these objects" (Wittgenstein 1967, §11). From this observation on the diverseness of our linguistic units, Wittgenstein proceeds to invite us to view language as a "system of language games." He uses this term to refer to the whole gamut of words used and activities surrounding the use of words.

Speaking is a way of acting; uttering sentences is part of our way of life. There are countless kinds of sentences. There is a colorful multiplicity of language games. Wittgenstein mentions examples as diverse as "giving orders," "reporting an event," "translating from one language into another," "thanking," "cursing," "greeting," "praying" (Wittgenstein 1967, §23). Different cultures produce different kinds of language games, but language games are part of all ways of life, parts of all activity.

American anthropologists Benjamin Lee Whorf and Edward Sapire show the relation between culture and language. There are many different expressions for "snow" among the Inuits; the Hopi language makes no distinction between past, present, and future but distinguishes among a fact, memory, expectation, and custom. Concepts reflect situations in which a culture felt compelled to draw a distinction and to mark this distinction. Our linguistic distinctions depend on our needs and interests. Our concepts and distinctions are embedded in everyday life. It is hardly possible to learn a language without knowing the culture. That is why we cannot simply introduce new concepts into particular contexts.[1]

Language games are part of life. The way we talk is linked with the way we live. Talking is a way of doing things. Concepts are always linked with use, with praxis, hence with culture. To give one example from a Pacific island:

> The word in Tobian for "baptize" usually refers to bathing (both swimming and washing), but it has two other meanings—one for the traditional cure for insanity, the other for a traditional disciplinary measure. Fathers punished their misbehaving sons by taking them to the sea and holding their heads underwater until they lost consciousness. Shamans chanting incantations used a similar technique to treat the insane (Black 1988, 58).

This language usage reflects the fact that the baptismal rite was linked with the cure for insanity and the punishment for transgressions. Language usage has an impact on the understanding of the meaning of a term when it is introduced. If our praxis changes, our concepts will change.

It is a powerful act to name something. It is powerful to be emancipated from the bonds of imposed language. It is an act of liberation to find one's own words and one's own names. Betty Friedan, for instance, wrote in *The Feminine Mystique* in 1963 about "a problem that has no name." Leny Mendoza Strobel[2] talks about faint memories about pre-colonial times "buried underneath an avalanche of foreign words. There were no words for what I felt in my bones—not in English anyway" (in Montgomery-Fate 1997, 89).

Concepts are powerful because they carry the whole force of cultures. Colonizers who have left their linguistic marks on colonies exercise power even after their departure. Kenyan novelist Ngugi Wa Thiong'o calls the linguistic colonization a "colonization of the mind." He observes that due to the traces of colonialism in language, "language and literature were taking us further and further from ourselves to other selves, from our world to other worlds" (Wa Thiong'O 1986, 12). Again, we see how implicit theologies are transported in our language.

---

[1] The advice of the British philosopher John Austin has not lost any of its significance: "Our common stock of words embodies all the distinctions men have found worth drawing, and the connections they have found worth making, in the lifetime of many generations: these surely are likely to be more numerous, more sound, since they have stood up to the long test of the survival of the fittest, and more subtle, at least in all ordinary and reasonably practical matters, than any that you or I are likely to think up in our own arm-chairs of an afternoon—the most favoured alternative method" (Austin, *Philosophical Papers* [Oxford: Clarendon, 1961], 130).

[2] Quoted in Montgomery-Fate, *Beyond the White Noise*, p. 89.

Concepts can be liberating. *Han* is an extremely powerful concept used in Korean *minjung* theology. *Han* is a psychological term that denotes the feeling of suffering of a person or a people who has been repressed or oppressed by others. "This feeling of *han*, the suffering and hopelessness of the oppressed, is a collective feeling in the collective social biography of the oppressed minjung of Korea" (Suh 1981, 24-25). This feeling of unresolved and unjustifiable suffering is the starting point and the point of reference of a local Korean theology.

Similarly, the term *lucha* plays an important role in liberation theology: "This word is used to counteract a passive and fatalistic stance towards the misery of the masses, and stress the urgency of an active—even aggressive—involvement in the war against poverty, oppressiveness, and exploitation" (Nouwen 1992, 138). Key terms in Hispanic theology—*pastoral de conjunto, teologia de conjunto, permitanme hablar, la comunidad, la fiesta*—have become means to give name to an important reality that cannot be properly grasped in the language of the oppressors.

Words develop against the background of a local culture. The very fact that the concepts are found within a local culture gives them a certain depth. The history of missiology and mission gives us many examples of the attempt to do mission work locally using the local language, local images, local concepts and distinctions. For example, the people of the Pévé in Southwest Chad use the word *Ifray* to talk about God. This word is derived from *Ya* (mother) and *fray* (heaven). The translation of the Lord's Prayer in this culture has to adjust to the local concepts found there. Local theologies must be sensitive to the nuances of a local language (see Sedmak 1997, 58).

THE FILIPINO CONCEPT OF *BAHALA NA*

Let us look at an example. In the context of the Lowland Filipinos the Tagalog expression *bahala na* is used frequently. *Bahala na* expresses a worldview, a general attitude, and has very strong theological implications; in fact, any major theological question can be linked with this expression. The Filipino way of life is condensed in this expression. The following (rudimentary) linguistic analysis of the expression *bahala na* has four steps: (1) examining dictionaries and possible translations; (2) collecting various contexts and ways of usage; (3) assessing the historical and social contexts of the expression; and (4) interpreting the expression theologically.

MEANING AND TRANSLATIONS

Bahala na is widely used to characterize an attitude of fatalism, acceptance of destiny, and trust in higher powers. It is translated in various different ways: "let come what may"; "never mind"; "God will provide"; "it is up to

God"; "what will be, will be"; "leave it to fate"; "whatever happens, happens."

It is significant that *bahala na* is a short expression that is, because of its intonation, phonetically attractive. This could indicate that the expression is part of the basic and elementary vocabulary. "Linguists tell us that *bahala na* does not refer to the god *Bathala*" (de Mesa 1987, 149); the root word of *bahala* means "responsibility," "concern," "management" (ibid., 161).

CONTEXTS OF USAGE

Bahala na epitomizes the Filipino attitude toward the world as a whole and toward life as such and toward God's rules within life. Let us take a number of situations when the *bahala na* might be used:

- A student, choosing between studying for an examination and going to a movie, chooses the movie, saying "Bahala na!"
- A married Filipino refuses to consider family planning, shrugs, and says "Bahala na!"
- People waiting in a shopping mall for the pouring rain to stop say "Bahala na!"
- People caught in traffic say "Bahala na!"
- A jeepney driver eyes his thin tires, his exhausted machine, and his third traffic violation and then tries to right things with some coffee money for the policeman at the corner. He sets out cheerfully with "Bahala na!" (de Mesa 1987, 161).
- Prisoners awaiting (political) trial and people suffering under the martial law of the 1970s and 1980s said "Bahala na!"

Because of the Westernization of the Philippines, *Bahala na* is also used on a meta-level; when the intellectual elite use it, they implicitly make fun of the concept and the social context. Students at the elite universities use the expression to talk about the traditional, rural Philippines. They see the *bahala na* as an expression of a way of life that is out of fashion, that is out of step with the speed and efficiency of the American culture that serves as the major model for the Philippines.

Affiliated expressions are frequently used in everyday life, especially when people have to "take care" of something, such as who should pay in the restaurant. The idea of having to take care of something that is expressed in *bahala na* with reference to God is also applied to humans. People use derivatives or affiliated expressions in the context of the father taking care of his family or the company boss taking care of his employees. In this sense it also connotes responsibility and solidarity.

The expression *bahala na* can be connected with proverbs like "Man's life is like a wheel, up now, down tomorrow" connected with the widely used expression *gulong ng kapalaran* (wheel of fortune). There is also the proverb, "Although I don't search for my fortune, it will come to me if it's really mine" (de Mesa 1987, 150, 152).

HISTORICAL AND SOCIAL CONTEXT

Bahala na points to experiences of powerlessness and dependence and is socially connected with colonialism and poverty that is not caused by individual failure and that cannot be changed through individual human efforts. According to José de Mesa, slum dwellers inevitably find themselves having to embrace the attitude expressed by *bahala na*: "Since so much of their lives is dominated by external forces, over which they have so little actual control, they easily assume an attitude of *bahala na*" (de Mesa 1987, 158). Historically, according to F. L. Jocano, the expression is closely tied up with ancient beliefs (Jocano 1969, 118).

THEOLOGICAL INTERPRETATION

There are two qualitatively different contexts of usage. First, there is a positive dimension. In this context *bahala na* connotes a "genuine trust or hope in God which includes human efforts and cooperation" (Gorospe 1978, 166). This is historically expressed in the resilience of the Filipinos in the face of adversities (the EDSA revolution of 1986 was called the "smiling revolution"). It is also connected with sentiments of solidarity, since individual independence is not as important a value as it is in the United States. It was used in this positive way by José Rizal, the national hero: "Bahala any may Kapa!" (God will provide) (ibid.). In this positive context, using the expression of *bahala na* is also connected with a sense of responsibility. No slum dweller following the *bahala na* attitude "is so utterly fatalistic as to wait for God's mercy and grace. Everyone, even the young, struggles for a place in life, for simple comforts, for a way to enjoy God's graces in little opportunities provided by the slum environment" (Jocano 1969, 194).

There is, however, a negative dimension. In this sense the attitude of *bahala na* is despised by the modern, urban, Americanized Filipino. It is taken to be an escape from involvement and responsibility and used in contexts of resignation. It connotes lack of motivation and effort, as well as laziness and resignation.

Our theological evaluation is based on local theological sources. In the *Catechism for Filipino Catholics* (CFC) we find the following contexts of usage: "If God creates and sustains everything, then *bahala na*, all is decided already" (CFC, 312). *Bahala na*, understood positively, relates the Filipino to God's providence (CFC, 260). The attitude of trust in God "is echoed in the traditional Filipino attitude of *bahala na*. Some claim that this has led to a certain fatalism, and a lack of the energy, discipline, and purpose needed for personal, familial, and national development" (CFC, 1158).

This attitude, according to the catechism, is based "on mistaken belief in some magic force or luck that supposedly renders our own efforts unnecessary or useless" (ibid.). This expresses a trustful dependence on God with a persisting belief that God provides for everything. This optimistic resignation, which can mean a commitment to do one's best while leaving to God what is not within one's control, is in line with Matthew 6:34, the first petition of the Lord's Prayer, and the invitation to seek first of all the kingdom of God. Theologically speaking, the *bahala na* is connected with religious convictions that the supernatural is heavily involved in the everyday life of individual people (Mulder 1997, 25ff.). The Second Plenary Council of the Philippines stresses the connection between *bahala na* attitude as trust in God and the social responsibility involved.

From the foregoing example drawn from the Filipino *bahala na*, we can gather the following:

- The emotional weight of concepts is revealed by their connotations.
- Everyday concepts are sources for doing theology.
- It should be part of the theologian's vocation to listen to the everyday language of people in everyday circumstances.

Exercise: Identify a key concept in your culture and try to conduct a linguistic analysis similar to the one on bahala na.

CULTURAL GAMES

THESIS 31: Culture can be analyzed by looking at cultural activities. We can call any identifiable cultural context a cultural game. Cultures can be characterized through their cultural games. Thus, we can view society as a community of players with different functions and different roles. We can view social life as a complex landscape of cultural games played. Important concepts to analyze are the distinction between competence (know how) and mandate (authorization) to participate in cultural games, the distinction between standardized and non-standardized games, and the concept of leading cultural games. The following questions can help to understand a particular local culture: Who is playing which cultural games? According to which rules? When and where? Why? Asking these questions systematically is a useful tool for local theologies.

The diffuse phenomenon of culture can be analyzed in much the same way as the complex phenomenon of languages. Eating, writing letters, making jokes, praying, traveling, watching TV, reading a book, undergoing a medical exam, and more are examples of cultural games. A cultural game is any social context that can be described by the rules that organize this particular social context. This can happen on a macro level (elections as a cultural game) and on a micro level (greeting as a cultural game).

A cultural game is any type of human activity that can be named and described and reproduced. Games are played in accordance with a canonical set of rules, and given this framework of rules, games can be reproduced and taught and played again and again. This kind of repetition and predictability is a basic element of our social life; we have to be able to count on the actions of our fellow human beings or we would completely lose our social orientation. Cultural games structure our lives.

There are three significant features that characterize games: (1) games are played in accordance with a set of rules; (2) games create a world of their own (very often special games are played in special locations only, for example, weddings, elections, graduations); and (3) games are limited (in space and time). Cultural games too take place in a special context; they follow specific rules; they have a beginning and a (more or less happy) end. In many cases we clearly mark the beginning and the end of a cultural game by rituals (think of a soccer game or a prayer service).

Cultural games can be learned (socialization) and handed down from generation to generation (tradition); cultural games can be introduced within a cultural context (innovation) or can be abolished after some time (obsolescence). Cultural games, like language games, have rules that determine whether the game is played properly. In order to participate in a certain cultural game, one has to meet specific requirements. Participation in cultural games presupposes (1) a certain type of competence (that is, knowing how to do it; for example, playing the piano, reading Aristotle in the original Greek); and (2) a certain type of mandate (society's permission or social authorization to play the game; for example, celebrating a Catholic Mass, announcing the date of national elections, or installing the electrical wiring in a new home).

The more cultural games a person seeks to play, the more intelligent, educated, and talented that person must be. The more cultural games a person is authorized to play, the higher the social status of that person. A kind of "social grammar," in other words, determines the mandate to enter a specific cultural game, though sometimes mandates and competencies seem to be out of order. The access to the cultural games reserved for Catholic priests, for example, seems to many to be a case of a formal mandate given to some rather than a matter of the competence of individuals to be effective priests. The point I am making here is that the question of the priesthood of women is not a question of competence, but exclusively a question of the mandate. When cultures are changing, the question of competence versus mandates often becomes a source of great disagreement in social groups. Other situations are less complicated and easier to understand. For example, anybody is welcome to learn to play the piano, but not everyone who tries to learn masters the instrument. This is a matter of competence, not of mandate. In this sense cultural games serve as social levelers, or—viewed from another perspective—as social stratifiers. The mandate to participate in cultural games organizes the different segments of society, allocates positions and status, distributes power and authority, and, if mandates are not given to all who are competent, keeps otherwise competent persons from moving upward into higher social strata.

Another important distinction lies between what have been called standardized and nonstandardized cultural games. Different local cultures standardize different sets of cultural games. Making telephone calls is a standardized cultural game in Austria but not in Bangladesh. Reading and writing are standardized cultural games in academic situations but not necessarily in a day-care center. Development in the context of adapting to a new culture entails being introduced to standardized cultural games (like the rules governing driving, communicating by telephone, gaining access to education, health services, and governmental administrative structures that can help solve a problem) in another culture. If you are an Arab in the United States or France, and if you want to take part in such Western cultural communities, you have to be able to participate in these standardized cultural games. "Outsiders," in such a context, are people who do not get the mandate to participate in standardized cultural games or people who do not have the skills to play the standardized cultural games. Each culture has interlocking sets of standardized games. Some games (like signaling welcome to visitors in Austria with a glass of schnapps) appear relatively minor and particular to a given culture. But extending or not extending such gestures is an important sign of whether one is truly accepted by members of that culture on the basis of reciprocal relations or is regarded as an undesired outsider.

Skill at playing standardized games defines cultural identities. Subcultures and minorities often struggle to get access to standardized games (think, for example, of the struggle for university education and entry to professions such as medicine, law, and ministry in the church by generations of women). Trying to change the interlocking set of standardized cultural games often causes bitter social conflict (think, for example, of the struggle to get German accepted as an official second language in Italian South Tyrol or to have Spanish accepted as a second official language in the United States). Hence, one must recognize that the question of standardizing cultural games is linked with questions of power. The answer to the question "Who has the influence and power to set the standards and change them?" reveals where ultimate authority lies. In every society we find outcasts, persons perceived to be socially deviant or simply not admitted to the full range of society's standardized games.

Sometimes it seems to be the vocation of an individual or a generation to break the rules.[3] Sometimes the rules that obtain—for example, when societies are undergoing major changes—are confusing.[4] Sometimes influential or creative people introduce new cultural games. Jesus may be described as a person who sought to bring new cultural games to a certain local cultural context. His reception by those with a stake in maintaining the traditional manner of running the society of his day is typical for those who seek to be agents of major change. Seeking to be a founding figure of a social movement is a dangerous occupation. Yet only such people truly change the games played within the framework of their culture.

Within the standardized cultural games of a culture we can identify the leading cultural games that dominate a particular culture. To understand them is to grasp the peculiarity of a local context. The leading games can be identified according to the amount of material and money devoted to them, the amount of time and space used by them, and by the number and prestige of people involved in them. Based on such criteria we see that soccer is a leading cultural game in Brazil; the celebration of Christmas is a leading cultural game in rural Austria; the presidential election is a leading cultural game in the United States; the fiesta is a leading cultural game in Hispanic cultures. The leading cultural games differ from culture to culture and are a good point of reference from which to assess local cultures.

There are key questions for the analysis of cultural games: *Who* plays *what* cultural games? *How* are they played? *When* are they played? *Where*

---

[3] Suppressive political regimes are characterized by a rigid body of rules and strict enforcement of these rules. Jean-Bertrand Aristide talks about Haiti, his country, in terms of rules and the need to break these rules: "Haiti is a prison. In that prison, there are rules you must abide by, or suffer the pain of death. One rule is: Never ask for more than what the prison warden considers your share. . . . Another rule is: Remain in your cell. Though it is crowded and stinking and full of human refuse, remain there, and do not complain. That is your lot. Another rule is: Do not organize. . . . Another rule is: Accept your punishment silently. Do not cry out. You are guilty. . . . I say: Disobey these rules. Ask for more. Leave your wretchedness behind. Organize with your brothers and sisters. Never accept the hand of fate. Keep hope alive" (Jean-Bertrand Aristide, *In the Parish of the Poor: Writings from Haiti* [Maryknoll, N.Y.: Orbis Books, 1991], 33-34).

[4] Dow Edgerton describes such a situation in a province of the Philippines: "In some ways it was worse than simple chaos. The knock at the door at midnight, the assassination at noon, the disappearance, the arrest, the accusation painted on the wall, the scooped-out grave—none of these were random and impersonal. Any and all of them were tied to reasons within reasons. Because you are Catholic, because you are Protestant, because you voted, because you didn't, because you have a job, because you don't, because you are in a labor union, because you are not" (Dow Edgerton, "Stand by Me," in *Beyond Theological Tourism: Mentoring as a Grassroots Approach to Theological Education*, ed. Susan B. Thistlethwaite and George F. Cairns [Maryknoll, N.Y.: Orbis Books, 1994], 18).

are they played? *Why?* With such questions we can analyze cultures and decipher their inner structure. *Who* is able and allowed to play a certain cultural game (be elected president, made a bishop, explain the theory of relativity)? *What* games are being played within a certain local culture? Among them, which are the most important? What are the games of a sub-culture or minority? What are the rules of the most important cultural games? What are the officially or unofficially allocated times and spaces for cultural games?

And finally, *Why?* This is the question of the "stories" behind the games. There is a story behind any initiation rite, memorial day celebration, Nobel Prize ceremony. Let us take a closer look.

Exercise: Think of a leading cultural game of your culture. Try to analyze this cultural game by answering the questions Who? What? How? When? Where? Why?

CULTURAL STORIES

THESIS 32: Why a certain cultural game is played is connected to a cultural story, which in turn is connected to a cultural worldview. The introduction of new cultural games is always and necessarily connected with the introduction of new cultural stories. Religions touch upon the deepest cultural layers, upon the worldviews. That is why cultural stories are especially important within the context of doing local theology.

There is more to culture than the layer of observable behavior, the cultural games. Behind many of the cultural games we find stories that show who is in power and how keeping "undesirables" down is maintained. This is especially true for leading cultural games. Let us take an example.

We cannot understand rituals without the story behind the cultural game. For example, the *lavabo* rite during the Catholic celebration of the eucharist calls for the priest to wash his hands. The priest did not slaughter a lamb prior to this ceremony. His hands are clean. He washes his hands not to get rid of dirt but to express a need and desire to be cleansed from his sins ("Lord, wash away my iniquity, cleanse me of my sin"). To an outsider, an external observer, this action does not make sense. Why would a person wash his already clean hands? The story is essential in order to make sense of this cultural game.

Similarly, we could consider the custom of washing the feet of a few chosen people on Holy Thursday. These people prepare, of course, by buying new socks and washing their feet meticulously before the ritual. The priest washes clean feet. Again, it does not make sense to an external observer who does not know the story behind the game.[5] The same condition applies to baptism, prayers, confirmation, ordination, and so forth. We need to have some understanding (background knowledge) in order to make sense of what we see. We need to know the cultural story.

The connection between cultural games and cultural stories is evident in the case of religious cultural games; there is a significant connection between the image of God and the ritualistic praxis at work. Behind our forms of worship we can trace an image of God. Flagellations in the Philippines, for example, depict an image of God demanding sacrifices, whereby grace is considered something that can be earned. In this sense local rituals reveal local knowledge (the local image) of God. The local image of God that is expressed in the ritual of flagellation is rooted in the religiosity of the Spaniards, introduced to the Philippines by way of colonization. There are cultural stories behind many of the cultural games we play.

There is a cultural story behind ceremonies and rituals, there is a cultural story behind many buildings, there is a cultural story behind our clothes and shoes, there is a cultural story behind our songs and behind the design of our keyboards.

A cultural story gives the background knowledge that one needs in order to place a cultural game within the cultural framework, to understand the roots of the game and the meaning of the symbols used. Cultures can be characterized not only through their cultural games but also through their stories. The creation stories in Egypt, Babylon, and Israel are colorful examples of stories that shape a culture. The stories of Francis of Assisi, Ignatius of Loyola, and Martin Luther King Jr. have influenced many people. The story of Austrian neutrality is a leading story for Austrian identity; the story of Jomo Kenyatta is a key story for Kenya.

---

[5] Sometimes we try to keep the cultural story without the cultural game: "In many American parishes the substitution of the quick, antiseptic and nonbiblical 'washing of the hands' for the inconvenient and messy, yet richly symbolic, foot-washing is an illustration. . . . I have even heard of parishes in which the foot-washing is replaced by a few moments of silence after a brief exhortation by the presider encouraging the assembly to 'imagine washing feet'" (Mark Francis, *Shape a Circle Ever Wider: Liturgical Inculturation in the United States* [Chicago: Liturgy Training Publications, 2000], 91). Obviously, it is difficult to preserve a story without expressing it! Dom Helder Câmara, when talking about John 11, makes this point: "I always feel a little uneasy when I see our twelve apostles offering themselves with their feet already well washed. The message ought to be: 'Dear brothers and sisters, we aren't here today to mime the washing of feet already carefully washed. . . .' Otherwise religion is in danger of being a mere theatrical spectacle. Religion has to be lived, not merely acted" (Dom Helder Câmara, *Through the Gospel with Dom Helder Câmara* [Maryknoll, N.Y.: Orbis Books, 1986], 136).

Different cultures are shaped by different stories. We talk about the paradigm story (Dyrness 1992, 147) of a culture or the founding myth of a religious community (Arbuckle 1988, 18ff.). The "American dream" is another famous and influential cultural story that shapes cultural identity.

Cultural stories can *be* the history. Henri Nouwen was introduced to the parish Ciudad de Dios in Lima. The parish was the result of a people's "invasion" on Christmas Eve 1954. On that night, thousands of people started illegally occupying barren land. Eventually, the present culture of this parish emerged. This is a cultural story behind the culture of this parish (Nouwen 1982, 5).

Hispanic theologian Virgilio Elizondo considers the story of Our Lady of Guadalupe to be the most significant cultural story of Hispanic identity: "I do not know of any other event in the history of Christianity that stands at the very source of the birth of a people like the appearance of Our Lady of Guadalupe. One cannot know, understand, or appreciate the Mexican people without a deep appreciation of Guadalupe" (Elizondo 1988, 59). Yet it takes a certain predisposition to understand and appreciate this cultural story: "To appreciate the story, it is necessary to see it through the categories of the ancient Nahuatl language—a language that expresses ultimate reality through image and poetry. The story begins with the *beautiful singing of the birds* and ends with *exquisite flowers*. For the native world, the expression for a divine message was precisely flower and song. Thus the entire story happens within the realm of a divine revelation" (ibid., 63).

The story of the Holocaust is, sadly, a key cultural story to understand contemporary Jewish cultural identity.

Different cultures are founded on different cultural stories, some incompatible (like the cultural story of American individualism and the cultural story of African family life). Guilt-oriented societies have different cultural stories than shame-oriented societies. Individual-centered societies have cultural stories that differ from community-oriented societies.

When two cultures meet, cultural stories are exchanged. When two cultural stories meet, established meanings (stories) and newly introduced ones mingle and overlap. A transformation of meanings takes place. This is when issues of truth become very complicated, and cultural identities have to be renegotiated in the face of different, perhaps incompatible cultural stories. For example, John Berthrong talks about an experience in Hong Kong:

> Early in our stay we were invited to attend the marriage of a young Chinese friend. I can't remember why we were going to send flowers to one of the events leading up to the ceremony, but we were. The flowers were white. Another Chinese friend . . . warned us that they were the wrong color entirely for a festive marriage. He told us that white in Chinese culture is the color of mourning and bereavement. . . . My mother and father were aghast and thanked our friend profusely for saving them from making such an intercultural social gaffe.

Where was the truth in this aborted giving of white flowers for a wedding? Were the flowers true or untrue? Was the color true or untrue?
(Berthrong 1999, 48).

The history of mission with its good share of syncretism is an especially
fascinating example of this mingling of cultural stories. We are well aware
of the problem of previous local theologies and previous cultural stories
when entering a culture. John Mahoney mentions the vertical and personal-
istic piety that he encountered when he arrived in Fiji. People were raised in
the ecclesiology of the French missionaries. Mahoney challenged their cultural story: "What surprised many people was that the 'French model' was
not a timeless, universal one but very specific in time and place" (Mahoney
1994, 5).

The confrontation of one cultural story with another can be a source of
conflicts as well as of enrichment. Popular religiosity is a rich source for
mixed cultural stories:

In the high pre-Columbian cultures of Mexico and Peru, the presence
of female divinities was bound up with fertility—especially in that we
are dealing with an agrarian culture, a culture of the earth. Tonantzin—
"our mother," for the Aztecs—was syncretized in the Virgin of
Guadalupe, a native American Virgin, just as the *Pachamama* (Earth
Mother) of the Quechua and Aymara has been syncretized with Mary
(as Mother). Clearly, in the first colonial era at any rate, the image of
the Virgin Mary, in the native and *mestiza* mentality, constituted the
syncretic elaboration of a female deity linked to cosmic rhythms, veg-
etation processes, and agrarian rites. But just as surely, the official
Catholic significate gradually imposed itself as the agrarian culture
lost its force. After all, the Virgin is Mother, no longer as goddess of
the fertility of the earth, but as refuge of the helpless (Parker 1996,
99).

The dynamics of globalization can actually be described as a movement
that tends to universalize not only a particular set of cultural games but also
a particular set of cultural stories. It has been observed, for example, that
TV presents the American dream to Hispanic children and hence destroys
their dream of equality because it always operates in categories of rich-
poor, powerful-powerless, and so forth (Bahr 1991, 68). Ironically, however,
the opposite is also true. Cultures that find themselves threatened by glo-
balizing uniformity tend to reassert their identity even more strongly by
emphasizing the wealth of their cultural games and cultural stories.

The introduction of new cultural games is always connected with the
introduction of new cultural stories. It isn't possible to introduce a casino
into a culture without introducing the story (greed, thrill, glitter) behind it.
One of the main tasks of the "image industry" is to produce cultural stories

that are connected with trademarks. There is a cultural story behind cars, watches, cigarettes, and dresses.

There is also a cultural story at the foundation of each and every religious community or political movement. Creating a new cultural story is a means of inculturation. Sometimes elements of the Christian story are rooted in a local culture by connecting it with local cultural stories. The parallels between the eucharist and the Javanese slametan festival, for example, or the parallels between the Christian liturgy and Shinto rituals can be used for the inculturation of the eucharist (see Immoos 1993, 228). The cultural game is slightly changed, and a new cultural story is attached to it.

That cultural stories behind the games can change is an interesting phenomenon. Let us look at an example. The traditional rule of abstaining from meat on Fridays was theologically justified by the participation in the universal sacrifice of Christ. Later this complicated theological cultural story lost credibility. An ingenious aid organization encouraged people to abstain from meat on Fridays and to give the money to the poor (a new story). Later this cultural story of solidarity lost its significance in the context of frustration over the politics of development, and an organization promoting healthy food suggested abstaining from meat for health reasons (a new story). The cultural game is the same, but the cultural story behind the game has changed.

Knowing the story does not mean that we have a rational justification. It would be naive to ask for a cultural story behind every cultural detail. Cultural change cannot be described in terms of rational choices. Why would we play the cultural game of using a fork? Using a fork is no more hygienic than using the hands. Similarly, why do we play the cultural game of using a handkerchief? German-Dutch sociologist Norbert Elias has pointed out that the use of forks and handkerchiefs was introduced in connection with ideas of etiquette and a self-understanding of educated urban people in the Middle Ages (Elias 1992-93). But one way is no more rational than another.

Cultures are not to be measured with the yardstick of reason. Every culture is a melting pot of cultural stories and cultural games. The fruit of any cultural analysis will not be a thorough documentation of the culture but a refinement of questions (Beattie 1964, 37f.). Where should we look? Local theologies attempt to look beyond the surface of a culture and to see the many faces of the particular local culture.

Exercise: Select a leading game of your community or choose a cultural game such as "praying" or "preaching" and try to identify the cultural story behind it.

5

Local Theologies
and the Social Situation

THESIS 33: Local theologies recognize that theology takes shape within a particular context. Theologies are developed in response to and within a particular social situation. Understanding the social situation is a necessary condition for understanding the genesis and validity of particular theologies.

Theology is done often and for particular times. A bishop preparing an official speech or a commission preparing documents on the celebration of the liturgy, for example, constitutes a context that is different from that of a professor preparing lectures and seminars. And all three are different from the pastoral context of a priest or deacon preparing homilies for liturgies or a catechist preparing a confirmation class. Doing theology from a wheelchair is different from doing theology from an armchair, and doing theology as a white man in Scotland is different from doing theology as a Sierra Leonean woman in the desolation of a city ruined by civil war.

Theology that tries to do justice to its place in culture and history is contextual. *Contextualization* literally means "weaving together" and is "thus an interweaving of the gospel with every particular situation" (Schineller 1990, 19). The process of contextualization includes the reflection on one's own place as person within a wider horizon. Obviously, there are more than merely religious features in a local culture that are of importance for doing contextualized theology—in the words of African theologian Mercy Amba Oduyoye: "Contextualization . . . expands to include the politico-economic aspects of life and seeks to produce symbols and language that are universal and inclusive of Africa's reality" (Oduyoye 1986, 54). That is why theology is called to take a look at the social situation.

When doing theology in a self-critical manner, we have to ask ourselves where we are. As Jon Sobrino writes, "Before one can theologize, one has first to be situated in a specific place. One's understanding of this place will determine how one understands theology and the theological task called for by one's place" (Sobrino 1991, 158). Vatican II, for example, changed the context of theology significantly: After Vatican II the context of theology was "in the world," reading the signs of the times rather than "outside of the world," rereading authoritative texts. Hence, after Vatican II, a whole new range of theological models evolved.

Doing local theology means doing theology in a way that is appropriate for the local cultural context. A theology for "Generation X," for example, will have to look into its particularities. Working with the Bible in this context may not be a matter of truth or use but a matter of general relevance: Where baby boomers asked, "Does it work for me?," Generation Xers raise the question, "Does it matter?" (Hahn and Verhaagen 1998, 67). The regional theologies developed in many parts of the world are examples of changing the context of theology and adapting to local situations.

DOING THEOLOGY WITHIN A PARTICULAR SOCIAL STRUCTURE

THESIS 34: Theology is always done within a concrete local social structure that provides rich resources for constructing local theologies and for developing a local identity as a theologian. The social, historical, cultural, and political context has an impact on the role of the theologian and his or her place in the context.

The theologian plays a certain role in a particular social context. Leonardo Boff speaks eloquently of the social location of theologians: "Theologians do not live in the clouds," he says, but are "social actors with a particular place in society." While they produce a theology that can often be quite technical, they also must address people in concrete situations. Because of this, Boff points out, "they find themselves situated somewhere within the comprehensive social fabric" (in Lois 1993, 169).

The role of the theologian depends on social and cultural circumstances. A teacher of theology has one role in Asia and another one in the United States. A theologian working for a Pontifical Council for Interreligious Dialogue has a different role from the editor of a theological journal. The place in the social structure in which one works is an important part of the theologian's life, greatly influencing what he or she thinks about a given question. No theologian can legitimately think he or she knows another situation without honest dialogue with concrete believers who live in that particular social location.

An honest attempt to read the signs of the times leads to a theology of social issues. Why? In the first place, a theologian is always working within a particular social structure; an institutional framework is part of the reality of doing theology.[1] Second, theology has to be honest to the social facts of human existence and to the facts of social reality. This is part of the "waking up" that being a theologian requires. Third, there is a theological duty to talk about injustice and the social faces of evil. In order to make theological judgments on social realities, one has to be able to give an account of these social realities. A theology of social issues is nothing new. From the very beginning the church fathers wrote and preached about justice, labor, and social structure (see Sedmak 2001, chap. 7). Theology fulfills a service function by ministering to a community.

We do theology in order to build community. Daniel Van Allmen has shown that in the New Testament the life of the community was the primary focus of religious life, while theology had a secondary, ordering function (Van Allmen 1975). Theology has the function of mediating in situations of dissent of a faith community (Braxton 1980). Therefore, "For whom are you doing theology?" is a key question in theological discourse.

According to Jesus, doing theology means doing "user-oriented" reflection, doing theology as if people matter. Local theology focuses on local people as its target audience in full awareness of the importance of context. According to David Tracy, there are three "publics" for theology—academy, church, and society at large (Tracy 1981, chap. 1). Theology must speak to each of these publics differently, for each audience has particular standards and needs.

Local theology is primarily done in response to a local community and a local church. The primary intention of local theologies is to provide service

---

[1] Awareness of this has been brought into relief in the context of political theology in Europe and liberation theology in other parts of the world. For an analysis of social context, see A. Roy, "The Socio-Economic and Political Context of Third World Theology," in *Irruption of the Third World: Challenge to Theology,* ed. Virginia Fabella and Sergio Torres, 87-112 (Maryknoll, N.Y.: Orbis Books, 1983); Enrique Dussel, "The Political and Ecclesial Context of Liberation Theology in Latin America," in *The Emergent Gospel: Theology from the Underside of History,* ed. Sergio Torres and Virginia Fabella, 175-92 (Maryknoll, N.Y.: Orbis Books, 1978); J. A. Calderón, "Peruvian Reality and Theological Challenges," in Fabella and Torres, *Irruption of the Third World,* 42-49. A communal effort to understand the context of doing Asian theology has been identified by a group of Asian theologians as follows: "We identified five common socio-economic and political realities in our different Asian countries: (1) colonial experience and debilitating structures; (2) poverty of the many and opulence of the few; (3) increasing marginalization of sections of our national communities; (4) the inferior and oppressed status of Asian women; (5) growing international militarism and repressive regimes in Asia" (Asian Report Group, "Toward a Relevant Theology in Asia," in Fabella and Torres, *Irruption of the Third World,* 61).

to a local community of faith. "Because theology springs from the faith of people, theology belongs to the people of faith. It is a social act" (Mueller 1988, 11). Theology is a community enterprise because theologians

- refer to a communal religious praxis of which they are a part;
- tackle questions and topics arising from religious praxis; and
- take their work to be part of their mission in sharing the life of a believer within a community of believers.

The orientation of theology toward a community determines the social significance of theology. A theology that wants to serve the people has to be socially significant, and therefore it needs to be close to people. In speaking of the Pacific, Sione Havea pointedly observes:

When I say "Pacific" it means to me a *focus on people*. People who are human and not puppets. They have tears, blood and sweat. When they are young they need care, when they are sick, they need treatment, and when they are "itchy" they want to be scratched (where it is itchy). They are people born to be free; they want to make their own decisions and list their top priorities (in Kabida 1987, 143-44).

SPECIAL ATTENTION TO THE POOR

THESIS 35: Jesus invites us to pay special attention to poor people, to make an option for the poor. This option will shape our theologies. Theological judgments on social situations are based on gospel values. There is no neutral theological stance.

Sometimes we cannot just sit and listen. Sometimes we cannot just lean back and watch passively. There are situations that require action. Pope John Paul II experienced such a situation when he was received in Lima. Victor and Irene Chero greeted the pope on behalf of the poor: "Holy Father, we are hungry." In his response John Paul II, deeply moved, exclaimed: "There is here a hunger for God. . . . There is here a hunger for bread. . . . Everything must be done to see to it that this daily bread is not lacking, for such bread is a right, a right expressed when we pray in the Our Father: 'Give us this day our daily bread'" (in Gutiérrez 1991, xi-xii).

A pastoral responsibility is a social responsibility. We cannot credibly talk about the eucharist in the midst of famine—the situation calls for more than words. We cannot credibly talk about anointing of the sick in the midst of unmitigated sickness—the situation invites us to care. We cannot credibly talk about liberation in the midst of political imprisonment—the situation urges us to look at the social reality of captivity.

Doing local theology requires that we keep our feet on the ground. Doing theology is about making an option. Jesus paid special attention to the poor, to the excluded, to the marginalized, to the "little ones," to the weakest members of society: the children, the sick, persons with handicaps. Theology is a way of following Jesus. That is why the theologian is called to pay special attention to the poor. This is challenging because we have to ask hard questions: Who are the weakest members of our society? Where are they? Why are they vulnerable and weak? Where is their strength?

Raising these questions means hard work. It is not at all romantic to pay special attention to those who do not fit into the ideals of our society. It is, however, important to be in touch with those who are excluded. This contact will change our attitudes. Encountering people who suffer is an experience that shapes our intuitions and sharpens our concerns.

Theology is a way of following an invitation. It is a way of being called. One of the mistakes in preaching (and in doing theology in general) is "preaching as though we get to choose what to say" (Untener 2001, 7). Theology is about answering a call and being faithful to a commitment. In a deep and important sense we cannot choose the message. The theological perspective is never neutral, never detached from experience and life.

Cardinal Bernardin changed his priorities in ministry after he had been diagnosed with cancer. Mother Teresa changed her ministry when she was confronted with the dying people in India. Josef Cardijn changed his priorities when he visited poor people in the hospitals of Brussels.

> In them [the hospitals] I saw the way those poor workers were treated, how their confessions had to be heard, how one had to help them in their last agony, the way they were abandoned, the heedlessness about the duty of letting their relations know of their death. I suffered greatly at seeing this immense distress of the working class (in de la Bedoyère 1958, 40).

That is why it is so tremendously important that theologians and church officials keep in touch with real life situations, with the reality of people who are less privileged. This educates our eyes to look at the world and see things and people in the world.[2]

---

[2] British philosopher Richard Hare used the word *blik* to refer to the basic intuition of values that determine how we see the world. Borrowing from Aristotle, Thomas Aquinas talked about the *habitus* that modifies how we think, act, and feel when we get rooted in a "habit" of mind and heart. Living among the poor is a school of life, a school that helps to acquire a Christian *blik* or *habitus* capable of seeing, hearing, judging, and acting in a Christian fashion (R. M. Hare, his contribution to "Theology and Falsification," in *New Essays in Philosophical Theology*, ed. A. Flew and A. MacIntyre, 99-103 [London: SCM Press, 1963]).

Theologians do not encounter a local culture with the attitude of a neutral observer but with empathy and respect. Theologians do not deal with social realities in a way similar to the approach of a butcher who deals with a piece of meat or a doctor who dissects a dead body. Theology is an invitation to care about people. Theologians are *interested* in local cultures and especially in the well-being of the local people. Jesus invites us to make an effort to see those who are hidden and excluded. In this sense doing theology means a deliberate choice of how to set our priorities.

Jesus calls us to examine our lives, our possessions, our priorities and desires, our motivations and gratifications. I know of a bishop who invited the people of his diocese to ask after every meeting the simple question: And what does this have to do with the poor? Even if the answer is "nothing," it is good to keep this question in mind. I know of a Latin American theologian who stood up at a conference that was filled with long and fruitless debates. He said: "This conference costs a lot of money. We are privileged to be in a position to debate all these issues. And this privilege is a call to set priorities. We have to serve. How can we serve the people in need?" This may sound romantic, but it is a simple way of thinking about priorities.

Jesus invites us to share the view of the excluded, to embrace an outlook on reality that is not the mainstream position. He invites us to look at the world with the eyes of the poor. This was expressed in very clear words in the pastoral letter *Economic Justice for All* by the U.S. bishops in 1986:

> The example of Jesus poses a number of challenges to the contemporary Church. It imposes a prophetic mandate to speak for those who have no one to speak for them, to be a defender of the defenseless, who in biblical terms are the poor. It also demands a compassionate vision that enables the Church to see things from the side of the poor and powerless and to assess lifestyle, policies, and social institutions in terms of their impact on the poor (no. 52).

Theology is called to look at society and culture "from below," with a special attention to the losers and the outsiders, the weak and the voiceless. Let us consider a few points of this special attention to the poor. It is a deliberate decision that implies commitments. This option requires us to make an effort to see and to hear.

Making an option is not an abstract undertaking. It is about faces and voices. We get to know the faces of individuals by sharing life with them. There is a clear distinction between "working for the people" and "working with the people." There is a clear distinction between "to live with" and "to do for" (Vanier 1989, 150). Sharing life means sharing the everyday struggle; that is why again and again throughout history Christians have chosen to be with the people. It is not always possible "to leave everything." We are bound by responsibilities. But we can make an effort to think about priorities, to discover the underside of our societies with the destinies and stories we encounter.

There are many faces of poverty. In the 1980s *Secours Catholique*, the French Catholic organization for emergency relief, addressed the issue of loneliness. The organization received many letters, not only cries for food and shelter, money and safety, but also letters crying for affection, crying for human company. The situation has not changed much since then. Many people have no home to go to. This is a face of poverty. The loneliness of old age, the daily harassment at the job—these are faces of poverty. Modern slavery, laborers in bondage, enslaved domestic helpers—these are faces of poverty.

Talking about poverty in general, in calm sociological terms, can give us "cold data" to process in the form of theories and conceptual frameworks. There is nothing wrong with that. But once we are confronted with faces and voices of poverty, we cannot rely on our cold data any longer. Instead, the data have become "warm" information about real people. We are talking about human beings with anguish and sorrows, hopes and joys. Talking about people with AIDS can be done in a very aloof, detached manner. In the same detached mode, without referring to any concrete faces and voices, we can talk of cases of exploitation, starving people, or refugees. This is the way many books and documents are written. But once we visit a refugee camp, once we see the pictures of war, once we listen to the story of people tortured by the police, we wake up.

Let us take an example. We can talk about modern slavery in learned terms. And this is important. But the whole treatment of the topic changes if we know that we are talking about real people with real lives. We are not talking about movies or novels. Kevin Bales starts out his book *Disposable People* with the account of a single life story, the story of Seba, who has been kept as a domestic slave in Paris for years, who has been exploited and mistreated, kept in captivity and even tortured. Telling that story, modern slavery becomes visible, gets a face. The whole impact, the whole status of the book changes. And Seba is one of perhaps three thousand domestic slaves in Paris, one of perhaps twenty-seven million slaves worldwide.

This is what making an option is about: seeing the faces and voices behind the data and figures. Every individual life has a message for humanity. Cardinal Bernardin notes, "A century ago Dostoyevsky said that the death of an innocent child was enough to destroy belief in God. Less dramatically, the suffering of innocent children is enough to indict the social priorities of a wealthy society" (Bernardin 1998, 58). Every single life counts. And every life has a face.

Making an option to pay special attention to the poor is about *making judgments*: As much as there is a gray zone in most theological discourse, a zone of careful assessment and cautious judgments, there is also black and white when it comes to taking an option. Grayness is not the basis for making a decision to act. It is the danger of intellectualizing to die the death of a thousand qualifications, to die the death of a thousand distinctions, to die the death of making everything gray.

Henri Nouwen learned this lesson from a priest in Peru:

> One of the temptations of upper-middle-class life is to create large gray areas between good and evil. Wealth takes away the sharp edges of our moral sensitivities and allows a comfortable confusion about sin and virtue. The difference between rich and poor is not that the rich sin more than the poor, but that the rich find it easier to call a sin a virtue. When the poor sin, they call it sin; when they see holiness, they identify it as such. This intuitive clarity is often absent from the wealthy, and that absence easily leads to the atrophy of the moral sense (Nouwen 1992, 159-60).

In his younger years Mahatma Gandhi, when he was still a lawyer in South Africa, wrote a letter to his fellow Indians in South Africa and asked them for financial support for a good cause. Again and again in this letter he uses the phrase "It will not do . . . ": It will not do to say, "I cannot make a difference"; it will not do to say, "I try my best, but I cannot really make a big contribution"; it will not do to say, "This is just a drop in the ocean." Paying special attention to the poor is based on the insight that it will not do to say, "Poverty is an unchangeable reality." It will not do to say, "There is nothing I can do about it." It will not do to stick our head in the sand and refuse to ask questions. It will not do to pretend that everything is all right.

Making an option is making a *commitment*, going beyond temporary and short-lived emotions. I would like to look at two things Jean Vanier said about this option for living with people with handicaps:

> Working and living with handicapped people does not become easier the longer you do it. In fact, it often becomes harder. . . . We have to move from feelings to conviction. As long as our relationship with handicapped people rests on feelings and emotions, a long-term, life-long commitment cannot develop. In order to stay with the handicapped even when we do not feel like staying, we need a deep conviction that God has called us to be with the poor, whether that gives us good or bad feelings (Nouwen 1988, 83-84).

It is not enough to be moved by the story of Seba. Warm feelings or hot emotions are not enough to make an option. It needs a commitment. This is the commitment of the Good Samaritan, who takes the responsibility to look after the person he found even beyond the immediate help he offered him.

Making an option requires the courage to accept *small beginnings*. Mother Teresa was not doing a lot of social analysis when she started ministering to the dying. Vinoba Bhave, who started the Bhoodan (land-gift) movement in India, was confronted with an appeal of landless peasants, and his address to the village people moved a rich farmer to donate a hundred acres of his land. After only three years more than two million acres of land had been donated, an achievement that outweighed any governmental land reform (Ellsberg 1997, 395). There is a danger to thinking of the lives of exemplary people only as a series of big and remarkable events.

Making an option is rarely spectacular. People working in hospitals, people working with the weakest members of our society testify to that. Henri Nouwen found the depth of this truth when he entered the Daybreak community. His fame, his books, his education, his travels—all that did not count to the people he lived with. "The unnoticed, unspectacular, unpraised life in solidarity with people who cannot give anything that makes us feel important is far from attractive. It is the way to poverty" (Nouwen 1988, 84). Making an option this radical forces us to see ourselves as we are— weak, vulnerable. Once all the protections of status, role, and prestige have been taken away, we are naked. This is how we encounter the faces of poverty. Henri Nouwen realized in Latin America: "Preaching for very poor people is an activity that forces you to be honest with yourself" (Nouwen 1992, 111). We cannot hide behind beautiful but shallow words. We have to get rid of all the protections. We have to get our priorities straight. Paying special attention to the poor is a concern that pervades many areas of our lives.

We are called to a special attention for the poor because the ethical quality of a society can be measured by the way it treats its weakest members. Who are the weakest members? Asking this question is already an important step in paying attention to the mechanisms of exclusion. Who are the poor? Those who suffer most are poor. Those who die before their time are poor. Those who do not know whether they will have enough food on the following day are poor. Making the option to pay special attention to those who are poor is a call to ask these questions and to draw the appropriate conclusions. Looking at poverty reveals a complicated and challenging social reality. Looking at poverty reveals not only weakness but power and energy. It is a colorful picture. There is no uniform group that can be called the poor. There is no homogenous set of innocent and holy people who are poor. There is a complicated social fabric to be discovered. That is why we need not only "theological eyes" but also "social glasses." It is not at all romantic to look at the underside of our social structure.

THEOLOGICAL EYES AND SOCIAL GLASSES

THESIS 36: Theology is called to analyze social realities. Talking about God is always, at least implicitly, talk about the social situation. Theology makes explicit judgments about key aspects of social situations (justice, labor, property). Theological analysis of social situations makes use of social analysis. There are, however, clear limits to social analysis. We can see these limits when we consider the mystical dimension in our lives. A theological analysis of social situations differs from an approach taken by social sciences in the option that is taken by the theologian.

Making an option for people requires both the processing of data and the warmth of personal engagement and vulnerability. Social analysis is a way of stepping back and taking a careful and courageous look. *Careful*—because we have to place our observations in a wider context. *Courageous*—because it takes a lot to face the truth: the truth of social evil, the truth of suffering, and the truth of a logic that makes the rich richer and the poor poorer.

Social analysis is an important tool for local theology because the local social structure determines the role and position of the theologian, the institutional range of faith communities, and the distribution of power. Because of the need to do justice to local contexts, social analysis is indispensable for the purposes of doing local theology. On the other hand, social problems cannot be solved without taking the theological dimension into account. Theology needs to dialogue with social and political analysis. Doing theology in a Palestinian context, for instance, cannot be done without a proper analysis of the socio-political situation (Ateek 1989). The case is similarly difficult in the situation of South Africa, where theologians are called to read the signs of the times, the historical and political realities (Nolan 1988, chap. 4).[3] In order to do justice to local social structures, we have to know

---

[3] A colorful example of the praxis of connecting social analysis and theological reflection on a local level is the development of different concepts of Basic Christian Communities. An African *Umunna* ecclesiology cannot be understood without a certain amount of social analysis. *Umunna* signifies the extended family and literally means "children of the father." "Thus *Umunna* ecclesiology is an understanding of the Church as constituted of members who can trace their origin from one father" (P. O. Iroegbu, *Appropriate Ecclesiology: Through Narrative Theology to an African Church* [Owerri, Nigeria: International Universities Press, 1996], 89).

the reality of local social contexts and not be carried away with a priori judgments and enthusiasms.

The theological dimension is indispensable both for the interpretation and for the solution of contemporary problems (*Centesimus annus,* no. 55). The concept of poverty seen through theological eyes differs from an economic analysis. We are not talking primarily about "lack of income" but about "quality of relationships" (Myers 1999, chap. 3). The concept of capital seen through theological eyes will differ from a purely economic view that sees deriving the most possible return from investments as the sole criterion for the use of capital. We are not talking primarily about the equipment, buildings, tools, and manufactured goods that we use to produce other goods and services but about the primacy of labor over capital. The theological account of development differs from development; it takes into account not progress, but human transformation. Theology looks at the concept of crime not only in a framework of deviant behavior and institutionalized sanctions, but also in terms of forgiveness, reconciliation and conversion. Theology analyzes the growing gap between rich and poor not only in economic terms of social balance and social stability but also in terms of responsibility and solidarity. There is a special way to look at the world with theological eyes. These eyes can be sharpened if we put on social glasses.

Looking through the instruments of the social sciences with theological eyes will present difficulties. Yet I don't believe that partnership between theology and social analysis is doomed to failure. As Joseph Holland says, theology and social theory are linked:

Behind every theology there is an implicit social analysis that is an interpretation of the society within which the theology functions. Behind every social analysis there is also an implicit theology that is an interpretation of the ultimate source, foundation, and goal of society (Holland 1983, 21).

We cannot speak about God without speaking, at least implicitly, about human society. We attribute properties to God that we treasure in our society. God's properties as established within a certain culture tell us a lot about the value system of that culture. In order to know which values are treasured within a certain society, there has to be an (at least implicit) analysis of the social order in question. If we talk about God as wise and depict God as an old man with a beard in our culture, this is a different idea of God from the idea of a young, healthy, virile man. Social values are depicted here.

Theology invites us to look at social reality from a special perspective. The social teachings of the Catholic church offer a theory of society and social life (see Sedmak 2001, 248-58). The tradition of Catholic social teaching deals with many issues of social life and gives an account of humans as social beings. The church teaches that due to their nature, humans live in community, that humans need a social world in order to realize their purposes and goals, that the individual is the engine of all social life. The church teaches that property has to be understood in the context of the dignity of the human person, that property has an individual and an undeniable social dimension, and that it is useful to distinguish between the possession and the use of property. The church teaches that the human person is the subject of labor, and that labor has to serve the common good. The church teaches that it is a human duty to strive for social justice that serves the dignity of all. These are glimpses into the church's statements on social reality. There is a genuine theological interpretation of social concepts and questions.

This perspective takes into account the conviction that God wants us to be liberated and saved. One example of an imminent need for a theological social analysis is the Indian caste system: The caste one belongs to is associated with the hereditary occupation of one's family and is a constitutive part of the social hierarchy in the Indian context, affecting all aspects of communal life. According to Indian theologian Michael Amaladoss, the caste reality is inexorably linked to all six of the most important aspects of life: economics, politics, social organization, the individuality of the person, culture, and religion (Amaladoss 1994, 34). Accordingly, understanding the social structure of Indian society requires understanding the caste system. The status of the individual is first and foremost determined by caste status. "In India, the caste system largely determines the function, the status, the available opportunities as well as the handicaps of an individual" (Desai 1969, 18). For Christians, Amaladoss and others suggest, the caste system has to be viewed as a *theological* problem along these lines:

- A basic claim of the Christian religion is the claim that all humans are equal.
- Religions in India have a stabilizing function vis-à-vis the caste system. Theology has to investigate whether contemporary religious praxis fosters and sustains the caste system.
- The caste system is part of a local culture. It cannot simply be eradicated if local cultures as a normative source are taken seriously.

The Dalit Christians have to be made a topic of local theology. According to John Webster, caste has even affected the way Indian Christians worship. At least until the 1960s, says Webster, Dalit Christians were assigned separate places of worship not only in the Roman Catholic church, but in the Mar Thoma church and the Church of South India as well (Webster 1996, 179-80).

The delicacy of the matter, of course, is revealed in the second and third items above. By what authority do we challenge a local cultural value? To what extent do we adjudicate how local cultures have "normative" value when they contradict other values? In this way, sociological knowledge and theological judgment lead to reasons to act and ways to live. Let us look at another example of a theological outlook on a social reality: the "Prison Statement from Sing Sing" produced by students at the New York Theological Seminary with their instructor John Eagleson. Fifteen students of theology, incarcerated in the Sing Sing maximum security prison in Ossining, New York, reflect upon their context. They reflect upon their situation, the larger picture of the "incarceration business" (who is in power, who is in prison, who is benefiting), the situation of their families. "We are sinners in the eyes of God, but repentant sinners. . . . Society, however, is not forgiving" (New York Theological Seminary Students 1990, 144). They know about God's care, their being created in God's image, the promise that all are one (Gal 3:28). They compare their situation with a situation in need of liberation and justice: "We are in exile, deported from our homes and our families" (ibid., 144). They believe in the liberating power of God and the human responsibility to make a contribution to that liberation. So they talk about consequences for actions and the changes that are due; the statement talks about the possibility of early parole, the possibility of contract parole (in which an inmate is given a list of obligations to fulfill), the possibility to get organized within the FIST (Families and Inmates Serving Time). The statement concludes: "This is our understanding of our situation, our reading of God's word for us, and our discernment of the commitment we are called to make" (ibid., 145). This is an example of local theology. Doing theology as an inmate changes many parameters of theology. We will see other examples in the context of regional theologies.

Reading social events with theological eyes is a task that is always open to divergent interpretations. Filipinos read the Smiling Revolution of 1986 as a sign of divine intervention. The fall of communism has been seen as a response to people's prayers. This is a genuinely theological way of reading social reality. But we need caution here and awareness that there are different readings.

Japanese doctor Takashi Nagai sees the dropping of the atomic bomb over Nagasaki's Catholic Cathedral on August 9, 1945, as providential. In Robert Ellsberg's words, he

> found it remarkable that as a result of heavy clouds obscuring the originally intended city, the bomb had been dropped that day on Nagasaki, an alternate target. As a further result of clouds, the pilot had not fixed his target on the Mitsubishi iron works, as intended, but instead on the Catholic Cathedral in the Urakami district of the city, home of the majority of Nagasaki's Catholics. He noted that the end of the war came on August 15, feast of the Assumption of Mary, to whom the Cathedral was dedicated (Ellsberg 1997, 13).

This theological reading (it is indeed a mystical reading) named Nagasaki as a place chosen for sacrifice, and this reading gave Takashi Nagai the strength to do work for peace and reconciliation.

German theologian Bernard Häring wrote his memories of World War II "to show that, even in the midst of all the crime and inhumanity of the war, there was so much goodness in people on all sides" (Häring 1976, vii). He tried to read his war experience, against all odds, as an experience of grace. This indicates the difference between a theological and a sociological view.[4]

These differences are also reflected in the limits of social analysis: plainly stated, social analysis does not give us the mystical dimension. The mystical dimension reminds us that there can be joy in the midst of suffering, that even in the midst of suffering there is the mystery of contemplation, that even in the midst of making an option there is the mystery of active indifference. The mystical dimension reminds us that making an option is not an end in itself. A mystical outlook on reality invites us to consider whether there is more to reality than the visible and tangible, that there is more to life than living day by day.

Jesus used not only prophetic language but mystical language as well. Prophetic language attacks the misery of a situation and addresses structural causes. "The language of contemplation acknowledges that everything comes from the Father's unmerited love" (Gutiérrez 1987, 97). Following Jesus is about finding God in all things and encountering Jesus in the poor. This is a dimension that cannot be grasped by way of social analysis. We can think of the example of Mother Teresa, who focused on Jesus: "It seemed that she saw only him and through him came to see the poorest of the poor to whom she has dedicated her life. She never answers the many psychological and socioeconomic questions brought to her on the level they are raised. She answers them with a logic, from a perspective and in a place that remains unfamiliar to most of us" (Nouwen 1992, 58).

---

[4] A useful model of doing social analysis from a theological perspective has been developed by the Jesuits Müller and Banawiratma in Indonesia (see J. Banawiratma and J. Müller, *Kontextuelle Sozialtheologie* [Freiburg im Breisgau: Herder, 1995]). Slightly adapting their model, we can think of ten steps to be considered in a theological approach toward social phenomena: (1) selection of the "field" and the subject of the analysis: What do we want to analyze?; (2) explication of our own point of view (value presumptions, theological criteria to be applied to social life); (3) social inventory: collection of data; (4) drawing up of a social map: identification of institutions and structures and mechanisms; (5) historical analysis (consideration of the beginning and historical development) of the social context; (6) systematization and formulating of assumptions about connections and dependencies; (7) prioritization of the theses put forward; (8) analysis using the theological criteria explained in point 2; (9) revision and examination of the analysis by the team; discussion of values and norms chosen; and (10) conclusions for our life praxis.

Social analysis does not give the whole picture. Social analysis cannot grasp the inner depth behind the faces and voices who are involved in the fight for social transformation. Gustavo Gutiérrez emphasizes "the importance of personal friendship, affective relationships, 'useless' prayer, and intimate joy as essential elements of a true struggle for liberation" (in Nouwen 1992, 145; see ibid., 172). Again, social analysis has to rely on facts and figures. It has to rely on the logic of numbers—the more projects, the better; the more social workers, the better; the more money, the better. But this is not the logic of Jesus. For him, every single life counts, and, in using that logic, sometimes one sheep deserves more attention than ninety-nine others.

One single person can make a difference. More often than not we are told that we cannot change anything, that we are too weak, that the big companies and the rules of globalization govern everything. Again, this is not the message of Jesus. Jesus wants his followers to be the leaven of society. Indian spiritual teacher Anthony de Mello, writes C. G. Valles, "knew that a liberated person is the greatest blessing to society in whatever field and whatever circumstance" (Valles 1987, 58f.). A similar insight is captured in Bernard Häring's reflection on the Second World War: "The question must be asked: Could so many people have been so easily manipulated by totalitarian regimes if they had been prepared for discernment and growth in freedom rather than trained for order and obedience?" (Häring 1976, 67).

THEOLOGICAL SOCIAL ANALYSIS IN PRACTICE: PASTORAL LETTER ON POVERTY IN ALABAMA (1990)

An excellent example of a theological social analysis is the pastoral letter "Make Justice Your Aim" issued by Archbishop Oscar Lipscomb and Bishop Boland in December 1990. The process of drafting the letter involved various offices, commissions, and experts from different fields (education, social work, business, economics, labor, religion, politics, medicine, and others). The social data were collected through questionnaires and consultations; an economic survey was used as a source. The history of the letter is significant as an example of interdisciplinary field work in theological analysis.

The letter begins by referring to the prophetic mandate to "make justice your aim" (Isa 1:17) and the responsibility connected with that mandate. Then a description of the local context of Alabama is given, naming the beauty and richness of the area. After briefly indicating that there is also a dark side to the social life of Alabama, the letter mentions the call of Jesus in Luke 14:13 ("When you give a banquet, invite the poor") and the directions given by the pastoral letter "Economic Justice for All," issued by the National Conference of Catholic Bishops in 1986.

The second part of the letter deals with poverty in Alabama using both a cultural characterization of poverty (inspired by the above mentioned national pastoral letter) and an official definition by the U.S. government. It offers eight reasons for the amount of poverty in Alabama: absence of economic development; poor educational system; unfair tax system; discrimination; political powerlessness of the poor; welfare dependency; lack of access to medical care; and negative attitudes. The letter describes some effects of this poverty.

The next parts of the letter give a phenomenology of poverty in Alabama and describe facts, figures, and faces of unemployment and education in connection with poverty in the state. Then the letter talks about the response to poverty, using biblical sources (Gal 2:10; Prv 17:5; Lk 19:1-10) and giving points of action (joining hands, lobbying, sharing). The seventh part of the letter calls for change in the Alabama economy. It specifies changes in attitude ("to move hearts from hardness toward the poor"); in various economic sectors (employers, job-training programs, child-care services, health care); and in the tax system, the welfare system, and the education system. After that, the letter challenges Alabama Catholics ("as our contribution") and encourages them to make concrete efforts to bring about social justice within church structures. Parish leaders, peace and justice commissions, priests, and deacons are urged to act in accordance with the concerns of the letter.

In its conclusion the letter refers to the experience of communal life of the early Christians (Acts 4:34) and the example of Jesus (2 Cor 8:9; Lk 4:18; Lk 6:20; Mt 25:35-36). "Empowered by God's spirit, we will 'make justice our aim.'" The conclusion is again a quotation from Isaiah: "Come now, let us set things right" (1:18).

This letter is an example of how theological social analysis should be done because it

- uses an interdisciplinary approach involving field work and methods of economic analysis and social research;
- draws from biblical sources and documents of theological social analysis as well as economic literature;
- considers a large variety of aspects, including both external and internal (attitudinal) factors;
- brings into relief the challenges of involvement and of self-awareness and of applying the social principles to the church itself;
- expresses a sense of commitment to action involving local parishes and church structures; and
- provides a vision that focuses concrete action.

Exercise: Think about a social problem of which you are aware, such as the problem of unemployment. How would you do a theological analysis of this social issue?

REGIONAL THEOLOGICAL SKETCHES

THESIS 37: Regional theologies try to do justice to the key features of a regional context. They pay special attention to key events, persons, and features. Regional theologies look at the social realities in which people live and try to highlight the core constitutive elements of the regional social setting.

When we talk about Filipino theology or Japanese theology or African theology, we are talking about regional theologies. The many islands in the Philippines, the many villages and towns in Japan, the many countries and tribes in Africa share significant features that invite us to construct such regional theologies. Regional theologies try to identify features that are significant for the identity of people living in this particular region. What is important in the life context of the Philippines, Japan, or Africa?

Regional theologies look at the social realities in which people live and try to point out constitutive elements of the regional social setting. The trauma of the Second World War is a key to German identity even today. We cannot understand the complex role Germany plays in the European context without this key feature of its regional identity. Political theology in Germany discusses the importance of "memory," "history," and "theology after Auschwitz." The establishment of communism and the Hungarian revolution in 1956 are still key factors that shape the regional identity of Hungarians. The unsolved questions in the coexistence of black and white is a key factor of Zimbabwean theology.

Any local theology will have to take into account aspects of the regional theology in question. When I do theology in a Tyrolean village, I should know something about regional theology for the Austrian context; when I do theology in a wealthy parish in North Chicago, I should know something about the regional theology for the United States and Chicago. It is always necessary to have this "bigger picture" at hand when working in a particular social setting.

Let us take a look at some examples for constructing regional theologies. In doing so, we have to take into account regional identities. For example, theology in the North American context will center around the message: "Disestablish ourselves!" "Disengagement from our status of cultural establishment is primarily . . . a work of theology" (D. J. Hall 1997, 41-43, 48). For Douglas John Hall, the greatest task of theology in the North American context is that of helping Christians "to provide a people indoctrinated in the modern mythology of light with a frame of reference for the honest exploration of its actual darkness" (D. J. Hall 1991, 36, 158). "The crisis of the dominant culture of North America is a particular species of the failure of the modern vision" (ibid., 158).

In Malaysia, according to J. J. Fung,

> God frequently manifests Himself through the signs of the times and a glaring sign today is the affluent lifestyle in Petaling Jaya and Kuala Lumpur. It is a way of life where the rule of the game is vying for more power, wealth and prestige. It is like an incessant whirlpool which slowly draws us until we are caught up in it, involuntarily. Through this and the signs of unbridled consumerism, I believe God is calling His people in Petaling Jaya and Kuala Lumpur for a "shoes-off" response (Fung 1992, 29).

In Holland, to give another example, theology may have to introduce a Jesus who will help people look deeper for meaning, since, as Henri Nouwen observed on a visit to his native land, people in Holland "are just very busy—eating, drinking, and going places. . . . The Dutch have become a distracted people—very good, kind, and good-natured but caught in too much of everything" (Nouwen 1988, 108).

Or, as Jean-Bertrand Aristide asks:

> If Jesus came to Haiti today, on August 23, what would he find? If he looked at the Catholic Church, if he looked at the Protestant Church, if he X-rayed the society, would he say again what he says in John 9:39-41? What reasons are there why Jesus would say of our society what he said of the Pharisees? (Aristide 1991, 85).

Regional theologies can be constructed by identifying general features in a particular area (*minjung* theology is an example of such a larger-scale theology). The point of departure is general cultural observations. In this sense, the theologically relevant cultural context of Vietnam might be that "we have *received a sense of the person, a sense of the family, a sense of the sacred, a sense of God*" (Thành 1993, 97). These observations based on repeated experiences can serve as a basis on which to construct regional theologies. A similar approach can be taken in Taiwan, where theologians analyzed theological challenges of the present situation considering the imbalance between lived values and material progress, the destruction of the family system, and isolation and loss of orientation (Chang 1981, 89-91). These factors serve as signposts for the construction of local theologies.

The theological imagination tries to discern deeper layers of meaning and challenge in a social reality. It tries to read the signs of the times to become conscious of the struggle to realize deeper values and the struggle for a full and happy life. I find Thomas Merton's account of Calcutta to be particularly apropos to illustrate this dimension of the theological task:

Calcutta is shocking because it is all of a sudden a totally different kind of madness, the reverse of that other madness, the mad rationality of affluence and overpopulation. America seems to make sense, and is hung up in its madness, now really exploding. Calcutta has the lucidity of despair, of absolute confusion, of vitality helpless to cope with itself. Yet undefeatable, expanding without and beyond reason but with nowhere to go. An infinite crowd of men and women camping everywhere as if waiting for someone to lead them in an ultimate exodus into reasonableness, into a world that works, yet knowing already beyond contradiction that in the end *nothing* really works, and that life is all anicca, dukkha, anatta, that each self is the denial of the desires of all the others—and yet somehow a sign to others of some inscrutable hope. And the thing that haunts me: Gandhiji led all these people, exemplified in the sense they might make out of their life, for a moment, and then, with him, that sense was extinguished again (Merton 1973, 28).

Merton peers beyond the visible and uses all the resources of his intelligence and his skill with the English language to make sense of his experience. He translates his experience into a picture of values and human struggles that makes it possible for others to enter into with their imaginations and their intelligence.

Looking at a social context, there is always, of course, the danger of oversimplification. One way to avoid the mistakes resulting from oversimplification is the attempt to give a thorough analysis of one particular local context as an example for a region. One of the most important proponents of rural development, Robert Chambers, used selected villages as "windows to regions" (Chambers 1994). Local theologies can indeed be windows to bigger theologies.

EXAMPLES OF THEOLOGICAL SKETCHES

Constructing regional theological sketches points out decisive factors in regional identities: events, persons (both past and present), and features. Developing regional theologies is a matter of knowing the local context (values, pressures, longings), as well as being aware of our theological "lens," the gospel values with which we evaluate a situation.

A regional theological sketch can be developed for a nation, city, district, village, parish, or religious congregation. Let us consider two examples. This is an invitation to learn by way of examples rather than by way of general guidelines. These examples will obviously not give a systematic theology, but simply directions "where to look."

Theological Questions in the Context of a Hospital

You find yourself in the strange world of a hospital. All your normal supports are gone. You wonder if you will walk back into the world healed.

Questions abound. Have you overcome the childhood idea that being in the hospital means you have done something wrong? Do you believe that being hospitalized means you have sinned against your body? Jesus was asked what a blind person had done wrong. He replied, "Neither this man nor his parents sinned; he was born blind so that God's works might be revealed in him" (Jn 9:1-4). Do you believe that? Do you create wonderful occasions for good things to happen, for people to help you to be transformed? Are you willing to believe that God invites good things to happen to sick people who need care and treatment? Are you convinced that God is not a God who repays deed by deed, sin by sickness? Are you convinced that God loves you the way you are, no matter whether you live up to the ideal of health and well-being that society sets as norms? Do you believe that the people Jesus healed experienced growth and transformation? Are you willing to see your sickness as an invitation to allow God to transform you? Are you aware that being transformed is also painful? Do you see a way to enter into the experience of being in God's hands?

After his stroke Pedro Arrupe prayed:

> More than ever I find myself in the hands of God. This is what I have wanted all my life from youth. But now there is a difference; the initiative is entirely with God. It is indeed a profound spiritual experience to know and feel myself so totally in God's hands.

Do you see sickness and weakness as an invitation to surrender?

Looking at Job and his sufferings, would you agree that Job did not find a theoretical answer to the question of why he was suffering? Don't you see that there is no theological "answer" that explains why you are hospitalized? Did you realize that Job found consolation the moment he turned to others? Are you able to see your illness as a chance to grow and not concentrate on your own suffering? Do you see that there is truth in saying that Jesus takes us—his disciples—as salt of the earth, light of the world, bread for the poor, and gives thanks for who we are, then breaks us, and gives us to be the life of the world as he gave himself?

Do you realize that Jesus wants you to become a "counter-symbol," a contrast to the ideals of our society, which takes the ideals of efficient functioning as the highest ideals? Henri Nouwen tells of a niece born with Down's syndrome:

> I cannot think about much else than this little child who will become the center of my brother and my sister-in-law's lives and will bring them into a world of which they have never dreamt. It will be a world of constant care and attention; a world of very small progressions; a world of new feelings, emotions, and thoughts; a world of affections that come from places invisible in "normal people." . . . Laura is going to be important for all of us in the family. We have never had a

"weak" person among us. We all are hardworking, ambitious and successful people who seldom have had to experience powerlessness (Nouwen 1992, 14-15).

Would you agree that people who are sick, people who are old, people with handicaps—that these people are tremendously important for our society? Don't they remind us of the need to slow our pace? To realize that the human body is not a disposable vessel to use and then throw out? To help us remember that the dignity of the human person cannot be measured by our efficiency, by what we have and by what we achieve, but by who we are as caring, loving, human beings?

The ministry of Jesus was enriched by people in need of healing. Isn't it amazing that the blind Bartimaeus sees what no one else in the scene seems to see, that Jesus is the "Son of David" (Mk 10:47)? Is illness the chance to understand those who do not fit into the ideals of society? Could it be wise for a religious community *not* to elect the healthiest persons as superiors, since they may not understand the slow, the sick, and the aging? If we glorify wellness and health, do we run the risk of deceiving ourselves by seeking to live in a "brave new world" where there is no pain, no deep questioning, no healing, and no need for religion to express our sense of living and dwelling in mystery? Would the ministry of Jesus have been possible if everyone were well educated and well provided for? Don't you see that healing and forgiving formed a unity in Jesus' ministry? Is your sickness a chance to be healed and forgiven all at once? Cardinal Bernardin, suffering from cancer wrote, "As a man of faith, I can really speak of pain and suffering only in terms of their redemptive, salvific qualities" (Bernardin 1997, 95).

Doing Theology in Hyde Park, Chicago

Hyde Park is a neighborhood on the south side of Chicago. It is the home of the University of Chicago, with its many brilliant scholars and its pride in its Nobel Prize winners. There are numerous fine bookstores in the area, even five theological schools. Hyde Park is, therefore, a faculty and student residential area and as rich in variety as the many restaurants that reflect its multi-cultural makeup.

Hyde Park, however, also struggles with its identity. It is part of a larger city that thought of itself as the railroad center of an industrial nation, "hog butcher of the world," as poet Carl Sandburg described it, a brash and muscular city in contrast to an East that Chicago viewed as effete and flabby. European ethnic groups flooded into the city in the years after the Civil War and through the 1920s. Most were Catholic, but Poles fought with Germans, and Italians fought with Irish. The Irish eventually triumphed over everyone, in the process dominating the Catholic church and engendering deep resentments among both the non-Irish Catholics and the Scotch-Irish Protestants who no longer counted in the political makeup of the city. In the years between World Wars I and II African Americans began to pour into the city, displacing the Irish, the Poles, and the Italians from their old neighborhoods. In 1892, thirty years before the African Americans started arriving in large numbers, money from the Rockefeller family was used to found the University of Chicago. The Rockefellers themselves were oil barons who had made their fortune by monopolizing the petroleum industry in several parts of the country. The university they founded quickly rose to the stature of the oldest of its Eastern rivals: Harvard, Princeton, and Yale. But it always had a "chip on the shoulder" attitude toward them, even when, by the 1960s, its number of Nobel laureates and recipients of other major distinctions clearly proved it was a world-class center of research and creativity.

Hyde Park faced a severe crisis in the 1960s. Racial unrest and severe economic dislocation faced the city as a whole and the whole Midwestern industrial zone, which was then becoming known as the Rust Belt of America. African Americans were hit disproportionately hard with layoffs from closing factories. Urban housing stock deteriorated as years of absentee landlords refusing to plow rent money back into refurbishing buildings began to take their toll. Expectations for social justice that had been kindled after the famous *Brown vs. the Board of Education* Supreme Court Decision of 1954 were not met. Despite President Lyndon Johnson's success in passing the 1964 Civil Rights Act, those expectations continued to be disappointed.

Race riots began occurring throughout the city, reaching a crescendo in 1968 after the assassination of Dr. Martin Luther King Jr. Crime rates rose. Throughout this period, but especially in the 1950s and early 1960s, elite whites who ruled and taught in the university began to fear that the low-income African Americans who had moved in were endangering the university's future. The university began to buy up available property, often paying premiums to owners of rundown buildings who had no interest in managing their properties. Families were put out into the streets. The Chicago Police Department and university security forces began making non-whites feel unwelcome.

Doing local theology in Hyde Park today involves taking all the above into account. In addition, by the 1990s the ethnic mix of African-American, Hispanic, Asian, and European-American had become more complex by increased religious pluralism and the presence of many persons who followed no formal religious path. At present, no religious tradition exerts hegemonic power in Hyde Park. Jews, Hindus, Muslims, Buddhists, Native American Traditionalists, and secular humanists all make a claim to be heard. Thus doing *Christian* local theology in Hyde Park provokes questions like the following, based on the premise that Jesus calls Christians to community building:

Has Jesus not told us that communities can be built by inviting people to share their gifts and talents? One is not dispensed from trying to do this by feeling inadequate. In his own day, didn't he call men and women who were not the most brilliant people of the day? And didn't he say to Peter, "You are Peter, and on this rock I will build my church" (Mt 16:18)? Yet, didn't

Peter betray Jesus (Mt 26:69-75)? And didn't Jesus ask Mary Magdalene to proclaim the news that he was risen from the dead (Mt 28:1-10)? She was a woman without a public voice in her society, yet Jesus revealed himself to her first and she believed. Jesus warned his disciples not to be proud because of social position, education, and power, and he advised his followers not to admire the Pharisees, who were paragons of virtue in that society. Don't we believe in a God who looks at the small things of life? Aren't we convinced that God will not ask us: How much money did you make? How many books did you write? Have you received a Nobel Prize?

A theology within an academic setting with its values of efficiency and success is well advised to ask: Is not the biblical God inefficient and slow? Did this God walk forty years in the wilderness? Did this God not speak through ox-cart history and the image of the crucified Christ (who is nailed down, and thus the ultimate symbol for immobility)? Is it possible that the experience of slowness is a salvific experience in the academic context? What kind of lifestyle, what kind of pastoral response would communicate salvation through a slow God?

The climate of competition engenders pressures and anxieties. We can ask theologically: Isn't our God a God of healing and compassion? Hasn't Jesus said: "Those who are well have no need of a physician. I have come to call not the righteous but sinners to repentance" (Lk 5:31-32). Doesn't healing mean making things well? Do we believe that Jesus will heal our fears of being a failure, of disappointing others, of not living up to expectations? Don't we believing that Jesus does not promote competition and the making of our reputation by leaving footprints on the backs of others?

What does it mean when Jesus said, "You received without payment; give without payment" (Mt 10:8)? Do you have a feeling for what *grace* means in a merciless world? Wouldn't you agree that God's grace means that God gives without asking anything in return? Do you have a lively sense of God inviting you to see that the lilies of the fields and the birds of the air have not achieved or accomplished anything yet are of inestimable value? And do you feel gratitude for the many people and events that have made you what you are now?

The social diversity in Hyde Park creates questions: Are you comfortable with the idea of the many gifts (1 Cor 12)? Are you comfortable with the idea that Jesus accepted a pluralism of ministries (Mt 11: 7-19), and that he encountered many different people in many different ways during his life time? Does not the Sermon on the Mount (Mt 5—7) invite us to change our social categories? Does not Jesus talk about those who mourn and about those who thirst for justice and about those with a pure heart (Mt 5:4-8)? Does not Jesus invite the rich young man to take the great step of sharing (Mt 19:21)?

If you appropriated the gospel message, wouldn't you see that God invites you to see the whole of life with eyes other than with business eyes? Do you remember the parable of the workers in the vineyard (Mt 20:1-16)?

They all received the same wage no matter how many hours they had worked. Isn't that unfair? Yet isn't that God's "logic"?

Hasn't Jesus said, "Strive first for the kingdom of God" (Mt 6:33)? What does that mean? What does the Letter of James say to you—do you agree with its message? Are you afraid? Don't you know that you are vulnerable, that your life can change at any time? Think of Jesus' parable of the man building a larger barn (Lk 12:13-21). Do you see that you are also in need of healing, in need of others? Do you hear God telling you not to be afraid? Do not be afraid, follow me!

If all these questions have a point, don't the Christian churches of Hyde Park need to develop a local theology that will articulate what God is offering both as resource and grace for transforming a neighborhood, and the challenge to transcend our fears that we are inadequate to deal with such a complex task?

Exercise: Sketch a regional theology for your region, religious community, or diocese. Collect data first, identify key features in a second step, and then give a theological interpretation/criticism.

6

Little Theologies

THESIS 38: Little theologies are theologies made for a particular situation, taking particular circumstances into account, using local questions and concerns, local stories and examples as their starting point. People should be able to recognize themselves in little theologies.

Once in a while my friend Jakob, a pastor in a small rural parish, calls me to talk about his pastoral concerns. "There is a ceremony for the second wedding of these two people. Both have children from their first marriages. The children will be there. How should I integrate them in the ceremony?" Or, "There is a baptism on Sunday. The parents are doing it just for the sake of the village, but they do not really care about 'churchy' things. They do not know anything about the sacrament. How could we try to make the ceremony meaningful, even to them?" Or, "I have a funeral tomorrow. The father of a girl I know from school. He was an alcoholic and brought much pain to the family. There is his wife and three kids. What should I do?"

In raising such questions, Jakob is not asking for a book or a prefabricated answer. He is not asking for a complicated theory. He is not asking for a simple "cookbook" ritual. Instead, he is seeking "little theologies" created for a particular occasion. I think most pastoral workers are looking for them, whether they know it or not.

These little theologies get their value not from flawless scholarship or good book reviews but from acceptance by the people. How should we prepare a mass for a high school in which there are many indifferent teachers and students? Which gospel should we choose to celebrate the fiftieth wedding anniversary of a particular couple? How should we talk about the Crusades with fifteen-year-old students?

119

If doing local theology means doing theology in a way that is appropriate to the local cultural context, then it goes without saying that the tools of local theology should be as flexible as possible. We are talking about a theological toolbox rather than a library, a leaflet rather than a book. As Robert McAfee Brown says, Today's theology should be done in looseleaf notebooks, so it is easy to add new pages or replace old ones.

Theology should grow where it is meant to serve a purpose—within the everyday life of a community. General approaches cannot substitute for little theologies. Each audience is different, there are unique aspects to every pastoral situation. We cannot talk about the exodus in Palestine in the same way we talk about the exodus in Latin America. We cannot talk about the sun as a symbol of love and warmth in a region of droughts and deserts. This is simple. Little theologies are user-oriented. Leonora Tubbs Tisdale makes this point when talking about the need to prepare a "user-oriented" sermon:

> Giving disciplined time and attention to the interpretation of one's listeners is critical for preaching. . . . No book of theology, even if it is addressed to the modern mind; no biblical commentary, even if it moves the text toward the pulpit; no volume of sermons, packaged and ready for delivery, has the Word winged for the hearts and minds of a particular group of listeners (Tisdale 1997, 26).

Little theologies become especially important when religious praxis is confused or self-destructive. Little theologies are needed in times of confusion, and confusion arises in times of change such as our own.

In times of change, theology has to respond to a new situation. Since local situations change constantly, theology is called to adapt to ever-new and ever-different circumstances. J. J. Mueller observes that in times past, theologians were more like homesteaders. There was land to cultivate, there were fences to be erected and mended, there were regular chores to do. Theology was about providing answers to regularly asked questions. But today, says Mueller, theologians are more like pioneers. "They have pulled up stakes, harnessed the wagons, and set off for new and unknown territories. Theology is moving, unsettled, searching for and discovering new territories and peoples" (Mueller 1988, 95).

The little theologies we are advocating are moving, unsettled—in the way Jesus was moving, unsettled as an itinerant preacher—yet rooted firmly in the God who is the ground of being and world process.

Definitive answers in a local context are not to be expected. Juan Luis Segundo tells us, "Everyday experience tells us that conscientious Christians of our day do not possess ready-made certitudes in their faith which enable them to evade the relativism that operates together with their faith in new and changing situations" (Segundo 1976, 183). Nothing can eliminate the element of risk in human actions. The outcome of our actions cannot be predicted.

Doing theology calls for sensitivity and a gift for subtly intuiting what is going on beneath the surface of people's lives. Everyday life is unpredictable and dynamic. Events occur unexpectedly, and many things are happening at the same time. Usually, there is not much time to carry out a thorough study in order to make a decision about what to do. Development expert Robert Chambers, talking about development reports written by experts, commented that these reports were, most of the time, "long, late, boring, and anyway not used." This might be true for many a theology as well. It is the very idea of local theologies to be useful and used "on the spot," "right here and now." I will try to give an idea of what little theologies are meant to be. Again, I will not give an elaborated theory but a series of examples.

LITTLE THEOLOGIES ARE NOT CHEAP THEOLOGY

THESIS 39: Constructing little theologies is a challenging task that demands cultural sensitivity, thorough knowledge, and respect for people. Little theologies are not "bumpersticker theologies." In fact, the criterion of a good theologian is whether he or she can do justice to the gospel while gaining the community's confidence that a little theology illuminates a particular situation.

Little theologies are not "cheap theologies" or "theology lite," without intellectual substance (or, for that matter, intellectual spice). When hearing the word *little* we might be tempted to think of saccharine spirituality and oversimplified textbooks. This is not what I intend. Charles de Foucauld chose the name "little brothers" and "little sisters" deliberately. He wanted to build a community of people who would walk along the road with people as companions rather than leaders, fellow travelers rather than guides.

Of course, there are situations in which taking on responsibility is a sign of the time. Every so often we mistake laziness, fear, or escape from responsibility for modesty and humility. This is not what I mean. Trained theologians have a responsibility to use their training for their community; using theological knowledge can sometimes mean challenging people, questioning established beliefs, shaking traditions. However, there are not only different roles of the theologian (speaker and listener, fellow traveler and guide), there are also different ways of exercising leadership.

The phrase *little theologies* emphasizes theological soundness and situational embeddedness. Widely known examples of "big theologies" by famous theologians, like Aquinas's *Summa*, Bernard Lonergan's *Method in Theology*, or Karl Rahner's *Foundations of Christian Faith*, are difficult books. They demand many hours of scholarly work, specialized knowledge, and imply far-reaching claims as to their validity and applicability. These are books with long texts and many footnotes. Little theologies, by contrast, are small contributions that serve a local community, on a certain occasion. A sermon, a letter, a conversation, a poster, or a sculpture could be a platform for a little theology.

Looking at what Leonardo Boff wanted to accomplish in his *Little Introduction to the Sacraments*, we can get an idea of little theologies. Boff used his personal experience to make sense of the concept of sacraments as signs of God's presence. Little theologies are modest theological reflections using "little concepts," "little examples," "little experiences." Little theologies only make sense with reference to a local cultural context. Little theologies are based on local experiences and local stories.

Ernesto Cardenal's *The Gospel in Solentiname* is an example of the development of little theologies. Cardenal collected the experiences of his Nicaraguan Bible group; the contributions of the different participants give a colorful range of examples of little theologies. Jesus found himself all the time in situations that provoked little theologies. It is significant that Jesus chose a child as a live parable to characterize the kingdom of God. Albert Nolan offers a little meditation on this surprising element in a key parable of Jesus:

> The child is a live parable of "littleness," the opposite of greatness, status and prestige. Children in that society had no status at all—they did not count. But for Jesus they are also people and they do count. That is why he is indignant when his disciples chase the children away. He would call them to him, put his arms around them and bless them by laying his hands on their heads. . . . It will be a *kingdom of "children"* or rather of those who are like children because in society they are insignificant; they lack status and prestige (Nolan 2001, 69).

Of course, there is a connotation to little theologies that makes them sound unprofessional or provincial and narrow. Referring to little theologies might sound slightly condescending or complacent. W. D. Campbell provides a homey example, however, that reminds us that this is not necessarily the case:

> I have a neighbor, an electrician by occupation, who is a theologian. He told me he would not teach his child to pray "Now I lay me down to sleep . . . " because, he said, the words could be a reminder to God to put her on his agenda that night. That is a theological statement because it is a statement about the kind of God God is. My neighbor is a "little theologian," as Barth put it (Campbell 1984, 42).

I would like more respect for the simple ways theology is being done by the people. All parents teaching their children how to pray are doing theology.

I think that constructing good little theologies is as demanding an enterprise as writing a theological book because to do so means making sense to
the people with whom we live.

Little theologies cannot copy other theologies or repeat those from the
past if they want to do justice to a particular context. We cannot use the
same sermon twice if it is to be a good sermon. We cannot tell the same joke
or the same story to the same person more than once. In this regard, the
construction of little theologies calls for the courage to say "I" ("I think,"
"I believe") and the creativity to come up with something new. We tend to
underestimate the impact a sermon, a letter, or a poster can have.

We certainly need specialists and scholars, people who can help the community with expertise; but we also need the freedom to "just do it." We
need frameworks in which to place our little theologies. We need coordi-
nates that tell us where we are with our little theologies. Both the local and
the universal, the little and the big, are vital. We do not want our little
theologies to oversimplify matters or play to people's prejudices. We want
little theologies to be taken as serious attempts to help people understand
their lives against the background of the gospel.

The famous principle of *subsidiarity* can also be read in terms of the
indispensability of local structures. The principle holds that nothing should
be done by a larger and more complex organization that can be done as
well by a smaller and simpler organization. It is not only that the higher
structure must not take over the functions of the lower structure; it is also
that the higher structure is incapable of doing so.

Little theologies can do justice to a local context in a way a big theology
cannot. It can talk to the hearts of particular people in a way a big theology
is not able to do. However, little theologies cannot be constructed without a
framework, and there are situations in which local theologies propounded
by agenda-driven preoccupations need to be reined in. Think, for example,
of the debates on the global church's position on the local theology called
liberation theology and about how the church should react to Archbishop
Lefebvre.

E. F. Schumacher reminds us that issues about how the local and the
universal relate are not found only in the church. Talking about the size of
economic units and social structures, he observes that when it comes to the
question of size, "there is no *single* answer. For his different purposes man
needs many different structures, both small ones and large ones, some ex-
clusive and some comprehensive" (Schumacher 1993, 49). What people find
most difficult, he says, is to keep two seemingly opposite notions of truth in
their minds at the same time. People clamor for a solution, forgetting that
the only truly final solution in human life is death!

Little theologies, therefore, are not about bringing about final solutions.
Little theologies are not long-term theologies. The question is not *either* big
theologies *or* little theologies (that is to say, solemnly defined dogmatic theologies *or* little theologies for a special occasion). Obviously, in the case of

theology we are not only talking about *size* but also about claims and quality, justification and legitimization. We need both—small claims for small
situations, far-reaching authority for general frameworks. The "size" of a
theology depends on the situation: What do we want to achieve? The points
Schumacher makes in his defense of small-scale economic structures are

- that large-scale structures have qualitatively different problems from
  local ones;
- that there is an "ideal size" for a certain structure according to the
  purpose it is to fulfill; and
- that disregard for the ideal size and allowing the proper degree of
  local autonomy leads either to the abuse of human beings to maintain
  structures or to the delegitimization and breakdown of structures being defended at the top by the powerful.

This is similarly true for theologies. Doing theology as if people matter
means choosing the right size for a theology. Little theologies can be the
appropriate way of doing local theology. The idea of little theologies tries to
do justice to the insight that the local culture is a theological source. The
church recognizes reading the signs of the times as a central task of theology.[1] The signs of the times manifest themselves in local social structures
and in local expressions of social life. Henri Nouwen wrote about the book
reviews in the *New York Times* that the books published, the topics treated,
are signs of the times. "Many books bring to mind forgotten treasures of
former generations, help find the world's few leftover quiet spots, or reveal
the simple life-styles of the past." Many titles suggest "that there were better times and that there were better places than our times and place" (Nouwen
1976, 176). This is a way of identifying burning issues and local topics. It is
a way of reading the signs of the times.

Looking at novels and movies, at paintings and sculptures, is a good way
of putting one's finger on the pulse that reveals what theologians have called
significant signs of the time. Human life is embedded in local cultures. "To
be a man means to live in a particular historical situation. *Particular*? Yes.
We do not live in some general idea of history. We live in a certain locality,
and each locality has a history, culture and language" (Koyama 1999, 32).
Because of that, we are looking for new places and new forms of theology
in order to do theology as if people matter (see Jossua and Metz 1979).
Local theologies are theologies made *from* and made *of* and made *within*
and made *for* local cultures: "Circumstances may require entry into the
process of constructing local theologies at different places. And experience

---

[1] See John XXIII, *Humanae salutis*, AAS 54 (1962), 5-13; John XXIII, *Pacem in
terris*, AAS 55 (1963), 257-304; Paul VI, *Ecclesiam suam*, AAS 56 (1964), 609-59;
P. Valdiers, "Signes de Temps, Signes de Dieu?" *Etudes* 335 (1971); Peter Schineller,
A Handbook on Inculturation (New York: Paulist Press, 1990), 52-56.

shows that local theologies tend to move by fits and starts" (Schreiter 1985, 23).

We find traces of little theologies throughout various local cultures. We call these a theology of everyday life, *situation theologies*, homemade theology, thinking-out-of-a-particular-situation or feet-on-the-ground theology. Clodovis Boff talks about "shade-tree theology—a theology that, far from the libraries and the offices, develops among brothers and sisters searching shoulder to shoulder with unlettered peasants for the sense of the word of God in situations in which this word touches them" (Clodovis Boff 1987). Similarly expressive is the idea and experience of doing theology under a tree in Africa, as Jean-Marc Ela has suggested (Ela 1986). The claim of these little theologies, even though they may and should have cross-cultural force, is a local claim.

We can think of some of the experiences related in Koyama's *Waterbuffalo Theology*. In this book Koyama coined the term "POT" ("particular orbit theology"): "Theological thinking cannot live outside the particularity of history, just as I cannot live outside the particularity of the Koyama family" (Koyama 1999, 45). This is the idea of little theologies. "Architects have a technical term for those structures that are designed and built by the people who live in them. They call this vernacular architecture" (Dyrness 1992, 15). People all over the world have used local material—rocks, grass, mud, wood—to build their dwellings. Similarly, William Dyrness suggests that vernacular theologies are the theological framework, the building materials, implicitly used by people to reflect on their faith and their religious life.

Little theologies use local materials for theological model making. Virtually anybody can do little theology out of his or her own life experience and local situation. Little theologies are a counterbalance to the big theological systems that have dominated the history of theology. The insight that history can be written as a history of little traditions as well as big events strengthens the idea of the power of the poor in history.

Little theologies look at the details and little things of life, knowing that these details always take on a local face. Second, little theologies arise out of little occasions, like Jesus' parables in reply to a question or Jesus' comment on God and Caesar out of the dynamics of a situation. Little theologies can be constructed using local theological resources like images, stories, or proverbs. Local theologies consider the local circumstances.

THREE TASKS OF LITTLE THEOLOGIES

THESIS 40: Little theologies are called to three tasks: (1) To point to the positive richness and goodness of local contexts; (2) to challenge the local context by inviting people to see and go be-

yond its limits; and (3) to inspire and encourage by opening eyes to previously unseen visions and ears to unheard sounds. Little theologies invite people to do theology themselves. When little theologies function properly, they empower.

When preparing a sermon, planning the liturgy on the occasion of first communion, or writing a letter to a friend in pain, we have to keep some key points in mind. Little theologies fulfill three tasks:

- they appreciate and relate to the local context;
- they challenge, relativize, and transcend the local context; and
- they inspire and encourage participants to live more deeply.

LITTLE THEOLOGIES APPRECIATE AND RELATE TO THE LOCAL CONTEXT

Little theologies are constructed for the here and now. They are meant to serve local needs. The first message of any theology is the good news of the original blessing, the news that all that is created is fundamentally good. This is the basis. Little theologies talk about the goodness of a particular congregation in rural Africa or suburban Chicago; little theologies talk about God's love for students in this particular class, parishioners in this particular parish, inmates in this particular prison. Little theologies are based on an appreciation of the local context. They are based on confidence in the local theological resources, and they are based on the optimism that a local context is full of the potential to grow and to be transformed.

People recognize themselves in little theologies! People want to be part of a sermon! We do not preach to "the whole of humanity." A person preaching to everybody does not reach anybody. Little theologies are not meant to be universal. Thus, it is advisable to be careful in using phrases like "We all believe . . . ," "All human beings . . . ," "We always . . . ," "Generally speaking, . . . " Little theologies are addressed to human people of flesh and blood, with experiences of their own, with local knowledge of their own.

The audience shapes little theologies. It makes a difference, Saint Augustine reminds us, "whether there are few or many; whether learned or unlearned, or a mixed audience made up of both classes; whether they are townsfolk or countryfolk, or both together" (in Tisdale 1997, 19). It is advisable not to have an abstract or overly simplistic picture of the audience. Cliches are a common trap in preparing sermons, as when one says to students, "At some point you will have a 'real job.'" Or to farmers, "Your life is lived within in the rhythms of nature, a hard life, a life that appreciates God's creation." The best little theologies are cautious about generalizations. Their articulators listen to people's concerns before talking.

Showing appreciation for local culture is especially important where the local culture has been denied the right to prosper. Filipino theologian José de Mesa talks of the task of "destigmatizing the local culture" as important for inculturation (de Mesa 1998). For the Philippines, with its long history of occupation and suppression, this is a very important aspect. Filipinos appreciate the use of Filipino examples, Filipino experiences, and positive allusions to the way Filipinos are.

Little theologies should be liberating. "Our first task in approaching another people, another culture, another religion, is to take off our shoes, for the place we are approaching is holy. Else we may find ourselves treading on men's dreams. More serious still, we may forget that God was here before our arrival" (Warren 1963, 10). Theologians should discover and reveal the beauty and depth of local resources. Leonore Tubbs Tisdale mentions a good example of appreciation of a local history: the sermon "Makers of Stone Soup" (Tisdale 1997, 111f.). It starts off with a well-known story of beggars who start cooking a soup with nothing but water and a stone. People become curious and are willing to add, one by one, more and more ingredients. In the end, because of everybody's contribution, there is a great soup. The pastor used that story to thank the parishioners for their wonderful contribution to the parish. This is a little theology of appreciation that shows that good things are not taken for granted. We tend to overstate the bad things in our lives and we tend to understate the good things. This is a strange psychological dynamic and a reason to keep in mind that little theologies are best when they help people appreciate what is good in a situation and to be grateful (see Leddy 2001).

LITTLE THEOLOGIES CHALLENGE, RELATIVIZE, AND TRANSCEND THE LOCAL CONTEXT

Little theologies are not mere reconstructions of a local situation but invitations to go beyond it. Jesus challenged the people profoundly. He challenged them because he cared for them and he loved them. Jesus challenged the rich young man, not for the fun of provoking him or out of anger, but because he loved him. Jesus challenged Peter, asking him about his commitment, not because he was conducting a job interview and wanted to make sure that his business would be run more efficiently, but because he loved him.

Challenges invite us, sometimes harshly, to look at things differently, to take a second look, to realize that there is more than one way of dealing with things, judging situations, encountering people, living life. For example: "'The poor are not our problem; we are theirs.' This epigram effectively stimulates a novel perspective" (Gittins 1994, 119). Little theologies (as much as theology in general) should invite us to embrace a new perspective.

Let us look at some examples. There was a priest preaching on Luke 18:9-13, the story of the proud Pharisee and the tax collector in the Temple.

He was addressing a crowd of pious people and started his sermon: "Frankly speaking, the tax collector is not appealing to me. I like people to walk with their head up, I prefer people with self-esteem." He challenged his hearers to rethink categories. Haven't we sometimes heard that humility is the opposite of self-esteem? And isn't the point of this story that humility is good and self-esteem is bad? No!

Similarly we should challenge theological or spiritual cliches; in the dissonance that such challenges create, sometimes something new can break through. In this vein, I recall a priest preaching to Carmelite sisters. He read the gospel on Jesus receiving the children and said: "Jesus invites us to become like children. But I assure you, he does not want us to become like children in every aspect. He does not want us to become helpless little creatures who cannot take care of ourselves and be parents only to dolls and teddy bears!" Such a break with saccharine cliches may be challenging in a community where the ideal of childlike innocence has been firmly established.

Little theologies fulfill this task of sensitive challenging. Dom Helder Câmara challenged us when talking about the parable of the prodigal son: "The one has awoken from his life of sin. When will the other awaken from his virtue?" (Câmara 1981, 71). Anthony de Mello asks in his retreats, "What is the difference between a terrorist and a saint?" Similarly, "we 'decent persons' differ from criminals . . . not in what we are but in what we do. At the heart we are the same" (Valles 1987, 64).

LITTLE THEOLOGIES INSPIRE AND ENCOURAGE PARTICIPANTS TO LIVE MORE DEEPLY

In the first chapter we talked about the need for empowerment. Jesus empowered people by his ministry to go their way, to continue his mission, to become ministers themselves. Little theologies, like theology in general, should help us to live and to live life more fully, to live a life in the face of God. That is why theology cannot stop at the challenge. We are people of anxieties and small dreams. We need to be reminded that we can dare to dream big dreams of transformation. We need to be reminded about the power of the mustard seed, the power of transformation that God gives us. Little theologies in this sense should inspire and encourage.

Dom Helder Câmara talked about the impossible dream and called for "men and women . . . ready to build a more just and more human world" (in Mary Hall 1980, 8). Little theologies should call those people of good will. They should open new horizons. They should stretch our imaginations. A wide imagination, a vision, can give us the courage to act and to walk the road less traveled. A vision of the face of the earth renewed is food for the soul that gives us strength to go on with our journey. The Bible calls this phenomenon faith (Clodovis Boff 1987, 47).

The famous "I Have a Dream" speech of Martin Luther King Jr. is an example of a little theology that inspires us and gives us encouragement:

When we allow freedom to ring , when we let it ring from every village and every hamlet, from every state and every city, we will be able
to speed up that day when all of God's children . . . will be able to join
hands and sing in the words of the old Negro spiritual: "Free at last.
Free at last. Thank God Almighty, we are free at last" (in Ellsberg
1997, 152-53).

Luis Espinal, a priest murdered in Bolivia, wrote these inspiring words:

Train us, Lord, to fling ourselves upon the impossible, for behind the
impossible is your grace and your presence; we cannot fall into emptiness. The future is an enigma, our road is covered by mist, but we
want to go on giving ourselves, because you continue hoping amid the
night and weeping tears through a thousand human eyes (in Gutiérrez
1987, 91-92).

We are a people of anxieties who need to be encouraged. In the Bible we
find many inspiring stories. Moses, Jeremiah, and Isaiah were afraid of becoming prophets. They did not feel able. Their imaginations were too small.
Abraham and Sarah and Zachariah did not believe God's message of a son
to be born. Their imaginations were not wide enough. Their God was too
small.

Little theologies remind us in a very simple way that God is great. Jesus
uses inspiring images to characterize the role of his followers: we are salt of
the earth, light of the world, sheep among wolves. Robert Ellsberg's *All
Saints* is full of examples of inspiring people who have given witness with
their lives. We need people who inspire us by the testimony of their lives.
Ignatius became a follower of Jesus after reading the lives of the saints.
Ellsberg writes, "I have learned far less about the gospel from studying
theology than I have from the lives of holy people" (Ellsberg 1997, 5).

Little theologies inspire people to do theology because they talk about
people's lives and questions and concerns. We all need to hear messages
that inspire us. We need to live in an open world, a world where the impossible is truly possible, a world of surprises. A friend of mine prays every
morning, "Jesus, surprise me." We can think of the attitude expressed by
the general superior of the Society of Jesus, Pedro Arrupe, on the occasion
of his golden jubilee: "The figure of Abraham has always been for me an
inexhaustible source of inspiration. 'Where is the Society heading?' men
have asked me. My reply has always been: 'Where God is leading it.' In
other words, I do not know" (in Becker 1992, 14). The figure of Abraham
gives us the vision of a promise, the promise that God is with us, that God
is leading us to a new land. We are inspired by people who were ready to
leave their homes and settle in a new, a promised land. Little theologies are
called to inspire and encourage.

CONSTRUCTING LITTLE THEOLOGIES

THESIS 41: Little theologies arise in concrete occasions and in response to specific needs; they are often evoked by simple questions. As personal answers to personal questions and particular reactions to local concerns, little theologies are developed face to face with the people without using "canned" answers. Constructing little theologies requires the ability to listen and learn. Articulating them requires both sensitivity to the realities of the concrete situation and basic knowledge of the gospel.

Little theologies respond to concrete occasions and needs. Karl Rahner, one of the most important theologians of the twentieth century, often did "occasional" theology. Many believe that the talks he gave on such occasions are his best work. For the most part, indeed, Rahner's work was produced as a result of accepting invitations to give talks and to write articles. Thus he produced hundreds of little but profound theological investigations rather than big books. This is a valuable example for little theologies—the enormity of what can be done over time if one uses particular occasions well.

The primary method of little theologies is the case study. Careful investigation of local situations on a case-by-case basis is the most promising and most serious approach to doing theology in a way that is appropriate to a local culture. Constructing little theologies is doing theology by way of examples. That is why the theologian should investigate cultural situations the way language philosopher Ludwig Wittgenstein investigated the many uses of language on a case-by-case basis: "Let us really think out various *different* situations and conversations, and the ways in which that sentence will be uttered in them" (Wittgenstein 1967, §592). Little theologies take the diversity of particular contexts seriously, the particularity of people and their lives, their stories, and their hopes. The method will be case studies,[2]

---

[2] The case study as a special technique is very useful for local theologies (see William A. Dyrness, *Invitation to Cross-Cultural Theology: Case Studies in Vernacular Theologies* [Grand Rapids, Mich.: Zondervan Publishing House, 1992]; Alice F. Evans, "Teaching and Learning with Cases," in *Human Rights: A Dialogue between the First and Third Worlds*, ed. Robert A. Evans and Alice F. Evans, 14-22 [Maryknoll, N.Y.: Orbis Books, 1983]; Robert A. Evans and T. D. Parker, eds., *Christian Theology: A Case Method Approach* [New York: Harper & Row, 1976]; G. D. Lewis, *Resolving Church Conflicts: A Case Approach for Local Congregations* [San Francisco: Harper & Row, 1981]; Robert A. Evans and Alice F. Evans, *Introduction to Christianity: A Case Study Approach* [Atlanta, Ga.: John Knox Press, 1980]).

and the result will be examples and "sketches of landscapes" (Wittgenstein 1967, v): sketches of dogmatic ideas, sketches of a theology of sacraments, sketches of a theology of everyday life.

Little theologies arise out of little occasions. Whenever we decorate a church, preach on a scripture passage, teach a class in a school, or answer a question, the dialogic pastoral worker, the priest, the theologian, or the catechist has an opportunity to develop a little theology. Little theologies deal with issues similar to the issues dealt with by big theological systems. A sermon can reveal an ecclesiological position, a work of art can point to a christological question, a letter can speak of our concept of God. Very difficult questions can come up during table conversation.

A farmer once asked me: "From the pulpit, I hear so much about the forgiving and loving God. Is that all true? Would that mean that a person like Adolf Hitler would come to heaven, too?" What do you say? In such a situation, you have to create a little theology. You are challenged to talk about heaven (place, process), God (God's freedom, human hope, God's justice, God's order of being), the meaning of forgiving (not to undo or make unhappened, no magic event). You might even want to challenge the hidden assumptions by saying such things as: "If we are truly saved and transformed, we will not be afraid of anybody anymore. No one will have the power to generate envy or hatred or fear in us." To the question of Hitler, what would be the response if you said, "There is a famous theologian who talked about our hope that hell is empty." Might one challenge overly concrete images of our state after death by saying, "You know, I don't think heaven or hell are places like Philadelphia or Chicago. What do you think?"

Once I was confronted with this question from a young student: "Why do we need priests? I do not need them!" The voice deserves being taken seriously. It calls for a little theology of priesthood, a theology of commitment and discipleship. I remember a little theology of priesthood of Dom Helder Câmara: "Priests! I believe we will always need priests with long years of training. But what we need most of all are priests with a thousand reasons for living" (in Mary Hall 1980, 80). This is a little theology of priesthood: priests as people with a thousand reasons for living. Similarly, we can recall the little theology of priesthood given to Dom Helder by his father: "Being a priest means not belonging to oneself any longer. A priest belongs to God and others" (ibid., 27).

Leny Mendoza Strobel, a Filipina woman, once said: "Nothing in my study of theology prepared me for God's silence to my many questions. If I'm a child of God, why do I feel intimidated by white people who are better-educated, talk faster, laugh louder? If I'm a child of God, why don't White Christians treat me like one? Why don't they ask me intelligent questions?" (in Montgomery-Fate 1997, 87). What do you say to such questions? We cannot give an answer from the catechism. We need a little theology that rises to the occasion, perhaps a little theology of listening, of silence, of attention.

Once I was asked by high school students about the meaning of intercessions: "Why do we always pray for peace in the world and good politicians and solidarity among the peoples if people don't pray with their heart anyway and if it doesn't do any good either?" An African friend asked me, "Wouldn't it be better to celebrate the eucharist only occasionally, let us say, once a month, to preserve the specialness of the occasion?" I couldn't help but remember the impact Oscar Romero's 1977 decision to celebrate only one mass for the whole archdiocese at the Cathedral had. This experience could help us to understand this person's point and concern and to take the question seriously.

All these questions provoke little theologies. In all these cases, it is highly appreciated if the person being questioned doesn't give a standard answer, especially if there are deep concerns involved. Theology is about waking up. It is a matter of looking in the right corners and asking the right questions. What questions should we ask? What are the problems we should spend our energy and ingenuity on? Can we justify our choice of questions? "Many of our problems are the problems of only one group, the well-to-do. They are often 'luxury' questions which are of no interest to those who live in misery and squalor. To be preoccupied with our own questions might mean death for the others. We live in our world so minimally aware of our connectedness that we don't even have the same problems or questions" (Donders 1986, 85).

We need to live *with* people in order to theologize *for* them, and we need to live *for* them to theologize *with* them. If the main local problems are economic problems, then that is what we need to address. If a theologian is confronted with a post-war trauma, as is the case of theology after Auschwitz in Europe or theology after Hiroshima and Nagasaki in Japan (Suzuki 1988), then this is where the theologian has to begin. The introduction of the Christian message to a new cultural context will give rise to new theological questions. "Christian theology in Africa will become truly indigenous as it struggles with the question . . . 'Is the God of our redemption the same as the God of our creation?'" (Oduyoye 1986, 75). This is a problem in a specific cultural context. Doing local theology means dealing with questions that are relevant in the local situation.

We are called to ask ourselves: What are the burning questions?[3] What are the key topics? It is a delicate task to identify burning issues. It is not a

---

[3] Philip Berrigan, writing in prison, talks about a fellow priest, a good and decent man. But "he, and others like him, are interested only in an updated liturgy, clerical freedom to marry, and official approval for birth control" (Philip Berrigan, *Prison Journals of a Priest Revolutionary* [New York: Holt, Rinehart and Winston, 1970], 70). Understanding priorities is a matter of understanding the social and cultural context: "From within situations of misery and struggle rise the questions that theology must take up. These are questions of the victimised people, questions posed by their poverty and experience and domination. They are not questions of the first world nor are they concerns of academic theology. These and metaphysical

task that can be carried out from an office. Understanding burning issues and topics is a question of listening. The first reaction of theologians has to be: You talk, we listen! Let the culture with its many signs and expressions talk. "Theologians must first be listeners and discoverers. Only in this way will they both find out the real questions being asked by the people and deal with the real issues alive in the socio-cultural context" (de Mesa 1979, 63). It is obvious that developing little theologies requires:

- *a listening ear*: What is behind the question? Is there an untold background?[4] What is the real concern of the person who raises the question? Am I willing to be challenged by the question? Am I willing to expose myself to the question without taking a ready-made answer out of my "theological refrigerator"? Am I willing to cook a "theological meal" just for this particular occasion?

- *insight and knowledge*: What should I know in order to give a well-balanced answer that does justice to the personal story, the local context, and the universal framework of our belief? What would I like the person asking the question to know? In what areas should I do more research and studying?

- *sensitivity*: The answer can have an impact. So I have to be aware of important issues. Which words do I choose? Which examples? How far can I go in challenging the person?

A Few Examples

Little theologies can give blood and flesh to the bones of well-known doctrines. Let me give you an example of a little eschatology that I found in Cardinal Bernardin's *The Gift of Peace*:

The first time I traveled with my mother and sister to my parents' homeland of Tonadico di Primiero, in northern Italy, I felt as if I had been there before. After years of looking through my mother's photo albums, I knew the mountains, the land, the houses, the people. As soon as we entered the valley I said, "My God, I know this place. I am home." Somehow I think crossing from this life into eternal life will be similar. I will be home (Bernardin 1997, 152).

---

and bourgeois questions would lead to a different kind of theology incapable of making significant contributions to the people's struggles and hopes" (Samuel Rayan, "The 'How' of Third World Theologies," in *Third World Theologies in Dialogue: Essays in Memory of D. S. Amalorpavadass*, ed. J. R. Chandran, 42-66 [Banagalore: EATWOT, W. Q. Judge Press, 1991], 51).

[4] Once a young woman asked me: "Do you think that God wants a woman to marry a particular man or are there many potential husbands for a woman?" It turned out that she was not asking an abstract question. She was struggling with doubts concerning her scheduled wedding.

German theologians Dorothee Sölle and Fulbert Steffensky create a little
theology of grace when they say, "The best thing in life [grace] is really
free" (Sölle and Steffensky 1985, 19). This little phrase captures important
moments of grace, its embeddedness in our lives, the many meanings of its
being free. Similarly, they created a little theology of the kingdom by char-
acterizing the kingdom of God as the "freedom from having and the freedom
for living" (ibid., 68). These simple words capture a whole theology of the
kingdom of God, a theology of farewell to consumerism and welcome to
life in its fullness. Jean Vanier, in an address at Lambeth Vigil in July 1998,
mentioned the example of Fareed, a severely handicapped man. Fareed had
his great moments when getting ice cream. Having a huge ice cream was
heaven on earth for him. If we told him that the kingdom of God is like a
big ice cream, Fareed would understand. This is a little theology, given to a
particular person under particular circumstances.

Little theologies can work with the details of life. We can think of the
theology of the sacraments. We all know that sacraments are special situations in which an encounter between God and humans takes place.
Sacraments are particular visible signs of the invisible, particular signs of
God's presence. This is part of the concept of sacraments. Again, it is very
important to know these things, but it is not enough. Little theologies try to
connect the concept of a sacrament with our life experience. Leonardo Boff
mentions the often quoted example of the drinking cup that his family used
for years and the last cigarette his father smoked before he died. Boff said
that these objects, the drinking cup and the cigarette, were sacraments for
him, signs of God's love.

Sacraments are signs of God's presence. Cardinal Bernardin tells us
about the cross above his bed. "It has been a constant reminder of Jesus'
death and resurrection" (Bernardin 1997, 128). This is a sacrament in a
certain sense. Dom Helder Câmara had a print in his room, a print in
black and white of an Andean shepherd boy playing a flute against a background of high mountains. This print was a sign of his being called by
God: "This shepherd boy has nothing but his flute, his song, and the gifts
of mountain and air. I like to think of myself as a shepherd for my people.
I too have a song, a song of God's love for each one" (in Mary Hall 1980,
18). These are examples that can help us to understand the meaning of
sacraments.

Little theologies invite personal answers to personal questions. A child's
beloved doll ("a sign of the love of your parents who gave you that doll")
can be a door to talk about sacraments to that child. Little theologies call
for respect of the situation. How would you illustrate the meaning of sacraments? What is for you a sign of God's loving presence? Winning the lottery?
A smile from the cashier when you go shopping? A letter from your beloved? A warm memory? Is it possible that partners in marriage can become
sacraments for each other?

Another instructive example are little theologies of the church. Quite often we use the image of the family to talk about the church. In the words of theologians Dorothee Sölle and Fulbert Steffensky: "This is our family. It is weird, and strange, but this is the family we have" (Sölle and Steffensky 1985, 93). More gently, this image is used by Cardinal Bernardin in his little theology of church shared with a person who was asking for reconciliation with the church:

> In every family there are times when there is hurt, anger, or alienation. But we cannot run away from our family. We have only one family, and so, after every falling out, we must make every effort to be reconciled. So, too, the church is our spiritual family. Once we become a member, we may be hurt or become alienated, but it is still our family (Bernardin 1997, 39-40).

This is a little theology of the church, a little ecclesiology.

Little theologies can be developed together in a community. There will be different voices. We can think of an example from Brazil: "Sister Nehida spoke with the community about models of church, illustrating with posters. One represented the church as a pyramid, with a rigid hierarchy. Another represented the church that dialogues, where everyone is heard and valued. Some people said they preferred the old way" (Rezende 1994, 40). It is significant to see little theologies at work in church decorations, in wedding invitations, at the party for an anniversary to the priesthood, in the parish bulletin. Leonora Tubbs Tisdale gives a wonderful example of how a little theology that shows itself in parish life can dominate the imagination of two different congregations:

> The first congregation—an old, historic church—always had an intergenerational gathering of children, youth, and adults playing the various assigned roles in the Christmas story. However, when it came to the role of the baby Jesus, the inviolable tradition was that no real baby or even a baby doll would take the part. Rather, this congregation, reflecting its metaphorical understanding of Jesus as "light of the world," placed a light within the manger—a light that shone forth and reflected the aura of God's own Son come to earth at Christmas. Obviously, the Christology in this church was high. Jesus may have appeared on earth in human form, but to this people he was primarily *God with us*. . . . In the second congregation, the expectation for the annual Christmas pageant was that a real, live baby would play the role of Jesus. However, it was also expected that the baby would be good: "The little Lord Jesus, no crying he makes." Jesus, then, was a human being, but he was also a superhuman being (not the kind who had messy diapers, cried when hungry, and shared other human limitations) (Tisdale 1997, 80f.).

When one thinks about examples such as these, it becomes clear, too, that a congregation's preference for certain songs needs to be considered carefully, and it is significant to observe preferred metaphors and images for Jesus (brother, shepherd, bread of life, son of God, teacher, savior, suffering servant). Many congregations have quite well-developed and specific local theologies that can be quite different from other congregations in the same town.

THE EXAMINED LIFE

THESIS 42: Little theologies look at the details of our lives. They try to look at these aspects from a theological perspective, weighing alternative ways of dealing with these details, reflecting on how to approach life theologically. Such a theologically examined life is both a task and a spiritual challenge.

Reading our lives is an important religious exercise. Practicing a "revision of life" invites to ask the question, How did I put my life in the service of the kingdom of God today? Looking back at the events of the day is important for the integrity of the heart. There are many aspects of our lives that we rarely think about.

Do we know where the clothes we wear were made or how toothpaste and cosmetics are made? Are the people making them receiving a living wage? Should we read two newspapers every day? Should we offer alcoholic beverages when we invite guests for dinner? Should inherited wealth be passed on from generation to generation? Is it irresponsible to have children in a world such as ours? How should children be educated? Can we imagine our life without books? Can we imagine our life without a television? Should we go to a doctor whenever we are in pain? Is politics necessarily dirty? Should we feel guilty about the poverty in many countries? Can a lie be justified?

The American philosopher Peter Unger wrote a remarkable book entitled *Living High and Letting Die: Our Illusion of Innocence*. In it he challenged our moral intuitions by using a series of examples. He asked, for instance, what is the difference between refusing to donate money to a charitable agency and refusing to help a drowning child in a pond as we pass by (Unger 1996). Another philosopher, Peter Singer, in *Animal Liberation* draws attention to the cruel ways animals are treated and asks whether eating meat is a moral issue (Singer 1975).

Questions of lifestyle are key questions for Christian identity. It matters how we live. When Henri Nouwen was searching for a proper way of life and spent seven months in a Trappist monastery in New York, the abbot asked him to prepare for time "after the monastery" by developing habits and schedules. He recommended especially the need for developing a habit of maintaining clear and fixed prayer times, because a life with well-defined boundaries makes for a better way of relating to people (Nouwen 1976, 114). Arranging the details of our lives is important for a fully conscious life. We need to keep a balance in mind, a balance between flexibility and uncompromising rigidity.

How we live matters. How we spend the precious first and last moments of our day matters. How we deal with commodities and possessions matters. The details of our lives should not be dismissed easily. In 1989 American philosopher Robert Nozick published *The Examined Life*. In this book Nozick reflects on life and what is important in life. It is a book in the tradition of Socrates, who encourages us to look at all the aspects of our life. Nozick deals with issues like parents and children, sexuality, selflessness, dying, wisdom, politics, enlightenment. He examines philosophically in order to clarify his own thinking and his own life.

Little theologies can take the form of theological reflections upon the little details of our life. There are so many things we take for granted. Do we need schools? Is there an alternative to having prisons? Is Jean Vanier's L'Arche an alternative to mental asylums? These are far-reaching questions that can be tackled from a theological angle.

How should we live? is the basic theological question. It is hard to deal with. In the 1950s Erich Fromm and Edward T. Hall, both teaching at Bennington College in Vermont, wanted to offer a course together entitled "How to Live Right." The course was turned down by the administration because such a topic, they were told, could not be dealt with in a scientific and serious manner. Yet, there is no doubt that reflection upon such issues is necessary. How should we live? What does a theologically examined life look like?

How should we live? What is it that counts in life? Mitch Albom, a journalist, had the chance to reconnect with his former college professor Morrie Schwartz in the last months of Schwartz's life. Knowing he was dying, Morrie visited with Mitch in his study every Tuesday. They were having "classes," lessons in how to live. Morrie Schwartz talked about life and what matters in life. As a person facing death, he was tuned to the essential. Morrie Schwartz was raising questions theology wants to address: how should we live? (Albom 1998).

A theological examination of important questions might ask: Would Jesus throw stones at abortion clinics? Is the multiplication of official church documents a positive development? Given the crises that periodically hit the church over issues such as clerical sexual misconduct, should there be a different model of appointing bishops? Should it be obligatory to give a certain amount of time and money to the public good? What should we do in solidarity with the poor? How should we celebrate God's bounty to us in the face of our knowledge of the crippling conditions of poverty and injustice under which so many live?

There are scores of questions concerning how one should follow Christ in a consumer society of relative mass affluence. Cardinal Joseph Bernardin talks about the concrete fruits of an examination of his life: "More than fifteen years ago I gave away all the money I had and said that I would never again have a savings account or stocks: I pledged that I would keep only what was needed to maintain my checking account" (Bernardin 1997, 10). We know of bishops who have given up their episcopal residences. These are questions of how to live that the laity also needs to face, for following Christ is not just for priests and religious.

A Jesuit friend of mine talked about the immense possibilities for changing things that large religious communities like the Society of Jesus could have if they were to buy certain products and boycott others, depending upon a corporation's policies in regard to establishing fair trade relations. Such ideas involve immense attention to details, however, and it is not always clear whether actions based on such ideas attain their goals. Nevertheless, Cistercian abbot John Eudes Bamberger is clearly right in saying about the business practices of his monastery that "even the prices of our products and the use of our money should be determined to the praise of God's mysterious presence in our lives" (in Nouwen 1976, 12).

Looking at the details of life is important when we talk about religious commitments. How should we express and live our religious commitments and our religious identity? What does it mean for members of religious communities to be poor, celibate, obedient? Poverty has a lot to do with "simplicity of life," chastity with "integrity of the heart," obedience with "solidarity and service to the community." These are all invitations to examine our life. Religious vows are an expression of an option. But they are not ends in themselves. If religious life is meant to be a witness to the rest of the church, what lessons are the laity to draw from the vowed life? Jesus' counsels to live a poor life are not intended as an end in themselves, so what does the counsel to embrace poverty mean for ordinary Christians? At one point in his life Anthony de Mello preached the need to embrace radical poverty. Later he changed his attitude: "I realized that my 'poverty' had become my 'riches,' that is, that I was attached to my image as a poor man and full of pride for it, so that poverty had defeated its purpose" (in Valles 1987, 13).

Looking at such details is a matter of developing a little theology. It is obvious that life is more complicated now than it was two thousand years ago. The forms to fill out, deadlines to remember, meetings to attend, laws to obey. The gospel gives us an orientation. We have to arrange the details of our lives ourselves. Looking at details of our life from a theological point of view—with an explicit reference to our relationship with God—is a matter of constructing little theologies.

In his theological reflections about ordinary things of everyday life, Karl Rahner invites us to keep three things in mind. First, he says, everyday life must be understood realistically; everyday life is just ordinary life. Second, it is within everyday life that we discover the mystery of God and God's silent grace. Third, we should treat the matters of everyday life in a "Sunday spirit"; the small is the anticipation of the great (Rahner 1964, 709). Thus, little things should be seen in proportion, as *little* things, with a level-headed mindset. Little things, however, carry traces of the divine and are our way to seek and find God in all things. "Often the theologian finds God—rather God finds the theologian—in ordinary events and symbols" (Mueller 1988, 93; see also Galilea 1998, 3-4).

It is a good theological exercise to look at various aspects of our life and think about ways to improve what we are doing. It might, for instance, be fruitful to spend twenty minutes a day thinking about how to "live right." Little theologies should lead us to honesty in our attempts to weigh options. It is useful to collect arguments for and against each choice we have before us. In this way we can look at time and money priorities, or possible service in community organizations, or our daily routine. Let us take a look at two simple questions with four different answers.

What Do You Do When a Beggar Asks You for Money?

1. Sometimes I give, sometimes I don't. It's like being with friends—sometimes you pay for a beer for them, sometimes you don't. It depends on my mood, it depends on how I feel toward that person, it depends on whether I have change in my pocket, and it depends on my schedule. Sometimes I am in a hurry. It is impossible to give something to every beggar.

2. I do not have much money, but I am not too busy most of the time. So I make it a point to take such a person to a restaurant where we can share something to eat and drink and talk a little bit. I don't think it is good just to give money. They might spend it on liquor.

3. I am a strong believer in the division of labor. If a person approaches me for money, how am I to know whether this person is genuine or not? There are so many cases of deception. I tell these people that they should go and talk to a social welfare aid agency. If they don't know it, I give them the address of the aid agency and give them directions. That does not mean that I am not willing to share. Sharing is important and a Christian duty. I regularly give money to charity, but I never give to individuals.

4. I make it a point always to have a few coins in my pocket when I leave the house. There are many beggars in the area where I live. I know that some of them are greedy and deceptive, but so what? Dorothy Day said, "It is better to be sometimes wrong than to be perennially suspicious." So I try to give a coin with a smile. I know it's not much and will not change their lives, but if everybody did that, it might make a difference.

Should We—as a Religious Community—Eat Organically Grown Food?

1. No. Organically grown food is much more expensive than the other food that you get in the supermarkets or the local markets. Ordinary people cannot afford expensive food. If you have children, you have to buy the cheapest food, and you cannot afford to ask where the food comes from and how it was produced. If we want to share life with the poor, we cannot buy organically grown food.

2. Yes. It is our responsibility to send out signals showing that a life in line with gospel values is possible. Following Christ in a consumer society means living a life of critical self-awareness and awareness of unjust and unhealthy economic systems. Being aware of your body, being aware of nature, being aware of your lifestyle are integral parts of that critical self-awareness. We cannot simply follow the mainstream, even if not doing so is a little more expensive. Organically grown food does not come from multinational companies. We should be willing to pay a little bit more to make a difference.

3. No. We should not pay so much attention to ourselves, to *our* well-being, to *our* way of life. We should not spend a lot of energy, time, and money on ourselves and on structures we can't change anyway. We are here to serve. With the money we save we could create a special fund to help people. It could become part of our ministry.

4. Yes. It could help us to be more aware of what we eat. Food is so basic, and we pray for our daily bread. Making this daily bread special is a great way to understand God's love and greatness. Food is a life source. It would be better to cut back on newspapers and magazines than on food expenses, as long as we are buying simple and healthy food.

Similarly, we can ask if a family or a religious community should have a TV? Should we subscribe to a variety of newspapers and magazines? How should we celebrate our birthdays? Where should we get our clothes? What should we give for Christmas? In asking such questions, there is no right or wrong answer, but I think it is important to ask them and reflect on the kind of life we want to construct on the basis of the answers. Not to do something like this means that we are not allowing the light of the gospel to illuminate the little, everyday things that make up 99 percent of life.

Little theologies encourage us to look at all the aspects of everyday life and try to reflect explicitly from a Christian perspective on issues that are normally taken for granted by our communities, our cultures, and our families of origin. Taking a step back and developing the little-theology orientation is especially important in complex contemporary societies and cultures. Conditions today differ vastly from the environment of the gospels in the first-century Mediterranean world. It is, though, a worthwhile challenge to see our cultural environment as a kind of "fifth gospel" from which to draw insights. It is challenging to see the sacramental nature of culture. It is challenging to find answers to the questions about how to live more deeply in the world of the twenty-first century. If we believe that God is present in all things and that we can find God everywhere, then no detail is unworthy to be looked at. How shall we live the little things of life so that we can find God?

The little things of life make a difference. How should we begin our day? How should we end it? It is the little things that show our faithfulness and care. The little things decide whether a marriage will fall apart or not. Little things keep a congregation's credibility high. How should we dispose of our garbage? Where should we do our shopping? Little things make a difference. Cardinal Bernardin observed at the end of his life: "The things people are naturally attracted to and remember most are small acts of concern and thoughtfulness. Years later, *that* is what they tell you about their priests and other clergy" (Bernardin 1997, 90).

God very often speaks in a gentle breeze, not in a storm, not in a dramatic fire (see 1 Kgs 19:11-13). In our own day, Henri Nouwen observes, "God, who is the creator of the Universe, comes to us in smallness, weakness, and hiddenness" (Nouwen 1992, 62). It is faithfulness in following the gospel in the care of little things—the *cura minimorum* of classical spiritual theology—that produces faithfulness in the greater things. Jesus was very clear about the importance of taking care for such little things.

Exercise: Choose an aspect of your life to examine or think about these questions or similar ones: Can I justify air travel in the same way I can justify traveling by car? Should I stop going to the movies? Should I dress fashionably? How should I spend my holidays? How should I choose the books I read? How should I talk about church officials and their performances?
Develop various possible answers and think of arguments for each position.

THEOLOGICAL OCCASIONS

THESIS 43: Little theologies arise in concrete occasions and places. Sometimes we are confronted with unpredictable, powerful events that provoke the need to develop afresh little theologies. Other occasions where little theologies are called for are regular pastoral situations such as the preparation of a homily. The criterion of a little theology is its appropriateness to the given situation and fidelity to the gospel.

Little theologies arise out of particular occasions. When Jesus is confronted with the question of innocent suffering, he presents a little theology as an answer: "Do you think that because these Galileans suffered in this way they were worse sinners than all other Galileans? No, I tell you; but unless you repent, you will all perish as they did" (Lk 13:2-3). Jesus presents a situational theology whereby individuals become symbols of suffering for a whole nation and in which suffering and evil are separated.

When Jesus observes the poor widow who donates money to the Temple, he uses this occasion to create a little theology of sharing. When Jesus sees the quarrel among his disciples about who will be the greatest, he creates a little theology of ministry. When Jesus sees the children, he uses the occasion to develop a little theology of the kingdom of God. Seen with theological eyes, life is full of theological occasions, occasions that call for theological reflection and theological judgment.

Sometimes the need for little theologies or serious theological reflection is provoked by events. September 11, 2001, has become a milestone in the history of religions. The tragic events around the World Trade Center in New York evoked many emotional theological debates. Many people talked about these events in waiting rooms, on trains, at street corners. There were many occasions and needs to forge little theologies. Whenever something unexpected or significant happens, we find ourselves in the position of having to ask questions and to give answers. These are occasions for little theologies.

Little theologies are not always provoked by events. Sometimes they are called for by the season. Preparing a sermon, decorating the church, writing a hymn, preparing a Sunday School class, all are occasions to construct little theologies. A wonderful occasion to construct a little theology is setting up a nativity set. Steve Bevans mentions an attempt in Korea in the 1980s: "The final design was a small cardboard shack against the background of tall hotels, apartment complexes, and office buildings, complete with signs advertising cabarets, health clubs, and bars" (Bevans 2002, 20).

In Austria, carving nativity sets is an art. Each parish is proud of its creche. Sometimes Joseph looks like an Austrian farmer; sometimes the three magi look like professors.

John Mahoney describes the representation of a nativity scene in Fiji:

Joseph was seated on the ground, clothed in the ordinary Fijian waistcloth or *sulu*. The magi were shown in full Fijian ceremonial garb, performing the customary ritual for visitors of very high rank. I asked Peni why he had changed Joseph's posture. He replied that Joseph was a man of royal descent; how could he do anything so low as to stand in the presence of distinguished visitors while they were performing the sacred welcome. . . . Mary is shown as a young Lau girl, dressed as an ordinary woman would be for her child's birth ceremonies. . . . The magi offer the traditional wealth: a polished whale's tooth, a root of *yaqona* (from which the chiefly drink will be prepared and offered) and mats. The ox is the Indian Zebu (Mahoney 1994, 20-21).

Making the biblical figures as natural as possible reveals a latent little theology of the incarnation. Similar accounts can be given of church decorations, house altars, Christmas cards, and so forth.

Little theologies grow in the soil of particular occasions. A good example is the way one prepares a good sermon. Every good sermon requires the homilist to create a little theology. Preaching is a way of doing local theology because it has to do justice to the text, the feast or special occasion, and the local context, including the needs of a particular audience and situation. If preaching is to announce authentic, meaningful good news, it has to touch the people's hearts. Leonora Tubbs Tisdale puts it this way: "Preaching that makes meaningful impact on lives has to reach persons at gut level, and it is at this level of communally stored wisdom and cultural affinity that such access to living souls is gained" (Tisdale 1997, 21).

We cannot prepare a good sermon without thinking of the audience. If I am to give a gospel reflection to a group of high school students I have to ask myself: What are their experiences, concerns, questions, hopes, and dreams? What language do they employ to speak of their own identity? If we are preaching in front of university students and professors about becoming like little children (Mk 10:13-16), we need to make our points very carefully. When preaching effectively, we choose examples that are familiar to the people we talk to. We refer to experiences that are familiar. The goal is to help people think and live more deeply because they understand these little things more deeply.

Jesus is an excellent example of how to create a little theology when proclaiming the good news. First, it is remarkable that Jesus chose parables, a literary form that is open to and requires interpretation and reflection, as his characteristic way of teaching. Second, it is remarkable that Jesus did not coin new terminology to express the new teaching he was trying to impart. Instead, he used the images of everyday life. The parables of Jesus offend our sensibilities and provoke questions. Take the parable of the laborers in the vineyard (Mt 20:1-16) or the parable of the prodigal son (Lk 15:11-32). They are short and to the point. It is remarkable, perhaps most remarkable of all, that preaching, nourishing, and healing formed a unity in Jesus, the Christ.

Preparing a homily, thus using an occasion for doing theology, requires the skills of a local theologian (see Untener 1999; idem 2001). Basic rules for developing little theologies in a homily include the following:

- Do not act as if you know it all and as if you are superior to or even the equal of your material.
- Do not give the impression that you having nothing more to learn and that your conversion is complete.
- Do not forget that less is more.
- Allow yourself to be challenged by texts and topics.

- Take a fresh look.
- Do not design your homily for the sake of effects.

Exercise: Prepare a sermon for a special occasion. What is most important in the occasion? What is going on in the lives of the people attending? What do you want to convey? What are the expectations and rules of the social situation? Discuss your little theology with others. Where do you experience agreement or disagreement? Are there points that need special attention?

DISCOVERING THEOLOGICAL OCCASIONS: THE ART OF LOOKING AT DETAILS

THESIS 44: Little theologies invite us to look at details, an art that has to be cultivated. Details in our lives or the lives of others, details in a text, can be the basis for illuminating little theologies. Little theologies highlight details by making simple observations.

Little theologies look at the little things of life, the details and aspects that do not get much attention. Looking at details, opening the eyes to small things, is an art that has to be cultivated and practiced. Practice sharpens our eyes and our ability to perceive what is beneath the surface. Little theologies can be invitations to look at the small things of life; they can be invitations to look at the details of a text; they can be invitations to look at the little circumstances rather than the big words in biblical texts.

Dorothee Sölle and Fulbert Steffensky, for example, in looking at the story of the healing of a paralyzed man (Mt 9:1-8), draw attention to the need to open a whole new horizon in the healing process: "Before his legs and arms are healed there is something else to do: his sins must be forgiven. That is, the invalid must be rid of his indifference towards his own future and be rid of his despair and hopelessness" (Sölle and Steffensky 1985, 24-25). This is a little theology of forgiveness, of being open to a new life. And this little theology developed organically by attending to a detail in the text that is easily missed.

I remember a sermon on December 26, the feast of Saint Stephen. The homilist concentrated on three words from the story: "Stephen, *full* of *grace* and *power*" (Acts 6:8). He drew the attention to the little point that there was Stephen, "full of grace and power." He invited the audience to picture that and concentrated on the three concepts: fullness, grace, power. He talked about the idea of fullness: fullness of life, abundance, God's generosity; God wants us to be overflowing vessels. He talked about the notion of grace and mercy in a merciless time, grace as the free gift in a time where everything has a price, grace as a talent, a gift, an invitation to take responsibility and act in the spirit of God. He reflected upon the idea of power as potential, force, and strength. Being a Christian does not necessarily mean to be powerless. There is the secular notion of power associated with wealth, weapons, pressure, and suppression. But there is also a power that challenges and edifies, encourages, and empowers people to realize their potential. The homilist's message was a little theology of encouragement developed out of attention to detail in the text.

A homily on the vocation of Samuel (1 Sm 3) drew attention to three simple points. First, God works through people like Eli, who is not described as an ideal priest. Second, God calls again and again. And third, God calls Eli by name. This little theology of vocation was addressed to university students who were about to make important decisions in their lives. The message was not to be afraid to find God even in people where you least expect to find God. Do not be afraid that you might miss your call, for God calls again and again. Do not think of vocation as a general thing. It is very personal, and God calls each of us by name.

Timothy Radcliffe, former master general of the Dominicans, makes three points about the Annunciation. First, in this mystery there is a moment of attentiveness (Mary listens to the good news); second, there is a moment of fertility (the fruit of Mary's attentiveness is the child she bears); and third, there is a moment of hope in the desert (God gives hope and the message of the kingdom in a situation of despair). The fact that such fundamental insights are what Christian theology and life really revolve around should help to keep the message of the text and the need for little theologies in mind. That insight should also help to discipline the pretenses of theologians who think their vocation demands "big thoughts." Such an insight can be the invitation to "bow down" and look for details and simple points. Essential truths are simple. This is an insight that we find in all the world religions. Little theologies cultivate this simplicity. Looking at details allows us to take a fresh look and to see new things, even in texts that we think we know very well.

There are many hidden treasures in the biblical text. Have you ever thought about this passage: "They returned to Lystra, then on to Iconium and Antioch. There they strengthened the souls of the disciples" (Acts 14:21)? What does that mean: "to strengthen the souls"? Or have you ever been surprised to read that Moses was tending the flock of his father-in-law when he was called (Ex 3:1)? Why was Jesus writing in the sand when he was confronted with the woman caught in adultery (Jn 8:6)? Why would the Proverbs say

> Those who mock the poor insult their Maker;
> those who are glad at calamity will not go
> unpunished (Prv 17:5)?

What does it mean to "mock the poor"? Isn't it amazing that the first words of Mary in John's gospel are spoken at the wedding at Cana: "They have no wine" (Jn 2:3)? Isn't it interesting that Jesus in his mission statement (Lk 10:1-9) advises his disciples not to greet anyone on the way, underlining the urgency of the mission, which was not to be hampered by the long ritual of greeting at that time? Isn't it meaningful that the prodigal son in Luke 15 returned to his father because he was hungry—and not out of love for his father (Lk 15:17)? Is it significant that Jesus, in the account of the man with dropsy (Lk 14:1-6), cured on the sabbath and thus was remembered as working on the sabbath? (see Schillebeeckx 1989, 2).

Drawing attention to details can shed new light on a text. This may be especially useful when we are dealing with well-known texts like the Christmas or the Easter gospel or the passion story. It can be a wise road to take: looking at details. Details strike us when we allow the text to be new to us; when we look at a text as if we are reading it for the first time. The experience of doing something or seeing something for the first time is indeed profound. Constructing little theologies can also be done by concentrating on small, memorable points, simple points that capture important aspects of a text.

INGREDIENTS OF LITTLE THEOLOGIES

THESIS 45: Little theologies use local sources of knowledge relevant for dealing with people's lives theologically. Ingredients of little theologies can be found in local rituals and everyday language, in local songs and proverbs, in buildings and works of art. Using such theological resources means doing "theological field work," living with the people and listening to their voices.

Jesus used soil, sand, and saliva to do theology. He used images and stories, expressions and thoughts people were familiar with. He referred to the local scriptures and the local religious tradition. He celebrated the local feasts and instituted the eucharist in the context of a local key memory. In all these Jesus was using local theological resources. Similarly, theologians do not create the ingredients of their theological cooking themselves. They use what is locally available.

A lot depends on the sources that theologians permit to serve as sources for their doing theology (see Oduyoye 1986, 51-55). Would you permit local superstition and local customs as a source of theological knowledge? Clodovis Boff describes how a Brazilian woman prayed over his bruised foot while he in exchange blessed some saints' picture in her house: "It was a chance for different religious procedures to mesh together. Our pastoral practice is unaware of, and hence overlooks, the religious resources of the people" (Clodovis Boff 1987, 13). How would you draw the line between faith and superstition?

How can theologians access local theological resources? The answer is simple: They have to leave their desk and go out among the people to listen to their songs and jokes, to see their daily life and their struggle to survive and to sustain their dependents (see Beltran 1987).[5] Theologians acquire the local culture as they acquire the local language. Proverbs and songs, stories and jokes, riddles and exclamations are part of oral tradition. And oral tradition, which reveals the deepest layers of a culture, is only to be traced in ordinary life.

Local theology can be found any place relevant questions are tackled. William Dyrness describes an experience with oral theology in Kenya:

> We occasionally visited the large independent church in Mathare Valley, Nairobi, called the Redeemed Gospel Church. There, each Sunday, several thousand believers crowded into a circus tent to hear Bishop Kitonga preach in English and Swahili. As I listened, I realized that I was hearing theology done in an oral mode that communicated directly to the people living in this vast and sprawling slum settlement. The bishop regularly related biblical passages to the problems of drugs, thievery, and alcoholism (Dyrness 1992, 16-17).

Life itself became the bishop's main source for doing theology with his people.

WORKING WITH IMAGES

THESIS 46: Little theologies can be developed around images rooted in the local culture. Such images reveal a way to capture the key points of little theologies. They help make little theologies concrete and colorful, and they can be a source of inspiration to think theologically. The use of images as a theological tool is an invitation to be creative.

[5] Beltran's *The Christology of the Inarticulate* describes a research project into the implicit christologies of some poor quarters in Manila. Beltran designed and organized an empirical research program to conduct that survey based on his own experience of living with the people.

Images are important ingredients of local theologies. Knowledge about locally used images is a key to local cultures. Images are invitations to capture truths. Images can easily be remembered. Years after people have forgotten everything the homilist said, they can still remember the image used.

Using images can provide simple and yet powerful messages that touch upon familiar life contexts. Images help us to focus on essential details. Images have been part of the Christian journey from the beginning. British theologian Alister McGrath enumerates biblical images for Christian spirituality—the feast, the journey, the exile, the struggle, the purification, the desert, the ascent, darkness and light, silence (McGrath 1999, chap. 5). These are familiar images that we find again and again in spiritual books and theological reflections.

The use of images is an invitation to be creative. Leonora Tubbs Tisdale uses the image of "beautiful feet" (Isa 52:7) and "labor pains" (Gal 4:19) to describe ministry (Tisdale 1997, 108). Little theologies can be captured with colorful images like these. The choice of a particular image is revealing. Which image, for instance, would you choose to talk about the kingdom of God? Is your image of the kingdom that of a class-free society? a social utopia? Or do you see the kingdom of God as a safe neighborhood where children can play on the street? Or as a party where everybody knows everybody? Or as a big resort, where all sorts of activities are possible and even facilitated? "The word 'Kingdom' is not one that Americans or many others are likely to even experience. Kings and kingdoms have negative connotations" (Mueller 1988, 28). Similarly, for Africans, talking about the Lord and his kingdom may stir associations of slavery, experiences of distance, and memories of exploitation.

Which image would you choose to illustrate entering the Christian way, of being reborn? A good shower after a long, hot day? Falling in love? Being able to see again after successful surgery? When can we use the image of a monarch to talk about the pope? Can we use the image of a great farm on which everybody earns the same as an image for the kingdom of God? (Cardenal 1984, 3:181). Such questions depend on the framework of theology and our understanding of the theological task and its relation to local culture. Images that communicate a clear message have to be rooted in a local experience, language, and culture.

But it may also be important to realize that sometimes the images we need to develop are images that show the insufficiency of local culture, that show how it can stultify and oppress. In such cases, how can one help wake people up without appearing arrogant?

A Filipino pastor learned that his parishioners usually used three images for God. The first was the image of a policeman. The second was that of a father who brings his children to school, leaves them there, and picks them up when the school day is done. Third, they employed the image of a magician (who can make people win the lottery). There are, then, times when little theologies have to challenge local images and help people develop more adequate images.

There is another challenge for those who read theological works produced in other cultures. Basic images have different connotations in different societies. Images take on different meanings from culture to culture. The images that can be used to explain the person and work of Jesus and how he relates to his followers, for example, are very culture specific. Just to give an example cited by P. O. Iroegbu:

> Among the Gbaya people of Cameroon and Central African Republic, there is a tree: the *Soreh (Soré)*. It is not extraordinary in size or appearance. But it is so in the reality that it portrays, and in the symbols it represents. . . . The *Soreh* cools hot situations: murder, conflicts and wars. When somebody is killed, willfully or accidentally, if the perpetrator party wants to prevent the offended party from savagely avenging, they will plant a branch of *Soreh* in between their border. On seeing that, the offended party will await a serious, quick and effective reconciliation. . . . *Soreh* represents new hope, new possibilities for reconciliation, peace, love, life and continuity. . . . Jesus becomes in Africa [in this part of Africa]: *Jesus Soreh-ga-mo-kee:* Jesus our *soreh*-cool-thing. Like the *Soreh*, Jesus is for making new villages, new families, new alliances and friendships. Like the *Soreh* also, Jesus becomes an antidote against death, suffering, disease and eternal loss. Above all, the *Soreh* creates the lieu [place] for life-together, for dialogue, for communication, for communion. It is a tree of life. It is a spring of living water (Iroegbu 1996, 96).

Studies of how things are classified in various cultures have shown that the best examples for illustrating a given idea differ from culture to culture (see Bowker and Star 1999). What constitutes the ideal of beauty in one culture is often quite different as well.

Local images can be very specific. They differ from one part of the world to another. Ricardo Rezende, for example, writes of a Brazilian farmer who speaks about the church as a cashew nut, with its seed growing separate from the fruit, growing on the outside of it. The church can also be like an avocado, the farmer says, with its pit inside the fruit but clearly separate from it. Perhaps the best way to talk about the church, however, is to compare it to an orange. As the farmer points out, the seeds of an orange are spread throughout the fruit and enter into each pulpy segment (Rezende 1994, 141). Without the farmer's insider knowledge about cashews, avocados, and oranges, the story makes no sense.

Dom Helder Câmara unfolds a local image for a global problem: "Looking at the goats with chains around their necks to stop them getting out of their pen and invading the plantation, I found the image I was seeking for the excluded, underdeveloped world" (Câmara 1981, 70). Karl Rahner, a European, uses the image of a warehouse to describe his soul:

> My soul has become a huge warehouse where day after day the trucks unload their crates without any plan or discrimination, to be piled helterskelter in every available corner and cranny, until it is crammed full from top to bottom with the trite, the commonplace, the insignificant, the routine (Rahner 1965, 36).

Exercise: Think of a special occasion—a wedding, a baptism, a Lenten reflection. Choose an image that can capture your thoughts. Unfold the image to present your message.

WORKING WITH PROVERBS

THESIS 47: Little theologies can be developed using proverbs as their ingredients. Proverbs reveal the flavor of local experience and values. Little theologies try to honor and utilize the wisdom contained in proverbs. They reflect on this wisdom in the light of gospel values.

Proverbs provide excellent insights into how a people understands the everyday life issues on which local theologies want to reflect. One type of proverb is a pithy statement distilling common sense and wisdom concerning a common experience or situation, often dealing playfully with well-known human foibles and the pitfalls to come if the wisdom distilled in the proverb is not followed. Another class of proverb speaks of the fates of those who do not follow the wisdom of the people. Proverbs reflect customs, social and legal matters, health, the weather, good and bad luck, typical things that take place between men and women, between young and old, between rich and poor. Proverbs are short and easy to remember.

The Wisdom literature of the Old Testament consists in great part of proverbs. There are numerous wisdom sayings that originated as folk proverbs (for example, Prv 10:6; 10:9; 10:15; 11:2; 11:13; 11:16; 11:21; 12:14; 13:24; 14:31; 16:18; 16:31; 17:28; 19:12; 27:1; 27:17; 28:2; Sir 13:1; 13:17; 27:26). There are also proverbs in the gospels (for example, Lk 14:11; Mk 10:31; 8:36; 10:43-44). Biblical proverbs have entered our culture and shaped our collective wisdom; for example, "A living dog is better than a dead lion" (Eccl 9:4); "The human mind plans the way, but the Lord directs the steps" (Prv 16:9); "Whoever digs a pit will fall into it" (Prv 26:27).

Proverbs are good sources for little theological reflections because they are easily accessible, they are simple, they refer to familiar events of life and use familiar images, and they express the values by which a community lives. The images contained in them reflect the everyday life of the culture and can be used to select locally meaningful images for theological occasions. They abound in Euro-American languages, but they are particularly powerful in other cultures and provide a window to the way we and others share a common humanity while using vastly different images to express ourselves. A Fulani proverb says, "You will not see an elephant moving on your own head, only the louse moving on another's." A Nigerian Yoruba proverb warns, "He who waits to see a crab wink will tarry long upon the shore." The African proverb, "Only a fool tests the depth of water with both feet," reflects the wisdom of people who know crocodiles may be nearby (Vithayathil 1992, 169). The Xhosa, talking about a man who is about to make a decision, say: "He is ripe inside, like a watermelon" (one cannot tell if a watermelon is ripe from the outside). Proverbs also reveal a people's understanding of the burdens of high social position, as in the Hausa proverb, "A chief is like a dust-heap where everyone comes with his rubbish and deposits it." Or their experience of foreigners, as with the Thonga proverb that says: "The white man has no kin. His kin is money."

Proverbs reveal local experience in the delicacy of relationships, thus the Asian proverb, "Debts can be repaid but not insults." Or ponder the wisdom of the ancient Chinese proverb, "Great winds are powerless to disturb the water of a deep well" (Vithayathil 1992, 90). Other Chinese proverbs deal with the social order, for example, "All ten fingers can't be the same length"; and the effects of unity, "A full bottle won't shake; a half-empty one will." They show wisdom gained from problems that arise from living together, as when one says, "It is easier to visit friends than to live with them," or "Let the host rest when his guests are gone."

Graffiti found in a university bathroom—for example, "Blessed are the pure, for they shall inhibit the earth"; "A pill a day keeps the stork away"; and "A friend with weed is a friend indeed"—show a much different vision of student values than the university catalogue. Using such graffiti can be a humorous way to delve beneath the sometimes pompous facades of institutions such as universities and churches. Skillful local theologians can exploit the knowing laughter of their audience and bring it to reflect more deeply. Graffiti and new cultural proverbs from one segment of a culture can bring very important insights to the questions we pose in local theological analyses of what our responses to situations should be. Can using such proverbs and graffiti help us avoid being too moralistic and thus losing credibility when we seek to ask challenging questions?

We are saying, then, that both classical and new proverbs can help us access the situation of a local culture. Such proverbs can help us see that the future is, in some ways at least, a continuation of the past. Some reveal to us the truth about power relationships and money, for instance, that are deep in Euro-American cultures. Think of the kind of grim values that the following two proverbs show lurk not far beneath the surface of life: "Money makes the world go round"; and what we tell our children, "Money does not grow on trees."

Similarly interesting are proverbs that talk about happiness (Vithayathil 1992, 91-92). These proverbs are especially revealing because they talk explicitly about values and life as such. There are proverbs that talk about happiness as an art ("Happiness is a thing to be practiced, like the violin"; "Happiness lies in being able to turn lemons into lemonade"). There are proverbs that teach us not to think happiness is to be found far off, such as the Austrian proverb, "Happiness is to be found at your own hearth, not in strangers' gardens." Or consider another, "Happiness has one advantage over wealth. No one can borrow it."

There are also proverbs, like the following, that express an admonition not to expect things to be easy: "No pain, no gain"; "Call no man truly happy till he dies."

The theological challenge in the use of proverbs is twofold. First, the theologian has to appreciate the depth of the proverb. What can we learn from the life experience expressed in a proverb for doing theology? And second, the theologian has to think about a theological response. Does the proverb confirm gospel values? Are we called to challenge the underlying message that we find in a proverb or an advertisement whose words gain common acceptance as truth?

A proverb like "The grass is always greener on the other side of the fence" could be used to drive home the point that we should be satisfied with what we have rather than always yearning for something different. Always comparing our situation to others and finding causes for dissatisfaction can lead to envy, clearly not consistent with gospel values. The proverb can be a little key to American culture, and this a key for a little theology (Mieder 1995).

A little theology based on this proverb would see the depth of this problem of dissatisfaction with one's lot in American culture. After acknowledging the depth of this proverb's little theology, could we, in a second step, help people ask whether they are crippled by the attitude criticized in the proverb? Are they unable to be grateful for the little things that are really more important?

When we think of Jesus' use of parables, how might he employ this proverb? How does Jesus deal with some of the attitudes this little proverb brings into relief? Think, for example of the parable of the laborers in the vineyard (Mt 20:1-16). How does Jesus deal with ambition and envy (see Lk 9:46-50)? Or greed (see Lk 12:13-21)? Why does Jesus recommend that we take the last seat rather than the seat of honor (Lk 14:7-14)? What does trust in God (Mt 6:25-34) mean in relation to this spiritual problem?

Example: Toward a Little Theology of Aging Based on Proverbs

When we look at some of the proverbs on old age in our culture, we quite frequently find a negative attitude. A proverb like "Enjoy life; you are only young once" shows that youth is the cultural ideal and that people dread aging. This attitude is sometimes taken as an excuse for certain types of behavior. Old age is seen as a point in life where no change is possible, as is expressed by two common proverbs: "You can't teach an old dog new tricks" and "You cannot transplant an old tree."

On the other hand, there are proverbs that talk about the experience and wisdom of old age; for example, "Old birds are not caught with chaff." A little theology of old age and aging could look at the insights we find in these proverbs. It could be important for a community to be reminded that youth are fragile and need to be treated with a certain tolerance in the community. The benefit of old age is experience and the knowledge and even wisdom that come with it. From the viewpoint of the young, the biggest handicap of old age is the lack of flexibility that some old people develop. That, though, is really a caricature. Is there anyone less open to changing an opinion in the face of a reality he or she does not like than a teenager? As a relatively young man, I know that I need the perspectives of older people to add depth to what could otherwise be a lot of "bright ideas" with little wisdom. And, isn't it true that the older person who stays close to young people often learns that there is frequently wisdom in their criticisms of the way things have "always" been done? The real issue, I think, is how a little theology can express the wisdom of common proverbs in ways that bring people together in gentleness and mutual support.

The unblinking theological eye turns to social reality. Theological reflection learns that the ideals of flexibility and mobility are preeminent in contemporary society. It will see the discrepancy between capability and experience in the job market and its prejudice for hiring the young, and it will seek ways to get people to reflect on such matters. It will see that advertisements use our desire to remain young as a marketing ploy to make us buy things. Is it a proper goal of local theologizing to get people to think about such things and draw lessons from such insights, lessons compatible with the gospel? In this and similar fashions, perhaps a little theology of aging will place these proverbs in a context, examine the values expressed, and help us draw lessons that might help us grow in the happiness that comes from being satisfied with who and what we truly are.

A little theology of aging will have to point out the danger of seeing old age as a period of life without possibility of change and development, but it will also need to acknowledge the particular gifts and tasks of youth. Ought the young not enjoy the possibilities that their energy, good health, and flexibility afford them? Youth *is* the time to experiment with one's identity, to try out different options for work, and to explore places one might want to live. It is a time to meet and become friends with different kinds of people in order to know with whom one is truly compatible. Acceptance and understanding of these characteristics of youth are also positive elements in a theology of aging.

A little theology of aging will, then, bring into relief the positive aspects both of youth and of old age. A wise little theology of aging will look at the reality of people's life experience and views rather than at cultural ideals created by advertising agencies' attempts to glamorize youth in order to sell products. In the Bible such a theology will find figures such as Simeon, Hannah, and Abraham, who are open to radical changes in their lives and opinions when they hear God's call. A friend once observed that one of the limitations of Christianity comes from having its founder die at a relatively young age. "Christ did not give us an example of how one embraces the different experience of life that is inherent with becoming a parent and needing to worry about community school policies, being middle aged and having to take care of both one's children and one's parents, being old and living on after many of one's contemporaries have died." She has a point. The Hebrew Testament and its many stories are undoubtedly an important resource for a little theology of aging. And we shouldn't forget the wisdom that can be garnered from religious ways as different as African traditional religion, Confucianism, and Islam. The wisdom we can derive from Jesus, the vigorous young man, needs to be complemented by other kinds of wisdom. Step by step, by looking at a variety of sources and by promoting cross-generational conversations, we can develop a more adequate theology of aging.

Exercise: Consider the proverbs of your culture about a particular life context (for example, children, sickness, family, love) and develop a little theology. Think about this proverb: "The big thieves hang the little ones." Develop a little theology of social justice.

WORKING WITH STORIES
AND EXAMPLES

THESIS 48: Little theologies can be developed using stories and examples. Stories connect to people's experiences. True stories have depth and authenticity that can be communicated, shared, and remembered. They become part of and reveal who people are. Sharing stories is an essential element in building community. It takes subtlety, intuition, and sensitivity to choose the right local stories and then to tell them well.

Little theologies make use of stories. Stories shape our lives. Being a Christian is to share in the story of Jesus. Telling who we are is telling a story, the story of where we come from and the story of where we are going. We grow into a culture by getting to know the stories that shape the culture. Sharing stories is an essential aspect of building a community. True stories are deep and authentic. Nobody can dispute an experience we have had, but in community discussions we can see if others may have light to shed on the *meaning* of our stories. Being open to such new meanings can become a major source of growth. Stories can capture difficult situations in a metaphorical way. They often make it possible for us to deal imaginatively with realities that are too fraught with raw emotion to bring up with parent, child, friend, or spouse at a given moment. Stories can give an ideal, colorful answer to a difficult question or situation. They allow space to move without being forced to give clear answers.

Clodovis Boff talked about his idea of "narrating the gospel." Instead of communicating the gospel by way of written texts, illiterate catechists, he showed, can be trained to narrate the gospel. This, he says, can be theologically justified on the ground that Jesus himself did not leave anything in writing (Clodovis Boff 1987, 28). Segundo Galilea reminds us that when we use the parables as Jesus used them, we are entering into a different kind of teaching and learning.

> When using a parable style, we do not treat the topics thoroughly and completely, nor do we follow a systematic order of presentation. The purpose of a parable is not to elaborate a doctrine, but rather to communicate symbolically a simple and essential message: Parables do not speak so much to the logical mind as to the heart" (Galilea 1998, viii).

Anthony de Mello's collections of stories have proven to be very helpful in ministry. Stories from the heart are powerful. They are authentic. They reflect life. Cardinal Bernardin recalls a memory from his childhood that shows the strength and self-forgetfulness of a loving father:

> My father had recently undergone cancer-related surgery on his left shoulder, and he was wearing a bandage under a white short-sleeved shirt. I was sitting on a metal railing on the porch of our friends' home, when suddenly I fell backwards, hit the ground and started crying. My father immediately jumped over the rail and picked me up. As he held me in his arms, I could see blood soaking through his shirt. He paid no attention to himself; all he wanted was to be sure that I was all right (Bernardin 1997, 62).

Stories such as this one are a very important means of doing local theology because they reflect personal experiences and local images (for a comprehensive account of the role of stories in theologizing, see Tilley 1985). A treasury of such stories can be found in the local oral tradition. A wise pastor or educator will exert great effort to become steeped in them. Mercy Oduyoye speaks of the importance of this principle in African narrative theology, which, she tells us, remains alive (Oduyoye 1986, 45 and chap. 3; see also Healey and Sybertz 1996). I suggest that this is not the case only in Africa. We will find that Norwegians, Canadians, Chinese, Pakistanis, Argentineans, and others will come alive if we exploit the memories of oral culture in skillfully doing local theology.

The stories used in little theologies may be little stories (as opposed to the "big story" of Christianity), but these little stories bring the big story closer to the people. Alex García-Rivera has used the so-called little stories about Martin de Porres preserved in legends and old stories to reveal a profound, liberating *mestizo* Christian identity that has helped people gain self-respect in the face of a brutal colonial experience (García-Rivera 1995). Doing theology by way of stories means doing theology by way of example. It is an art to choose appropriate examples, an art that requires experience, sensitivity, and an eye for details. Again, we have to be awake to do good theology and to do theology well. We need a balanced diet of examples for our theologies. The use of tired stories and metaphors has weakened many theologies. The still valid truths those theologies often contain seem trite and unexciting. At least part of the reason for this is that standard, prepackaged examples are boring, worn out, and meaningless. We need vital, local examples that spring up spontaneously and help people connect with the deeper implications of everyday events. Local theology is above all concerned with direct experiences expressed in personal examples. Little theologies use little examples; they try to find local examples for theological reflection, local parallels to biblical stories.

Choosing good examples is a matter of sensitivity to cultures, and the choice of examples by an individual is perhaps the best sign of where that person really comes from. Someone who spends most of her time in an office will give different examples from a person who works in a hospital or in a slum. Listen to yourself talking to a group. If most of your examples come from books, you may be out of touch. The examples we use to illustrate the point we want to make say a lot about who we are. It is also in this sense that the little theologies we try to articulate reveal a lot about us.

Example: A Little Theology of Burning Hearts

There was a big missionary youth gathering. It was about setting hearts on fire, inspiring people to "bring fire to the earth" (Lk 12:49). Young people from thirteen nations had gathered. At a special eucharist, the gospel was the prediction of the passion by Jesus (Mt 16:21-23). In the homily the priest told the story of two candles, one new, beautiful, and untouched, a second burnt, trails of wax spilling down the sides. The young candle said to the old one, "Look at you! You are ugly, ugly and old. I am beautiful and young!" The old candle replied, "True, you are young and unused. I am old and ugly, but I have burned for many hours, and I have endured the burning to give warmth and light." This simple little theology brought home the wisdom that if we want to give light to the world, we have to endure heat. This little theology is easily connected with the little theology of aging and the proverbs mentioned above. In the homily this little story was connected with the experience of the two disciples on the road to Emmaus, as they said, "Were not our hearts burning within us while he was talking to us on the road?" (Lk 24:32).

Experiences of the cross and of resurrection make our hearts burn. This is how a mature human heart is formed. It takes in all the smiles and tears, the chatter and the silence, the long loneliness and the fleeting moments of intimacy, the hopes and anxieties of those with whom it walks on the way. All this is part of the story of a human soul growing deeper in the ability to be present with others. All experiences of height and depth make our hearts burn, and we know that we are alive. We feel pain and vulnerability, too, but it is only the burning heart that sheds light and warmth. And in attempting to share light, we are transformed in the joyful hope of resurrection.

Exercise: Select a gospel passage such as the story of Jesus' encounter with the sinful woman who anoints his feet (Lk 7:36-50), one that shows how the openness of Jesus to outcasts upsets conventionally minded people. Try to think of a story from life today that connects with the passage you have chosen. On the basis of the story, develop a little theology of love.

Epilogue

A Culture of Hope

THESIS 49: Doing theology entails cultivating the art of hope; it promotes a hopeful culture. Doing theology means walking the path of the promise inspired by God's word: "For surely I know the plans I have for you, says the LORD, plans for your welfare and not for harm, to give you a future with hope" (Jer 29:11).

Doing theology is an attempt to create a culture of hope. Juan Luis Segundo tries to make clear that "a theology worthy of the attention of the whole human being is not the outcome of abstract scientific or academic interest. It stems from a pre-theological human commitment to change and improve the world" (Segundo 1976, 39). The ultimate aim of thinking about our lives is the desire to make the world a better place and to instill hope that this is possible in the people around us.

This hope is born out of the Christian belief that we are created in God's image and therefore called to be "for others" as Jesus was. The theological vision of hope is a vision of peace and justice, respect for the dignity of the other person, and concerned respect for human rights and the future of our planet.

Theology strives to articulate the reasons to hope in the face of so much negativity (1 Pt 3:13-15). The gospels talk about life and the promise of life (McFague 2001). We do theology because we see that people suffer and out of the conviction that new life can blossom. We do theology in order to make people's lives better. The good news is a story about good life and about new life.

French writer Anais Nin talked about the cancer treatment she had to undergo in New York in 1970. She had to have radiation treatments every day for two weeks. She managed to endure this experience by thinking of all the happy moments in her life. She found that she had enough happy

moments both to cope with the whole two weeks and to grow in the ability
to love life and embrace the beauty of the moment. We need joyful people,
people who can smile at a beggar and take the time to exchange a few
words; people who can tolerate the inevitable disappointments and failures
in day-to-day life; people who can be patient with talkative or narrow-minded
persons; people who have space in their hearts to look at others and respond to their concerns.

New life has small beginnings. Theology asks for the humility to embrace small beginnings. It asks for the courage to make mistakes. A few
people can make a difference. In 1961 the English lawyer Peter Benenson
introduced the famous newspaper article that led to the founding of Am-
nesty International with these words:

> Open your newspaper any day of the week and you will find a report
> from somewhere in the world of someone being imprisoned, tortured
> or executed because his opinions or religion are unacceptable to his
> government. . . . The newspaper reader feels a sickening sense of im-
> potence. Yet if these feelings of disgust could be united into common
> action, something effective could be done (Benenson 1961).

This was the beginning of a global movement, a movement rooted in a
small beginning and the conviction that individual people can make a difference.

The ultimate test is what people *do*. As Robert Chambers pointedly notes:

> Social change flows from individual actions. By changing what they
> do, people move societies into new directions and themselves change.
> . . . Most of the time, the soundest and best way forward is through
> innumerable small steps and tiny pushes, putting the last first not once
> but again and again and again. Many small reversals then support
> each other and together build up towards a greater movement (Cham-
> bers 1994, 217).

Theology is an invitation to become part of the solution rather than remain-
ing part of the problem. Our hearts, spirits and intellects need to be
awakened. They need to be nourished and touched. Mindful people are
awake. They see the people around them. They discover their capacity to
give hope to others, to instill the love of life in others.

**THESIS 50: Theology is an expression of the hope that a few
people can make a difference. Theology cultivates the art of hoping. There are at least seven important features of hope: Hope
rises in the darkness of a crisis; hope can give reasons to keep**

believing; hope paradoxically both requires and engenders patience and endurance; hope means wideness and openness and also risk and the willingness to change; hope is stubborn and endures long periods of delayed fulfillment; hope admits small beginnings; and the message of hope is the promise of life.

Theology is about hope, the hope that individual people can make a difference. The Jewish and Christian tradition's archetypal story of hope lies in the Book of Genesis. It is the familiar story about Noah and the flood, about the construction of an ark in which Noah, his family, and all the animals on earth are saved. In the few verses (Gn 8:5-12) we find deep insights into the nature of hope. I would like to capture these ideas in seven points:

First, the story of the ark tells about a particular hope that arises out of a crisis, after a terrible disaster. This hope blossoms in the middle of the storm. Hope is the child of a crisis. Times of crisis are critical times. Critical times are moments in which we know life to be at the crossroads. Hope rises in the middle of confusion and anxiety.

Second, as the flood begins to recede after some months, Noah and his family can see the tops of some mountains. This experience of hope is described in verse 5. Hope grows because they see "signs of the times" that ground their hope. Hope is not blind. Instead, hope listens to the voices of promise and sees signs of new life.

Third, in verse 6 Noah opened the window of the ark after forty days, a symbolic length of time and completion. A propitious time had arrived, and hope had its *kairos*, its "favorable moment." The story of the patient Noah reminds us that hope is patient and endures long periods of waiting.

Fourth, Noah opened the window of the ark. What does the open window symbolize? Hope is associated with openness and wideness, but also with risk and vulnerability. Hope rises when we are constricted and isolated. Hope overcomes this constriction but also challenges the security that goes with being closed in a familiar environment. To attain the fruit of hope, we need to change and renew. Noah opens the window of the ark and lets in sunshine and fresh air. He is hopeful and thus able to accept the invitation to be disturbed.

Fifth, Noah sends out a raven and three times sends out a dove. Noah had to make several attempts to be sure that the flood had gone. Hope is stubborn. Hope cannot easily be discouraged. Again, this is an invitation to be patient.

Sixth, Noah has to wait seven days between the first and the second mission of the dove. After its second flight, the dove returns to the ark in the evening, carrying an olive branch. This olive branch becomes a symbol of hope down through the centuries, a sign that life continues to be possible, a promise of a future. The message of hope is the promise of life.

Finally, in verse 12, we learn that the dove did not return from its third mission. Hope brings about changes that cannot be reversed and calls for an attitude of letting go. Hope needs the courage to let life develop if it is to attain its ends. From the story of Noah, we learn that hope rises in the darkness of crisis. Hope is not mere optimism; it can give reasons. It requires patience and has its *kairos* in due course for those who are open to risk and willing to change. Finally, hope springs from small beginnings and is a promise of life in abundance in concrete, local situations. It is in those situations that we do theology to bring about a culture of hope.

Fifty Theses
for Doing Local Theology

THESIS 1: Theology is an invitation to wake up: to be mindful and attentive.

THESIS 2: Theology is done locally. In order to be honest to the local circumstances theology has to be done as local theology, as theology that takes the particular situation seriously. Local theology can be done with basic theological means. It can be done by the people, and it is done with the people.

THESIS 3: Doing theology is a way of following Jesus. Theology seeks friendship with Jesus and communion with God.

THESIS 4: Theology talks about life. It looks at our lives as if how we live makes a difference.

THESIS 5: We do theology because we share a vision and we experience wounds.

THESIS 6: There are many ways of doing theology. Theology is like a family of many different activities centered around friendship with God.

THESIS 7: Since doing theology is as natural as walking and talking, we all do theology, both as individuals and as a community. There is, however, a difference between explicit and implicit theologies, between trained and untrained theologians.

THESIS 8: Theology is always done from a certain perspective within a particular context.

THESIS 9: Many different images capture the work of a theologian. The idea of local theologies can be expressed through the image of the theologian as village cook. Doing local theology is like cooking with local ingredients.

THESIS 10: Jesus is our great teacher. Since he was talking about God, he was doing theology. It is helpful to look at the way Jesus did theology. We will take this look without an elaborate Christian theology. We will look at Jesus "B.C."

THESIS 11: Jesus' life is described as a human existence within a certain local culture. He was rooted in the religious traditions of his time and place. Jesus' life is described as a sequence of face-to-face actions on a local (especially rural) level. Jesus is, however, also described as a person challenging local cultural standards and raising a universal claim.

THESIS 12: Jesus did theology with authority that was not his. The basis of Jesus' doing theology was his relation with God. That is why he sought out spaces for prayer and solitude. He did theology as one sent, and he used this authority to serve God and the people.

THESIS 13: Jesus was doing theology with common sense. He invited people to use their own judgment and trusted in the capabilities of human reasoning. This can be illustrated by the parable of the good Samaritan.

THESIS 14: Jesus did "situational theology." He had an eye for detail, the small things and the "little people." Jesus used occasions to do theology, and he respected the dynamics of particular situations. We could see this as an invitation to do "leaflet theology" rather than "book-length theology."

THESIS 15: Jesus did theology to build up community. He called everyone into community, a community that is constantly "on the move." Doing theology as Jesus did is a community-building enterprise.

THESIS 16: Jesus did theology with self-respect and with respect for others; he did theology "as if people matter." Healing and feeding, forgiving and teaching formed a unity in Jesus' way of doing theology. We can see this feature of Jesus' way of doing theology as an invitation to theologies that are vulnerable, modest, and a response to people's questions and needs.

THESIS 17: Jesus talked about the criteria for good theology. The most obvious criterion is the criterion of the good fruit, but he also saw this fruit coming from modest beginnings. Jesus taught that the full variety of good fruits came from a variety of sources or ministries (theologies). Jesus did theology according to the criteria of sustainability, appropriateness, empowerment, and challenge.

THESIS 18: An important tool for doing local theology is taking "a third look at Jesus." It is an invitation to ask the question: Who is Jesus for you? This question can be answered by identifying the key moments in the life of Jesus as depicted in the gospels.

THESIS 19: Doing theology is a way of following Jesus. We follow Jesus as a community of believers, a community built on a tradition. In order to do local theology we have to reappropriate the tradition of our community. This is a challenging task because there is a series of little traditions rather than one great tradition.

THESIS 20: Reappropriating our tradition means seeing its relevance for our contemporary situation. We need to ask these questions: What is the key message of our tradition? How do we understand this message today?

THESIS 21: Events in the life of Jesus can serve as a reference point for our judgments in the present. When thinking about ideas, concepts, or values of our own culture, we can assess these elements by looking at how Jesus responded to facets of his own culture and times. This is a useful theological tool to connect contemporary challenges with the praxis of Jesus.

THESIS 22: Our community of faith has developed a theological tradition. It is a matter of intellectual honesty to respect this tradition when doing theology. As theologians we are members of a community and accountable to this community. That is why we are called to make an effort to reappropriate the theological tradition of our community. It gives guidelines and norms on how to do theology. It is an important theological task to "translate" the theological tradition into a local context by looking at the concern of a particular element of this tradition.

THESIS 23: The main source of Christian tradition is the Bible. In order to see the relevance of the Bible for present-day contexts we need to reappropriate biblical texts. In order to do that we need basic knowledge of the Bible and sensitivity toward the concrete concerns of a given biblical text.

THESIS 24: The tradition of our community of faith is a living tradition. It "lives" because there are people who realize the message of Jesus in their own lives. It is inspiring to look at the example of these people who have reappropriated the message of Jesus in their particular situation.

THESIS 25: Reappropriating our tradition cannot be done without good theology. Chief among the criteria of good theology are reality, fidelity to the founder, and the practical consequences that follow from a particular theological "work."

THESIS 26: Local cultures are expressions of God's continuing creation. Theology begins with the human situation. It is a "second step." The human situation has a cultural face. The concept of culture, which touches all levels of human existence, is one of the most difficult and yet basic concepts and needs to be considered in local theologies.

THESIS 27: Doing theology is a matter of being honest with ourselves and others. We do theology because we are inevitably faced with burning questions of life (beginning, end, purpose, choices) in our human situation. Everybody is confronted with these questions and develops "implicit theologies," which can be dangerous and should be made explicit for the sake of the community.

THESIS 28: A way to unveil biases or to trace hidden values and implicit theologies is through the use of stories that present ambiguous situations with actors who act on the basis of different value systems. These "value stories" are a useful theological tool when we ask which actors in this story are justified in acting the way they do.

THESIS 29: There is a need for a dialogue between our understanding of theology and our concept of culture: Theology reflects upon culturally embedded forms of religious life. Theology has to reappropriate the message of Jesus from its cultural context into local cultural context. There is, however, no "supercultural theology" or "universal Christian culture."

THESIS 30: Local theologies need to pay attention to the particularities of local language. Concepts are powerful because they reveal a culture's way of seeing the world. Concepts convey value systems. An elementary linguistic analysis is a useful tool for local theologies. Using local language is a sign of respect for the local culture.

THESIS 31: Culture can be analyzed by looking at cultural activities. We can call any identifiable cultural context a cultural game. Cultures can be characterized through their cultural games. Thus, we can view society as a community of players with different functions and different roles. We can view social life as a complex landscape of cultural games played. Important concepts to analyze are the distinction between competence (know how) and mandate (authorization) to participate in cultural games, the distinction between standardized and non-standardized games, and the concept of leading cultural games. The following questions can help to understand a particular local culture: Who is playing which cultural games? According to which rules? When and where? Why? Asking these questions systematically is a useful tool for local theologies.

THESIS 32: Why a certain cultural game is played is connected to a cultural story, which in turn is connected to a cultural worldview. The introduction of new cultural games is always and necessarily connected with the introduction of new cultural stories. Religions touch upon the deepest cultural layers, upon the worldviews. That is why cultural stories are especially important within the context of doing local theology.

THESIS 33: Local theologies recognize that theology takes shape within a particular context. Theologies are developed in response to and within a particular social situation. Understanding the social situation is a necessary condition for understanding the genesis and validity of particular theologies.

THESIS 34: Theology is always done within a concrete local social structure that provides rich resources for constructing local theologies and for developing a local identity as a theologian. The social, historical, cultural, and political context has an impact on the role of the theologian and his or her place in the context.

THESIS 35: Jesus invites us to pay special attention to poor people, to make an option for the poor. This option will shape our theologies. Theological judgments on social situations are based on gospel values. There is no neutral theological stance.

THESIS 36: Theology is called to analyze social realities. Talking about God is always, at least implicitly, talk about the social situation. Theology makes explicit judgments about key aspects of social situations (justice, labor, property). Theological analysis of social situations makes use of social analysis. There are, however, clear limits to social analysis. We can see these limits when we consider the mystical dimension in our lives. A theological analysis of social situations differs from an approach taken by social sciences in the option that is taken by the theologian.

THESIS 37: Regional theologies try to do justice to the key features of a regional context. They pay special attention to key events, persons, and features. Regional theologies look at the social realities in which people live and try to highlight the core constitutive elements of the regional social setting.

THESIS 38: Little theologies are theologies made for a particular situation, taking particular circumstances into account, using local questions and concerns, local stories and examples as their starting point. People should be able to recognize themselves in little theologies.

THESIS 39: Constructing little theologies is a challenging task that demands cultural sensitivity, thorough knowledge, and respect for people. Little theologies are not "bumpersticker theologies." In fact, the criterion of a good theologian is whether he or she can do justice to the gospel while gaining the community's confidence that a little theology illuminates a particular situation.

THESIS 40: Little theologies are called to three tasks: (1) To point to the positive richness and goodness of local contexts; (2) to challenge the local context by inviting people to see and go beyond its limits; and (3) to inspire and encourage by opening eyes to previously unseen visions and ears to unheard sounds. Little theologies invite people to do theology themselves. When little theologies function properly, they empower.

THESIS 41: Little theologies arise in concrete occasions and in response to specific needs; they are often evoked by simple questions. As personal answers to personal questions and particular reactions to local concerns, little theologies are developed face to face with the people without using "canned" answers. Constructing little theologies requires the ability to listen and learn. Articulating them requires both sensitivity to the realities of the concrete situation and basic knowledge of the gospel.

THESIS 42: Little theologies look at the details of our lives. They try to look at these aspects from a theological perspective, weighing alternative ways of dealing with these details, reflecting on how to approach life theologically. Such a theologically examined life is both a task and a spiritual challenge.

THESIS 43: Little theologies arise in concrete occasions and places. Sometimes we are confronted with unpredictable, powerful events that provoke the need to develop afresh little theologies. Other occasions where little theologies are called for are regular pastoral situations such as the preparation of a homily. The criterion of a little theology is its appropriateness to the given situation and fidelity to the gospel.

THESIS 44: Little theologies invite us to look at details, an art that has to be cultivated. Details in our lives or the lives of others, details in a text, can be the basis for illuminating little theologies. Little theologies highlight details by making simple observations.

THESIS 45: Little theologies use local sources of knowledge relevant for dealing with people's lives theologically. Ingredients of little theologies can be found in local rituals and everyday language, in local songs and proverbs, in buildings and works of art. Using such theological resources means doing "theological field work," living with the people and listening to their voices.

THESIS 46: Little theologies can be developed around images rooted in the local culture. Such images reveal a way to capture the key points of little theologies. They help make little theologies concrete and colorful, and they can be a source of inspiration to think theologically. The use of images as a theological tool is an invitation to be creative.

THESIS 47: Little theologies can be developed using proverbs as their ingredients. Proverbs reveal the flavor of local experience and values. Little theologies try to honor and utilize the wisdom contained in proverbs. They reflect on this wisdom in the light of gospel values.

THESIS 48: Little theologies can be developed using stories and examples. Stories connect to people's experiences. True stories have depth and authenticity that can be communicated, shared, and remembered. They become part of and reveal who people are. Sharing stories is an essential element in building community. It takes subtlety, intuition, and sensitivity to choose the right local stories and then to tell them well.

THESIS 49: Doing theology entails cultivating the art of hope; it promotes a hopeful culture. Doing theology means walking the path of the promise inspired by God's word: "For surely I know the plans I have for you, says the Lord, plans for your welfare and not for harm, to give you a future with hope" (Jer 29:11).

THESIS 50: Theology is an expression of the hope that a few people can make a difference. Theology cultivates the art of hoping. There are at least seven important features of hope: Hope rises in the darkness of a crisis; hope can give reasons to keep believing; hope paradoxically both requires and engenders patience and endurance; hope means wideness and openness and also risk and the willingness to change; hope is stubborn and endures long periods of delayed fulfillment; hope admits small beginnings; and the message of hope is the promise of life.

Bibliography

Abesamis, C. H. 1991. "Why a Third Look at Jesus?" In *Third World Theologies in Dialogue: Essays in Memory of D. S. Amalorpavadass*, edited by J. Russell Chandran, 132-42. Banagalore: W. Q. Judge Press.

Albom, Mitch. 1998. *Tuesdays with Morrie*. New York: Doubleday.

Amaladoss, Michael. 1984. "Ein Inder liest das Evangelium des heiligen Johannes." In *Wir werden bei ihm wohnen: Das Johannesevangelium in indischer Deutung*, edited by George Soares-Prabhu, 19-34, Freiburg im Breisgau: Herder.

———. 1994. *A Call to Community: The Caste System and Christian Responsibility*. Anand Gujrata, India: Gujrat Sahitya Prakash.

Arbuckle, Gerald A. 1987. *Strategies for Growth in Religious Life*. New York: Alba House.

———. 1988. *Out of Chaos: Refounding Religious Communities*. New York: Paulist Press.

Aristide, Jean-Bertrand. 1991. *In the Parish of the Poor: Writings from Haiti*. Maryknoll, N.Y.: Orbis Books.

Asian Report Group. 1983. "Toward a Relevant Theology in Asia." In *Irruption of the Third World: Challenge to Theology*, edited by Virginia Fabella and Sergio Torres, 61-76. Maryknoll, N.Y.: Orbis Books.

Ateek, Naim. S. 1989. *Justice, and Only Justice: A Palestinian Theology of Liberation*. Maryknoll, N.Y.: Orbis Books.

Austin, John Langshaw. 1961. *Philosophical Papers*. Oxford: Clarendon.

Bahr, H.-E. 1991. "Jeder einzigartig, nie dagewesen, nie wiederkehrend. Die Reise zu den streunenden Kindern von La Paz." In *Augen für die Anderen. Lateinamerika. Eine theologische Erfahrung*, edited by H.-E. Bahr and Johann Baptist Metz, 63-81. Munich: Kindler.

Baillie, John. 1962. *The Sense of the Presence of God*. Oxford: Oxford University Press.

Balasuriya, Tissa. 1980. "Towards the Liberation of Theology in Asia." In *Asia's Struggle for Full Humanity*, edited by Virginia Fabella, 16-27. Maryknoll, N.Y.: Orbis Books.

Bales, Kevin. 2000. *Disposable People: New Slavery in the Global Economy*. Los Angeles and Berkeley: University of California Press.

Banawiratma J., and J. Müller. 1995. *Kontextuelle Sozialtheologie*. Freiburg im Breisgau: Herder.

Beattie, John. 1964. *Other Cultures*. New York: Free Press.

Becker, Joseph M. 1992. *The Re-Formed Jesuits: A History of Changes in Jesuit Formation during the Decade 1965-1975*. San Francisco: Ignatius Press.

Bedoyère, M. de la. 1958. *The Cardijn Story*. London: Longmans, Green and Co.

Beltran, Benjamin P. 1987. *The Christology of the Inarticulate: An Inquiry into the Filipino Understanding of Jesus the Christ*. Quezon City: Divine Word.

Benenson, Peter. 1961. "The Forgotten Prisoners." *The Observer* (London). May 28.

Berger, Peter. 1979. *The Heretical Imperative: Contemporary Possibilities of Religious Affirmation*. New York: Anchor Press.

Bernardin, Joseph. 1997. *The Gift of Peace: Personal Reflections*. Chicago: Loyola Press.

———. 1998. *A Moral Vision for America*. Edited by John Langan. Washington: Georgetown University Press.

Berrigan, Daniel. 1971. *The Dark Night of Resistance*. Garden City, N.Y.: Doubleday.

———. 1979. *Lights on in the House of the Dead: A Prison Diary*. Garden City: Doubleday.

Berrigan, Philip. 1970. *Prison Journals of a Priest Revolutionary*. New York: Holt, Rinehart and Winston.

Berthrong, John H. 1999. *The Divine Deli: Religious Identity in the North American Cultural Mosaic*. Maryknoll, N.Y.: Orbis Books.

Bevans, Stephen B. 2002. *Models of Contextual Theology*. Revised and expanded edition. Maryknoll, N.Y.: Orbis Books.

Black, P. W. 1988. "The Apotheosis of Father Marino: Foundations of Tobian Catholicism." In *Culture and Christianity: The Dialectics of Transformations*, edited by G. R. Sanders, 47-72. New York: Greenwood Press.

Boff, Clodovis. 1987. *Feet-on-the-Ground Theology: A Brazilian Journey*. Maryknoll, N.Y.: Orbis Books.

Boff, Leonardo and Clodovis. 1984. *Salvation and Liberation: In Search of a Balance between Faith and Politics*. Maryknoll, N.Y.: Orbis Books.

Boff, Leonardo. 1978. *Jesus Christ Liberator*. Maryknoll, N.Y.: Orbis Books.

———. 1987. "Jesus, a Person of Extraordinary Good Sense, Creative Imagination, and Originality." In *Third World Liberation Theologies: A Reader*, edited by Deane W. Ferm, 109-22. Maryknoll, N.Y.: Orbis Books.

Bonhoeffer, Dietrich. 1953. *Letters and Papers from Prison*, edited by Reginald Fueller et al. London: SCM.

Bowker, G. C., and S. L. Star. 1999. *Sorting Things Out: Classification and Its Consequences*. Cambridge: Harvard University Press.

Braxton, Edward. 1980. *The Wisdom Community*. New York: Paulist Press.

Brockman, James. 1985. "The Passion and Death of Maria and Felipe." *America* (December 7).

Brown, Raymond. 1994. *An Introduction to New Testament Christology*. New York: Paulist Press.

Burrows, Millar. 1977. *Jesus in the First Three Gospels*. Nashville, Tenn.: Abingdon Press.

Calderón, J. A. 1983. "Peruvian Reality and Theological Challenges." In *Irruption of the Third World: Challenge to Theology*, edited by Virginia Fabella and Sergio Torres, 42-49. Maryknoll, N.Y.: Orbis Books.

Câmara, Helder. 1981. *A Thousand Reasons for Living*. Philadelphia: Fortress Press.

Campbell, W. D. 1984. "Nit-picking on a Fine Book." *Christianity and Crisis* 44/2 (February): 42-43.

Cardenal, Ernesto. 1984. *The Gospel of Solentiname*. 4 vols. Maryknoll, N.Y.: Orbis Books.

Carr, Anne. 1990. *Transforming Grace: Christian Tradition and Women's Experience*. San Francisco: Harper & Row.

Casaldáliga, Pedro, and J. M. Vigil. 1994. *Political Holiness*. Maryknoll, N.Y.: Orbis Books.

Chambers, Robert. 1994. *Rural Development: Putting the Last First*. London: Darton, Longman and Todd.

Chang, A. B. 1981. "Taiwan: Kulturelle Vielfalt und theologische Arbeit im freien China." In *Den Glauben neu verstehen: Beiträge zu einer asiatischen Theologie*, edited by L. Wiedenmann, 85-100. Freiburg im Breisgau: Herder.

Chang, A. B. 1984. *Dann sind Himmel und Mensch in Einheit: Bausteine chinesischer Theologie*. Freiburg im Breisgau: Herder.

Chupungco, Anscar J. 1992. *Liturgical Inculturation: Sacramentals, Religiosity, and Catechesis*. Collegeville, Minn.: The Liturgical Press.

Cobb, John B., Jr. 1967. *The Structure of Christian Existence*. Philadelphia: Westminster.

Cunningham, Lawrence. 1980. *The Meaning of Saints*. New York: Harper & Row.

Cunningham, P. 1988. *Jesus and the Evangelists: The Ministry of Jesus in the Synoptic Gospels*. Mahwah, N.J.: Paulist Press.

Cupitt, Don. 1977. "The Christ of Christendom." In *The Myth of God Incarnate*, edited by J. Hick, 133-47. London: SCM; Philadelphia: Westminster.

Day, Dorothy. 1978. *From Union Square to Rome*. New York: Arno Press.

Denzinger, Henricus. 1991. *Enchiridion Symbolorum Definitionum et Declarationum de Rebus Fidei et Morum*. Edited by Peter Hünermann. Freiburg im Breisgau: Herder, 37th edition.

Desai, A. R. 1969. *Rural Sociology in India*. Bombay: Popular Prakashan.

Dodd, C. H. 1970. *The Founder of Christianity*. New York: Macmillan.

Donders, Joseph. 1986. *The Global Believer*. Mystic, Conn.: Twenty-Third Publications.

Dulles, Avery. 1992. *The Craft of Theology*. New York: Crossroad.

Dussel, Enrique. 1978. "The Political and Ecclesial Context of Liberation Theology in Latin America." In *The Emergent Gospel: Theology from the Underside of History*, edited by Sergio Torres and Virginia Fabella, 175-92. Maryknoll, N.Y.: Orbis Books.

Dyrness, William A. 1992. *Invitation to Cross-Cultural Theology: Case Studies in Vernacular Theologies*. Grand Rapids, Mich.: Zondervan Publishing House.

———. 1997. *The Earth Is God's: A Theology of American Culture*. Maryknoll, N.Y.: Orbis Books.

Edgerton, Dow. 1994. "Stand by Me." In *Beyond Theological Tourism: Mentoring as a Grassroots Approach to Theological Education*, edited by Susan B. Thistlethwaite and George F. Carins, 16-33. Maryknoll, N.Y.: Orbis Books.

Ela, Jean-Marc. 1986. *African Cry*. Maryknoll, N.Y.: Orbis Books.

Elias, N. 1992-93. *Über den Prozess der Zivilisation*. 2 vols. Frankfurt/Main: Suhrkamp.

Elizondo, Virgil. 1988. *The Future Is Mestizo: Life Where Cultures Meet*. Bloomington, Ind.: Meyer-Stone Books.

Ellsberg, Robert. 1997. *All Saints: Daily Reflections on Saints, Prophets, and Witnesses for Our Time*. New York: Crossroad.

Evans, Alice F. 1983. "Teaching and Learning with Cases." In *Human Rights: A Dialogue between the First and Third Worlds*, edited by Robert A. Evans and Alice F. Evans, 14-22. Maryknoll, N.Y.: Orbis Books.

Evans, Robert A., and Alice F. Evans. 1980. *Introduction to Christianity: A Case Study Approach*. Atlanta, Ga.: John Knox Press.

Evans, Robert A., and T. D. Parker, eds. 1976. *Christian Theology: A Case Method Approach*. New York: Harper & Row.

Foucauld, Charles de. 1964. *Spiritual Autobiography of Charles de Foucauld*. Edited by J. F. Six. New York: Kenedy & Sons.

Francis, Mark. 2000. *Shape a Circle Ever Wider: Liturgical Inculturation in the United States*. Chicago: Liturgy Training Publications.

Freire, Paolo. 1998. *Teachers as Cultural Workers: Letters to Those Who Dare Teach*. Boulder, Colo.: Westview Press.

Fresacher, B. 1998. *Anderl von Rinn. Ritualmord und Neuorientierung in Judenstein 1945-1995*. Innsbruck: Tyrolia.

Fromm, Erich. 1963. *The Art of Loving*. New York: Bantam Books.

———. 1969. *Escape from Freedom*. New York: Avon Books.

Fuchs, Ottmar. 1990. *Heilen und Befreien*. Duesseldorf: Patmos.

Fuellenbach, John. 1998. *Throw Fire*. Revised edition. Manila: Divine Word Publications.

———. 2002. *The Church: Community for the Kingdom*. Maryknoll, N.Y.: Orbis Books.

Fung, J. J. 1992. *Shoes Off: Barefoot We Walk*. Kuala Lumpur: Longman Malaysia Sdn. Bhd.

Galilea, Segundo. 1998. *The Music of God: Parables of Life and Faith*. Oak Park, Ill.: Meyer Stone.

García-Rivera, Alex. 1995. *St. Martin de Porres: The "Little Stories" and the Semiotics of Culture*. Maryknoll, N.Y.: Orbis Books.

Gittins, Anthony J. 1994. "A Matter of Homelessness." In *Beyond Theological Tourism: Mentoring as a Grassroots Approach to Theological Education*, edited by Susan B. Thistlethwaite and George F. Carins, 109-20. Maryknoll, N.Y.: Orbis Books.

Goizueta, Robert. 1999. "Fiesta." In *From the Heart of Our People*, edited by Orlando Espín and M. Díaz. Maryknoll, N.Y.: Orbis Books.

González, Justo L. 1990. *Mañana: Christian Theology from a Hispanic Perspective*. Nashville, Tenn.: Abingdon Press.

Gorgulho, G. da Silva. 1993. "Biblical Hermeneutics." In *Mysterium Liberationis: Fundamental Concepts of the Liberation Theology*, edited by Ignacio Ellacuría and Jon Sobrino, 123-49. Maryknoll, N.Y.: Orbis Books.

Gorospe, V. R. 1978. *The Filipino Search for God: Philosophy in a Philippine Context*. Manila: Jesuit Educational Press.

Gravrand, H. 1986. "Afrikanisches Gebet und afrikanische Spiritualität als Quelle christlicher Spiritualität und christlichen Gebetes." In *Afrikanische Spiritualität und Christlicher Glaube. Erfahrungen der Inkulturation*, edited by M. C. Musharhamina, 93-111. Freiburg im Breisgau: Herder.

Grollenberg, L. 1978. *Jesus*. London: SCM.

Gutiérrez, Gustavo. 1973. *A Theology of Liberation: History, Politics and Salvation*. Maryknoll, N.Y. Orbis Books.

———. 1984. *We Drink from Our Own Wells: The Spiritual Journey of a People*. Maryknoll, N.Y.: Orbis Books.

———. 1987. *On Job: God-Talk and the Suffering of the Innocent*. Maryknoll, N.Y.: Orbis Books.

———. 1991. *The God of Life*. Maryknoll, N.Y.: Orbis Books.

Hahn, T., and D. Verhaagen. 1998. *GenXers after God: Helping a Generation Pursue Jesus*. Grand Rapids, Mich.: Baker Books.

Hall, Douglas John. 1991. *Thinking the Faith: Christian Theology in a North American Context*. Minneapolis, Minn.: Fortress Press.

———. 1997. *The End of Christendom and the Future of Christianity*. Harrisburg, Pa.: Trinity Press International.

Hall, Edward T. 1959. *The Silent Language*. Greenwich, Conn.: Fawcett Publishers.

———. 1982. *The Hidden Dimension*. Garden City, N.Y.: Doubleday.

Hall, Mary. 1980. *The Impossible Dream: The Spirituality of Dom Helder Câmara*. Maryknoll, N.Y.: Orbis Books.

Hare, R. M. 1963. His contribution to "Theology and Falsification." In *New Essays in Philosophical Theology*, edited by A. Flew and A. MacIntyre, 99-103. London: SCM Press.

Häring, Bernard. 1976. *Embattled Witness: Memories of a Time of War*. New York: Crossroad.

Healey, Joseph, and Donald Sybertz. 1996. *Towards an African Narrative Theology*. Maryknoll, N.Y.: Orbis Books.

Helminiak, D. A. 1986. *The Same Jesus: A Contemporary Christology*. Chicago: Loyola University Press.

Holland, Joe. 1983. "Linking Social Analysis and Theological Reflection: The Place of Root Metaphors in Social and Religious Experience." In *Tracing the Spirit: Communities, Social Action, and Theological Reflection*, edited by James E. Hug, 170-91. New York: Paulist Press.

Hope, Anne, and Sally Timmel. 1995. *Training for Transformation: A Handbook for Community Workers*. 3 vols. Reprint. Gweru, Zimbabwe: Mambo Press.

Illich, Ivan. 1970. *Celebration of Awareness: A Call for Institutional Revolution*. Garden City, N.Y.: Doubleday.

Immoos, T. 1993. "Die Harfe, die von selber tönt. Überlegungen zur Inkulturation in Japan." In *Der eine Gott in vielen Kulturen. Inkulturation und christliche Gottesvorstellung*, edited by K. Hilpert and K.-O. Ohlig, 215-32. Zurich: Benziger.

Iroegbu, P. O. 1996. *Appropriate Ecclesiology: Through Narrative Theology to an African Church*. Owerri, Nigeria: International Universities Press.

Jennings, T. W., ed. 1985. *The Vocation of the Theologian*. Philadelphia: Fortress Press.

Jocano, F. L. 1969. *Growing Up in a Philippine Barrio*. New York: Holt, Rinehart, and Winston.

Jonas, R. A. 1996. *Rebecca: A Father's Journey from Grief to Gratitude*. New York: Crossroad.

Jossua, Jean-Pierre, and Johann Baptist Metz, eds. 1979. *Doing Theology in New Places*. *Concilium* 115.

Kabasélé, François Lumbala. 1994. "Africans Celebrate Jesus Christ." In *Paths of African Theology*, edited by Rosino Gibellini, 78-94. Maryknoll, N.Y.: Orbis Books.

Kabida, J. 1987. "In Search of a Melanesian Theology." In *The Gospel Is Not Western: Black Theologies from the Southwest Pacific*, edited by G. W. Trompf, 139-47. Maryknoll, N.Y.: Orbis Books.

Knox, Ronald, ed. 1958. *Autobiography of a Saint* [Thérèse of Lisieux]. New York: Kenedy & Sons.

Koyama, Kosuke. 1976. "Thailand: Points of Theological Friction." In *Asian Voices in Christian Theology*, edited by Gerald H. Anderson, 65-86. Maryknoll, N.Y.: Orbis Books.

————. 1999. *Waterbuffalo Theology*. Revised and expanded twenty-fifth anniversary edition. Maryknoll, N.Y.: Orbis Books.

Leddy, Mary J. 2001. *Radical Gratitude*. Maryknoll, N.Y.: Orbis Books.

Lewis, G. D. 1981. *Resolving Church Conflicts: A Case Approach for Local Congregations*. San Francisco: Harper & Row.

Lois, J. 1993. "Christology in the Theology of Liberation." In *Mysterium Liberationis: Fundamental Concepts of the Liberation Theology*, edited by Ignacio Ellacuría and Jon Sobrino, 168-93. Maryknoll, N.Y.: Orbis Books.

Mahoney, J. D. 1994. *Mission and Ministry in Fiji*. Edited by F. Hoare. Samabula, Fiji: Columban Fathers.

May, Rollo. 1998. *Power and Innocence: A Search for the Sources of Violence*. Rev. ed. New York: Norton.

McFague, Sallie. 2001. *Life Abundant: Rethinking Theology and Economy for a Planet in Peril*. Minneapolis, Minn.: Fortress Press.

McGrath, Alister E. 1999. *Christian Spirituality: An Introduction*. London: Blackwell.

Meland, Bernard E. 1962. *The Realities of Faith*. New York: Harper & Row.

Merton, Thomas. 1973. *The Asian Journal*. New York: New Directions.

————. 1996. *Turning toward the World: The Pivotal Years*. Edited by V. A. Kramer. San Francisco: Harper & Row.

de Mesa, José. 1979. *And God said "Bahala na! The Theme of Providence in the Lowland Philippines*. Quezon City: Maryhill School of Theology.

————. 1987. *In Solidarity with Culture: Studies in Theological Re-Rooting*. Quezon City: Maryhill School of Theology.

————. 1996. *Following the Way of the Disciples: A Guidebook for Doing Christology in a Cultural Context*. Quezon City: East Asian Pastoral Institute.

————. 1998. "Tasks in the Inculturation of Theology: The Filipino Catholic Situation." *Missiology* 26/2: 191-200.

de Mesa, José, and Lode Wostyn. 1984. *Doing Theology*. Quezon City: CSP Book Shop.

Mieder, W. 1989. *American Proverbs: A Study of Texts and Contexts*. New York: Peter Lang.

————. 1995. "The Grass Is Always Greener on the Other Side of the Fence: American Proverb of Discontent." *De Proverbio* 1/1.

Montgomery-Fate, Tom. 1997. *Beyond the White Noise, Mission in a Multi-Cultural World*. St. Louis: Chalice Press.

Moon, C. H. S. 1985. *A Korean Minjung Theology: An Old Testament Perspective*. Maryknoll, N.Y.: Orbis Books.

Mueller, J. J. 1988. *What Is Theology?* Wilmington, Del.: Michael Glazier.

Mulder, N. 1997. *Philippine Society: Interpretation of Everyday Life*. Quezon City: New Day Publishers.

Mullins, Mark R. 1998. *Christianity Made in Japan: A Study of Indigenous Movements*. Honolulu: University of Hawaii Press.

Murphy, Nancey. 1990. *Theology in the Age of Scientific Reasoning*. Ithaca, N.Y.: Cornell University Press.

Murray, John Courtney. 1960. *We Hold These Truths: Catholic Reflections on the American Proposition*. New York: Sheed and Ward.

Mveng, Engelbert. 1979. "Black African Art as Cosmic Liturgy and Religious Language." In *African Theology en Route*, edited by Kofi Appiah-Kupi and Sergio Torres, 137-42. Maryknoll, N.Y.: Orbis Books.

Myers, Bryant L. 1999. *Walking with the Poor: Principles and Practices of Transformational Development*. Maryknoll, N.Y.: Orbis Books.

Nagel, Thomas. 1974. "What Is It Like to Be a Bat." *Philosophical Review* 83/4 (October): 435-50.

———. 1986. *The View from Nowhere*. New York: Oxford University Press.

Nam-dong, Suh. 1981. "Historical References for a Theology of Minjung." In *Minjung Theology: People as the Subjects of History*, edited by the Commission on Theological Concerns of the Christian Conference of Asia, 155-82. Maryknoll, N.Y.: Orbis Books.

New York Theological Seminary Students with Instructor John Eagleson. 1990. "Prison Statement from Sing Sing." In *Yearning to Breathe Freely: Liberation Theologies in the U.S.*, edited by M. Peter-Raoul, L. R. Farcey, and R. F. Hunter, 143-45. Maryknoll, N.Y.: Orbis Books.

Nolan, Albert. 1988. *God in South Africa: The Challenge of the Gospel*. Claremont, South Africa: David Philip.

———. 2001. *Jesus before Christianity*. Twenty-fifth anniv. ed. Maryknoll, N.Y.: Orbis Books.

Norris, Kathleen. 1998. *Amazing Grace: A Vocabulary of Faith*. New York: Riverhead Books.

Nouwen, Henri. 1976. *The Genesee Diary: Report from a Trappist Monastery*. Garden City, N.Y.: Doubleday.

———. 1988. *The Road to Daybreak*. Garden City, N.Y.: Doubleday.

———. 1992. *¡Gracias!* Maryknoll, N.Y.: Orbis Books.

Oduyoye, Mercy Amba. 1986. *Hearing and Knowing: Theological Reflections on Christianity in Africa*. Maryknoll, N.Y.: Orbis Books.

Parker, Cristian. 1996. *Popular Religion and Modernization in Latin America: A Different Logic*. Maryknoll, N.Y.: Orbis Books.

Paton, Alan. 1996. *Ah, But Your Land is Beautiful*. New York: Simon and Schuster.

Popper, Karl R. 1973. *Objective Knowledge: An Evolutionary Approach*. Oxford: Clarendon Press.

Radcliffe, Timothy. 1996. "The Identity of Religious Today." Rome: Curia of the Order of Preachers.

Rahner, Karl. 1964. *Alltägliche Dinge*. Einsiedeln: Benziger.

———. 1965. *Encounters with Silence*. Westminster, Md.: Newman Press.

Rayan, Samuel. 1984. "Jesus und die Armen im Vierten Evangelium." In *Wir werden bei ihm wohnen. Das Johannesevangelium in indischer Deutung*, edited by G. Soares-Prabhu, 81-98. Freiburg im Breisgau: Herder.

———. 1991. "The 'How' of Third World Theologies." In *Third World Theologies in Dialogue: Essays in Memory of D. S. Amalorpavadass*, edited by J. R. Chandran, 42-66. Banagalore: EATWOT, W. Q. Judge Press.

Rezende, Ricardo. 1994. *Rio Maria: Song of the Earth*. Edited by M. Adriance. Maryknoll, N.Y.: Orbis Books.

Rohr, Richard. 1992. *Simplicity: The Art of Living*. New York: Crossroad.

Roy, A. 1983. "The Socio-Economic and Political Context of Third World Theology." In *Irruption of the Third World: Challenge to Theology*, edited by Virginia Fabella and Sergio Torres, 87-112. Maryknoll, N.Y.: Orbis Books.

Ruiz, J.-P. 1998. "The Bible and U.S. Hispanic American Theological Discourse: Lessons from a Non-Innocent History." In *From the Heart of Our People: Latino/a Explorations in Catholic Systematic Theology*, edited by O. O. Espín and M. H. Díaz, 100-120. Maryknoll, N.Y.: Orbis Books.

Schillebeeckx, Edward. 1989. *For the Sake of the Gospel*. London: SCM Press.

Schineller, Peter. 1990. *A Handbook on Inculturation*. New York: Paulist Press.

Schreiter, Robert J. 1985. *Constructing Local Theologies*. Maryknoll, N.Y.: Orbis Books.

———. 1991. "Some Conditions for a Transcultural Theology: Response to Raimon Panikkar." In *Pluralism and Oppression: Theology in World Perspective*, edited by Paul F. Knitter, 23-28. Lanham, Md.: University Press of America.

Schumacher, E. F. 1993. *Small Is Beautiful: A Study of Economics as if People Mattered*. London: Vintage.

Sedmak, Clemens. 1997. *Was wird gespielt? Die andere Seite der Entwicklungshilfe*. Thaur/Wien: Druck- und Verlagshaus Thaur.

———. 1999. *Theologie als "Handwerk."* Regensburg: Pustet.

———. 2001. *Sozialtheologie: Theologie, Sozialwissenschaft und der Cultural Turn*. Frankfurt/Main: Peter Lang.

Segundo, Juan Luis. 1974. *Capitalism-Socialism: A Theological Crux. Concilium* 96.

———. 1976. *The Liberation of Theology*. Markynoll, N.Y.: Orbis Books.

Senior, Donald. 1992. *Jesus: A Gospel Portrait*. New York: Paulist Press.

Sheets, J. R. 1981. "Profile of the Spirit: A Theology of Discernment of Spirits." In "Notes on the Spiritual Exercises of St. Ignatius of Loyola," edited by David L. Fleming. *Review for Religious*: 214-25.

Sheldrake, Philip. 1987. *Images of Holiness: Explorations in Contemporary Spirituality*. London: Darton, Longman and Todd.

———. 1992. *Spirituality and History: Questions of Interpretation and Method*. New York: Crossroad.

Shorter, Aylward, ed. 1980. *African Christian Spirituality*. Maryknoll, N.Y.: Orbis Books.

Singer, Peter. 1975. *Animal Liberation*. New York: Random House.

Smith, Charles W. F. 1969. *The Paradox of Jesus in the Gospels*. Philadelphia: Westminster.

Soares-Prabhu, George M. 1988. "Jesus, der Lehrer: die befreinde Päsdagogik des Jesus von Nazareth." In *Verlaß den Tempel. Antyodaya - indischer Weg zur Befreiung*, edited by Felix Wilfred, 96-115. Freiburg im Breisgau: Herder.

———. 1992. "The Liberative Pedagogy of Jesus: Lessons for an Indian Theology of Liberation." In *Leave the Temple: Indian Paths to Human Liberation*, edited by Felix Wilfred, 100-115. Maryknoll, N.Y.: Orbis Books.

Sobrino, Jon. 1985. *Spirituality of Liberation: Toward Political Holiness*. Maryknoll, N.Y.: Orbis Books.

———. 1991. "Theology in a Suffering World: Theology as *Intellectus Amoris*." In *Pluralism and Oppression*, edited by Paul F. Knitter, 153-77. Lanham, Md.: University Press of America.

Sölle, Dorothee, and Fulbert Steffensky. 1985. *Not Just Yes and Amen: Christians with a Cause*. Philadelphia: Fortress Press.

Sofola, Zulu. 1979. "The Theatre in Search for African Authenticity." In *African Theology en Route*, edited by Kofi Appiah-Kupi and Sergio Torres, 83-94. Maryknoll, N.Y.: Orbis Books.

Stolzmann, William. 1986. *The Pipe and Christ: A Christian—Sioux Dialogue*. Chamberlain, S.Dak.: Tipi Press.

Suh, David Kwang-sun. 1981. "A Biographical Sketch of an Asian Theological Consultation." In *Minjung Theology: People as the Subjects of History*, edited by the Commission on Theological Concerns of the Christian Conference of Asia, 15-37. Maryknoll, N.Y.: Orbis Books.

Suzuki, S. 1988. "Kirche und Theologie nach Hiroshima und Nagasak." In *Brennpunkte in Kirche und Theologie Japans: Beiträge und Dokumente*, edited by T. Yoshiki and H. E. Hamer, 69-74. Neukirchen-Vluyn: Neukirchener Verlag.

Tanner, Kathryn. 1997. *Theories of Culture: A New Agenda for Theology*. Minneapolis, Minn.: Fortress Press.

Thành, M. 1993. "Aspects of Christianity in Vietnam." In "Any Room for Christ in Asia?" edited by Leonardo Boff and Virgil Elizondo, 95-109. *Concilium* 1993/2. London: SCM Press.

Thompson, William. M. 1996. *Fire and Light, the Saints and Theology: On Consulting the Saints, Mystics, and Martyrs in Theology*. New York: Paulist Press.

Tilley, Terrence W. 1985. *Story Theology*. Wilmington, Del.: Michael Glazier.

Tisdale, L. Tubbs. 1997. *Preaching as Local Theology and Folk Art*. Minneapolis, Minn.: Fortress Press.

Tracy, David. 1975. *Blessed Rage for Order*. New York: Seabury Press.

———. 1981. *The Analogical Imagination*. New York: Crossroad.

Ukpong, Justin S. 1994. "Christology and Inculturation: A New Testament Perspective." In *Paths of African Theology*, edited by Rosino Gibellini, 40-61. Maryknoll, N.Y.: Orbis Books.

Unger, Peter K. 1996. *Living High and Letting Die: Our Illusion of Innocence*. New York: Oxford University Press.

Untener, Kenneth. 1999. *Preaching Better: Practical Suggestions for Homilists*. New York: Paulist Press.

———. 2001. "The Fundamental Mistakes of Preaching." *New Theology Review* 14/1: 5-13.

Valdiers, P. 1971. "Signes de Temps, Signes de Dieu?" *Etudes* 335: 261-79.

Valles, C. G. 1987. *Unencumbered by Baggage: Tony de Mello, a Prophet for Our Times*. Gujarat: Gujarat Shitya Prakash.

Van Allmen, Daniel. 1975. "The Birth of Theology," *International Review of Missions* 64: 37-52.

Vanier, Jean. 1989. *Community and Growth*. 2d ed. London: Darton, Longman and Todd.

Vithayathil, P. 1992. *Proverbs and Wise Sayings*. Cochin, India: Vithayathil Publications.

Wa Thiong'O, N. 1986. *Decolonizing the Mind: The Politics of Language in African Literature*. Nairobi: Heinemann Kenya.

Walls, Andrew F. 1996. *The Missionary Movement in Christian History: Studies in the Transmission of Faith*. Maryknoll, N.Y.: Orbis Books.

Warren, Max A. C. 1963. "Introduction." In J. V. Taylor, *The Primal Vision: Christian Presence amid African Religion*. Philadelphia: Fortress Press.

Webb, Val. 1999. *Why We're Equal: Introducing Feminist Theology*. St. Louis: Chalice Press.

Webster, J. C. B. 1996. *The Dalit Christians: A History*. Delhi: Indian Society for Promoting Christian Knowledge.

Wiles, Maurice. 1975. *The Making of Christian Doctrine: A Study in the Principles of Early Doctrinal Development*. Cambridge: Cambridge University Press.

Williams, L. L. 1994. *Caribbean Theology*. New York: Peter Lang.

Wittgenstein, Ludwig. 1967. *Philosophical Investigations*. Oxford: Basil Blackwell.

Worsnip, Michael. 1996. *Priest and Partisan: A South African Journey, the Story of Father Michael Lapsley*. Melbourne: Ocean Press.

Young, B. H. 1995. *Jesus the Jewish Theologian*. Peabody, Mass.: Hendrickson Publishers.

Index